AF413364

Sungi Mlengeya

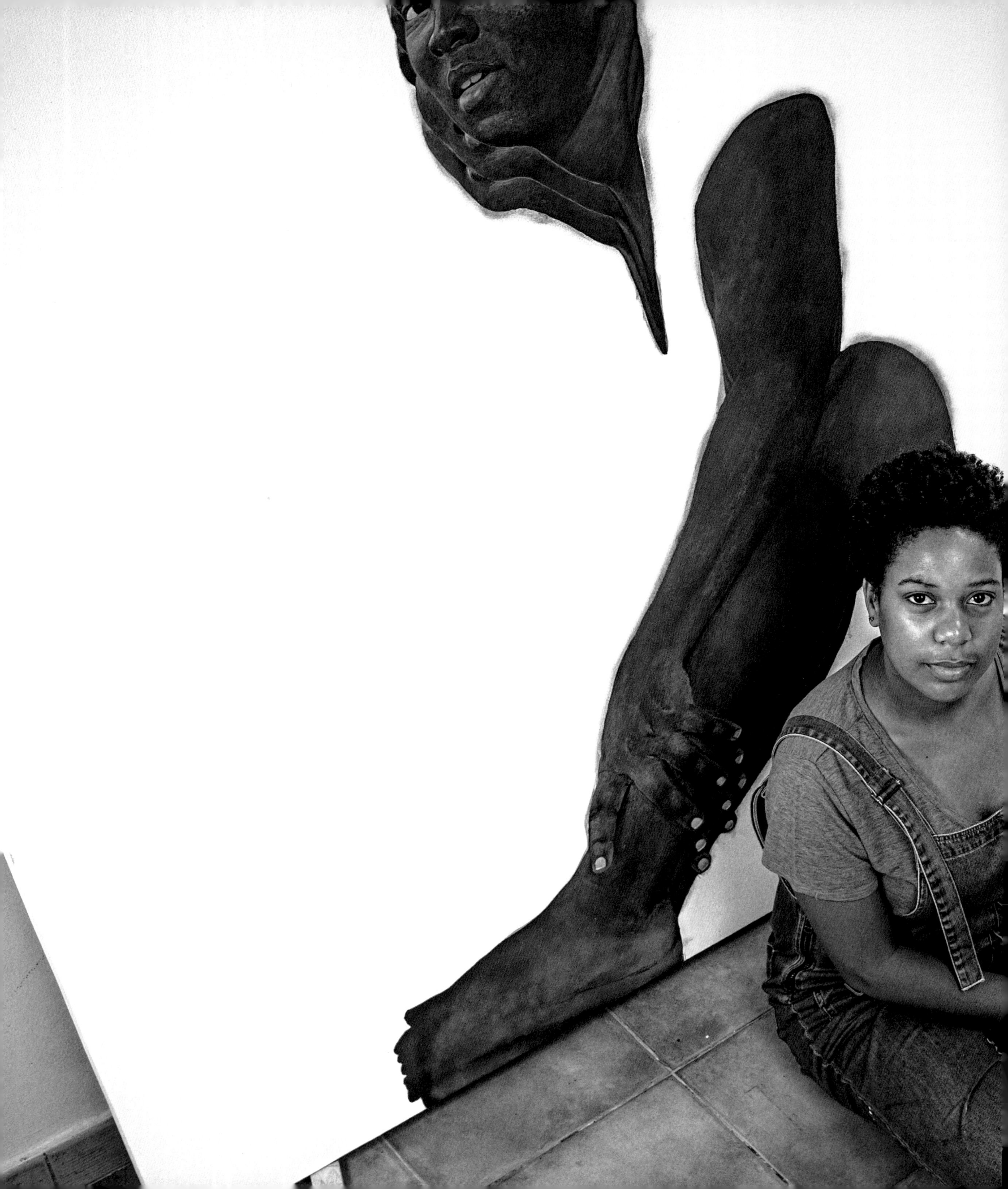

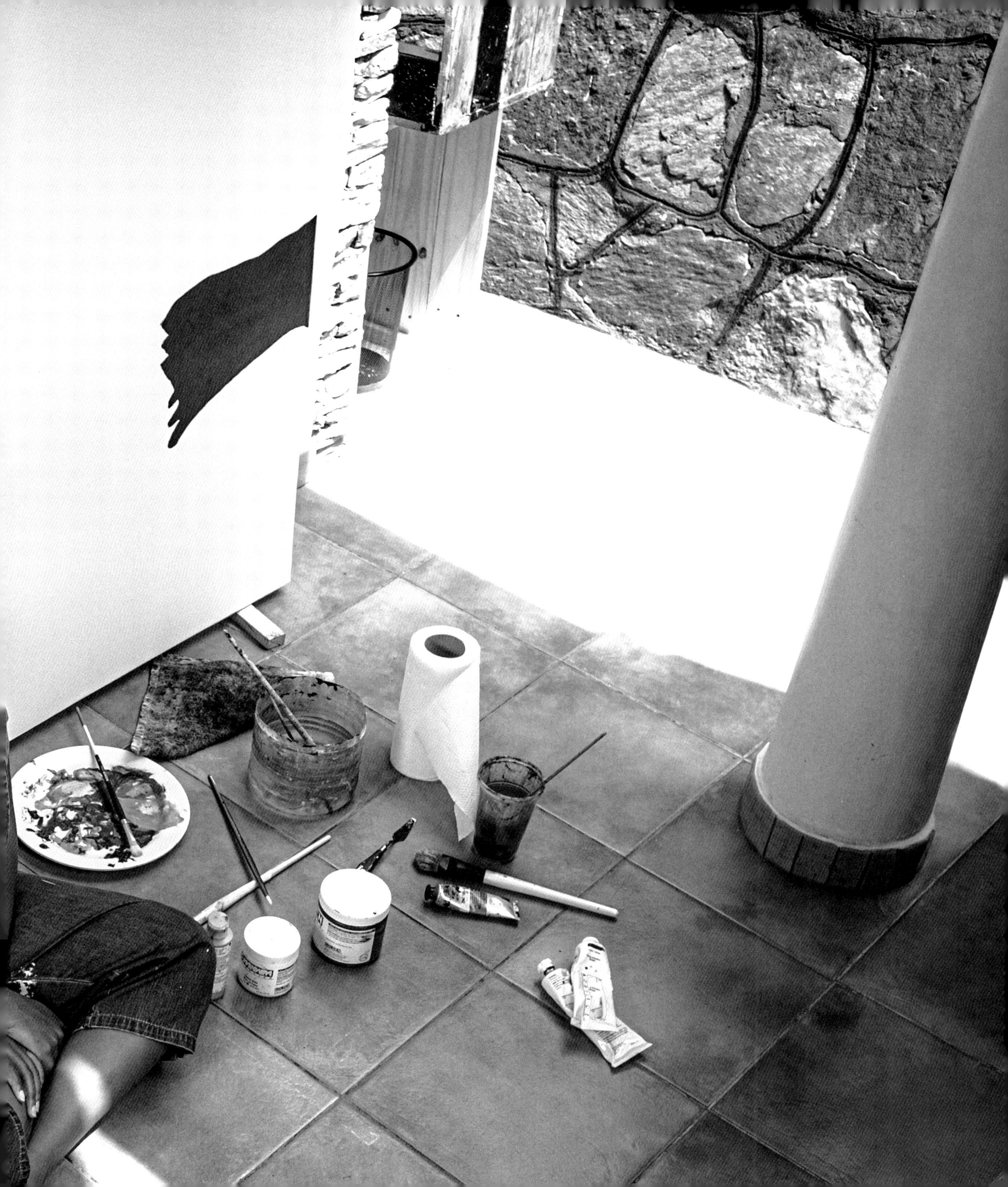

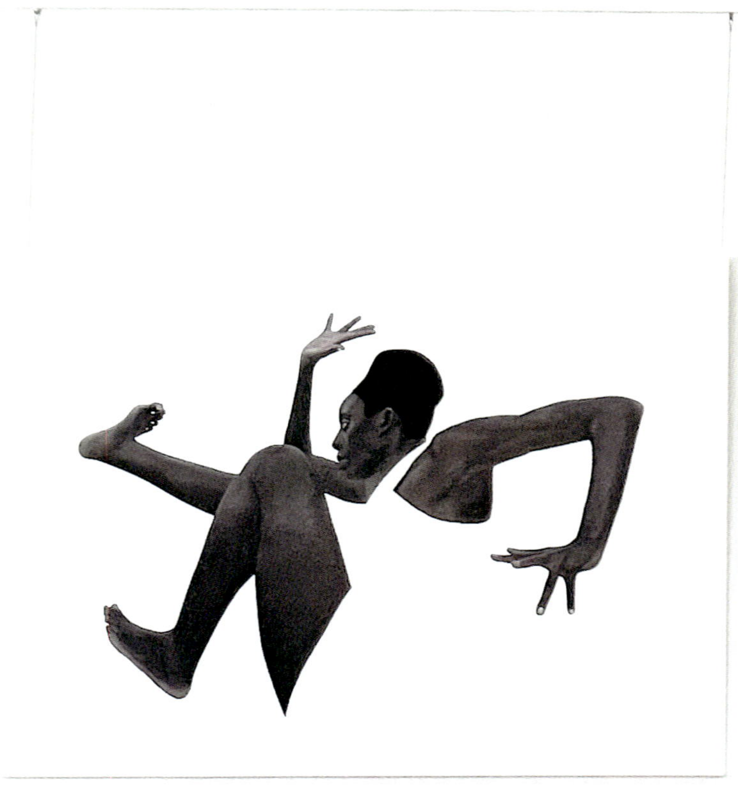
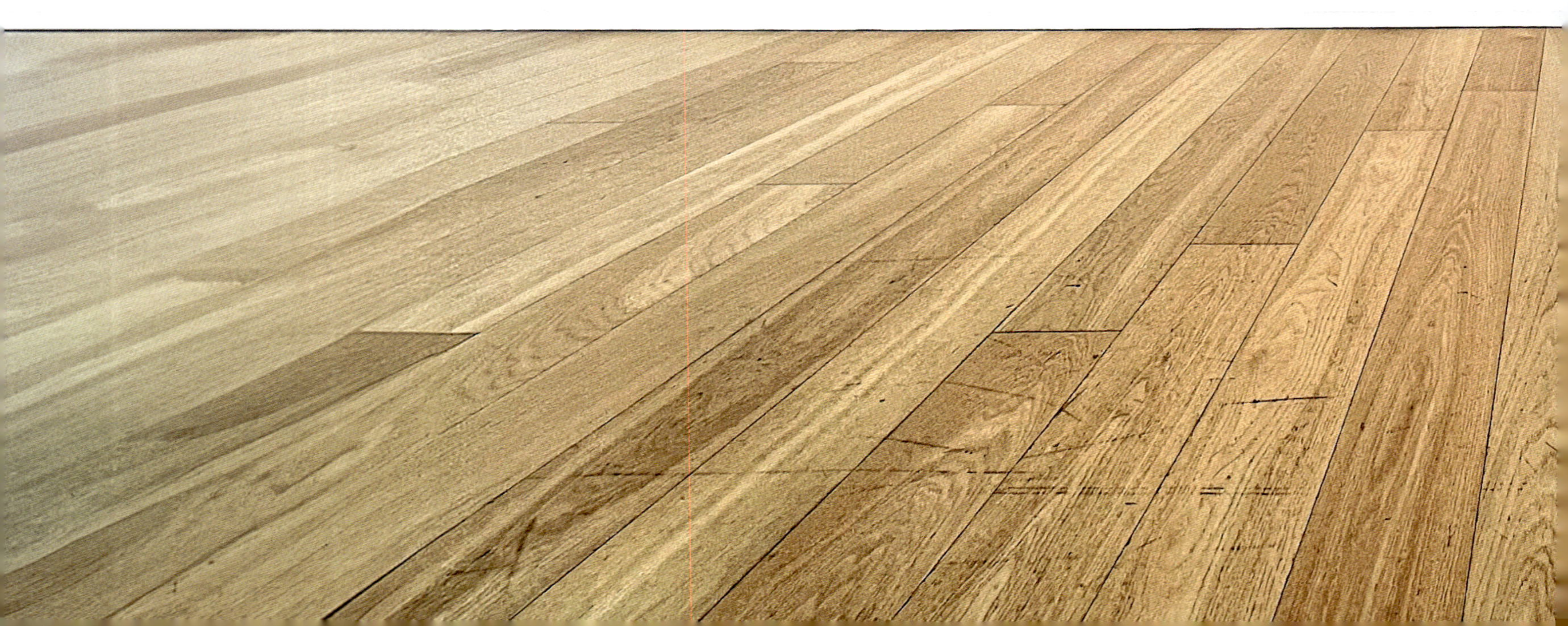

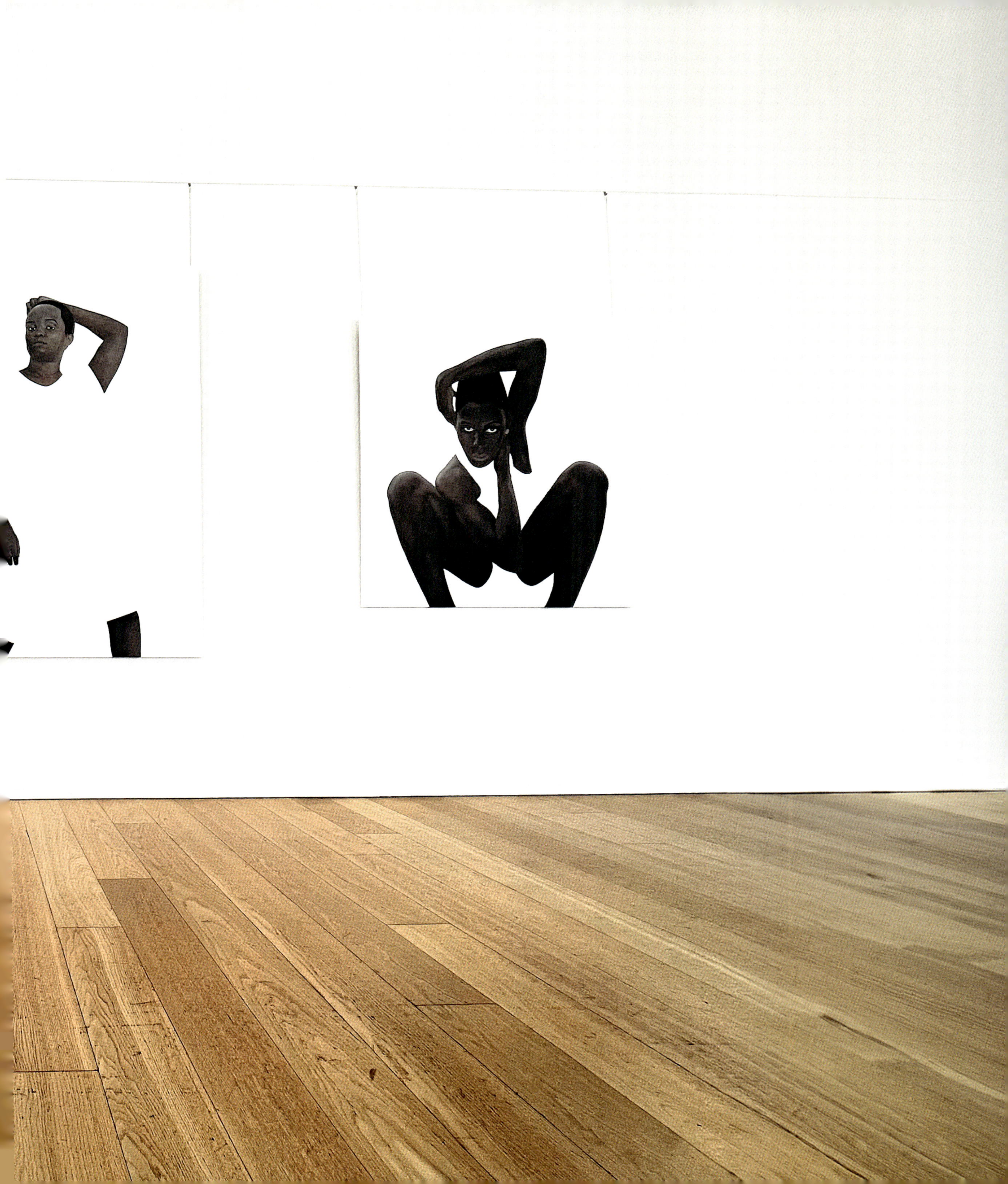

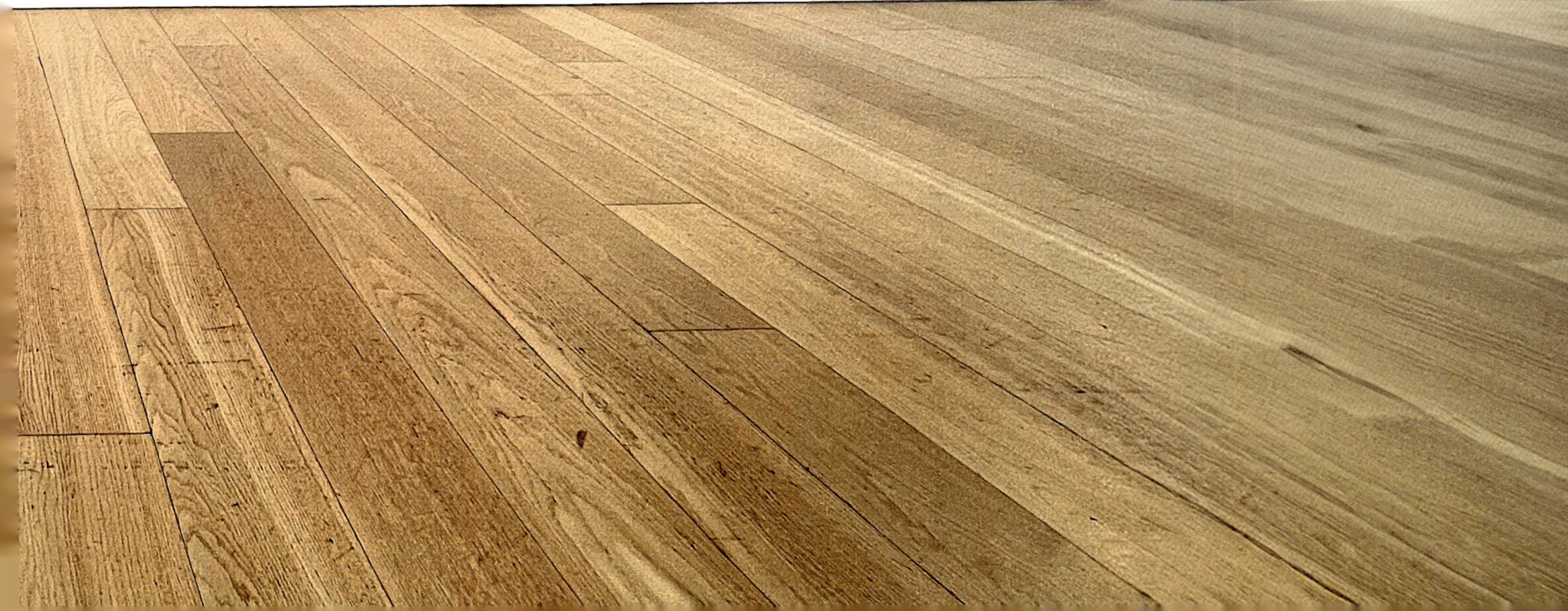

Sungi Mlengeya

AAG

SKIRA

Summary

11 Encountering the Work of Sungi Mlengeya

Suzanne McFayden

13 Painting "Normal": Africanity, Womanhood & Blackness in the Work of Sungi Mlengeya

Tandazani Dhlakama

21 Works

50 *Ruka*, presented by Katherine Alcauskas

82 *Spring*, presented by Birgit Lauda

123 In Conversation with Sungi Mlengeya

Sungi Mlengeya – Jemima Michael

131 Biography

134 List of Works

141 Acknowledgements

Pages 2-5:

Portrait of the artist
in her studio
February 2022

Don't Try. Don't Not Try
B.LA Art Foundation, Vienna, Austria
2022

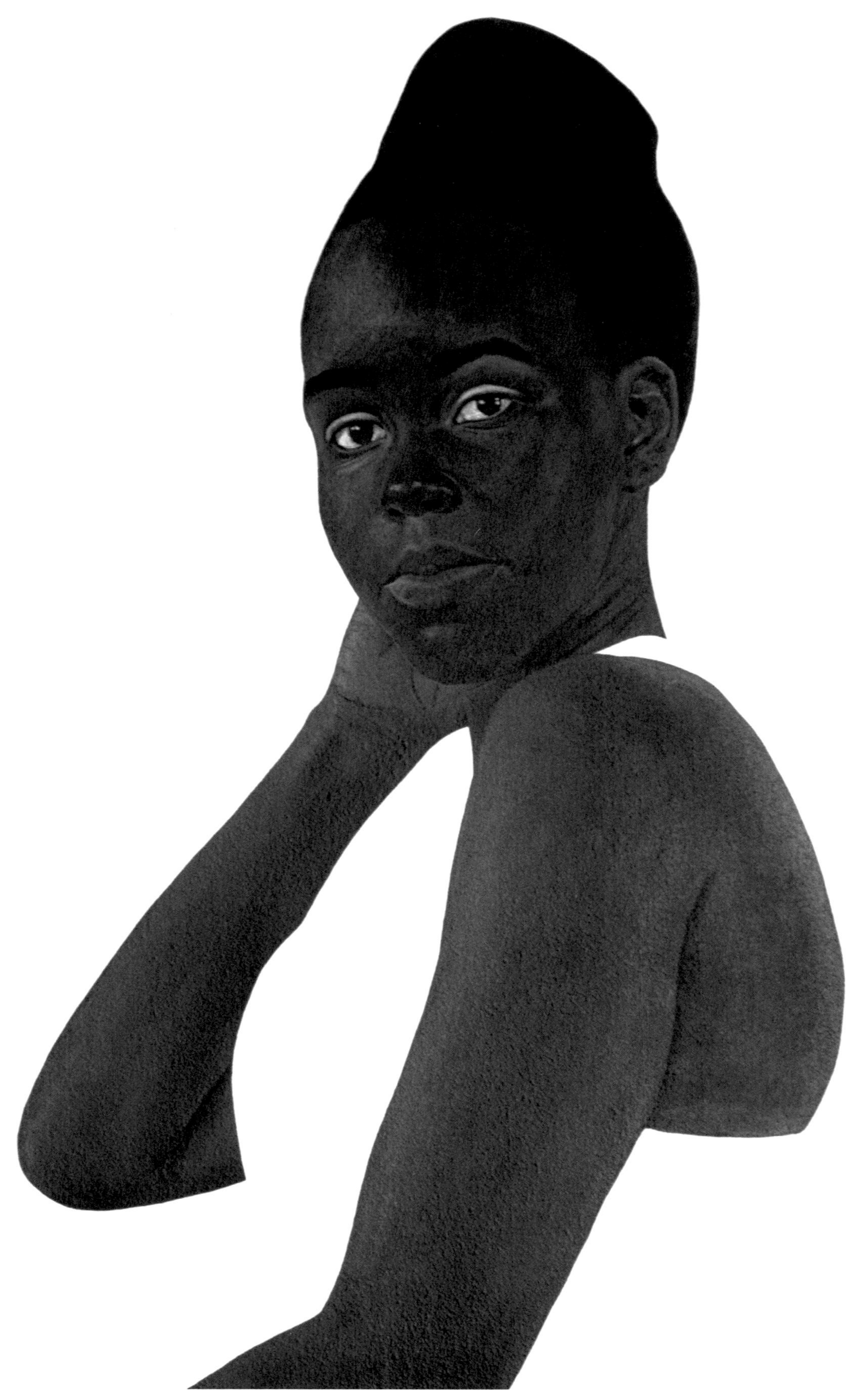

Encountering the Work of Sungi Mlengeya

Suzanne McFayden

1. Poet and sister of the artist.

"I shade no skin, I like mine with scars; sugu and burns…" Ngollo Mlengeya[1]

My first encounter with Sungi Mlengeya's paintings was mesmerizing. Her deceivingly simple palette of chocolate skin against white dresses allowed my focus to remain fully on the women she paints, their outstretched limbs, the grace of their bodies in motion, the steady calm of some faces, the joy breaking through in others' smiles. Each woman seemed free, safe and full of her own possibility.

I wanted to be one of them.

2. With Ayla Angelos for *It's Nice That*.

My early life in Kingston, Jamaica, taught me much was expected from Black women. We were to be Godly first and foremost. When some in my generation chose to be Dance Hall Queens instead, there were expectations there, too. Both models were equally performative, rigid spins on the trinity of virgin/mother/whore. As for any art I saw, there was the "acceptable" as portrayed in my Encyclopedia Britannica; classical portraiture where the subject is turned slightly to the side, the gaze fixed somewhere in the distance. Other supposedly more real-life art depicted market women, baskets between their legs or on their heads. Where were the women of my life? Where was I?

I wish I had had Sungi's paintings then. They represent what it looks like to fully inhabit one's being. Growing up, I didn't fit into any singular version of womanhood held out to me by my society or in the art I saw. Sungi has described a similar experience to mine of feeling restricted by societal constructs before bravely stepping away from the script in 2018 – her career in finance – and instead turning to art, the thing that feeds her being. I see the same bravery in her subjects. They are unconcerned with the thoughts of others. They express tenderness towards and connection with the other subjects. There is undeniable sisterhood in her work and it shows another possibility of and for Black women.

Sungi usually knows her subjects and creates poses that reflect multiple ways of being. Thus, in her work *Huru* (the Swahili word for 'free'), the subject is floating. Sungi's paintings will forever remind women that they are allowed to choose. In a previous interview,[2] she said,

I'm painting women into (…) a place where it is possible to go through life pursuing true preferences and being whoever you want to be. I'm celebrating that rebellious woman (…) and also shedding a light on the frightened one (…) – encouraging her to come forward and make her own statement.

As a Black woman who has chosen writing as my departure from the script, I am happy to see "us" represented in this way. In Sungi's art, we are no longer fixed. We can be limitless, strong and tender.

Liirwa I, 2020
acrylic on canvas
86 × 60 cm

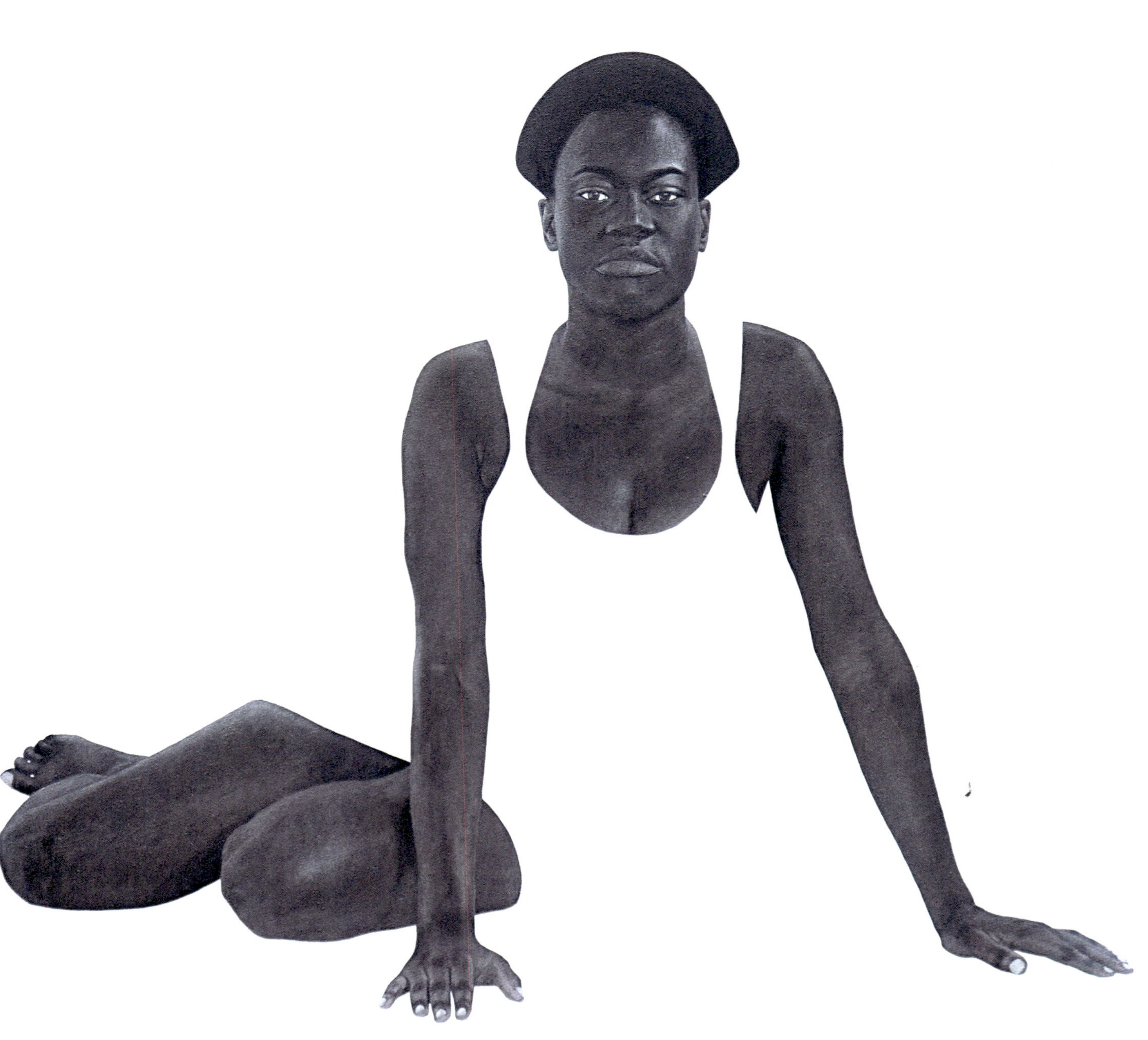

Painting "Normal": Africanity, Womanhood & Blackness in the Work of Sungi Mlengeya

Tandazani Dhlakama

"[Jesus Christ] used to have blue eyes but I painted them brown like mine and everybody's, to make him normal".[1]

NoViolet Bulawayo in *We Need New Names*

1.   Bulawayo, NoViolet, *We Need New Names* (London: Vintage, 2014), p. 25.

In NoViolet Bulawayo's novel, a young child innocently makes an artistic alteration to a hanging image of a white Jesus in a neighbour's home. To make this depiction of Christ relatable, the little girl felt that her saviour ought to resemble the Black people around her, who looked like her. As we read on, we find out that, unfortunately, the girl gets "walloped" for her comical efforts to make Christ look "normal".

This moment in Bulawayo's text, which is both poignant and humorous, begs us to think more broadly about image and representation. Why do we brighten up when we see elements familiar or similar to ourselves in art? Why does a painting like *Nyamgana* (2024) draw us in? This is because for those who have been historically marginalized, to be reflected in film, portraiture or song speaks to the soul, evoking a sense of dignity and desire for legacy, which are all elements that make us human. When representation has been limited, erased or obscured, seeing oneself documented or one's story amplified can be emboldening. Suzanne McFayden's anecdotal introductory text in this publication beautifully elaborates on this.

Perhaps this is why many find Tanzanian-born Sungi Mlengeya's painting so moving. Her figures look like us people of colour. Her paintings resemble Black, African or African Diasporan persons. In many ways, the individuals depicted look like our mothers, aunties, friends, siblings and ancestors. They reveal the 'normal' yet multi-layered elements of who we are. They offer intimate, broad and celebratory perspectives as opposed to the limiting tropes that have historically been projected onto us.

In the last five years, there has been much coverage of Black figuration from different Black geographies. However, I am cautious of any attempts to position Sungi's painting as part of a 'new' trend of Black figuration, for I think to do so would be too reductive. Though her primary mode of expression is figurative, I prefer to think of her practice as one that stems from an important African art historical continuum as opposed to one that emerges from a current fad. Sungi is part of a Black art canon, an artistic lineage informed by diverse practices and countless figurative artists, ranging from Belkis Ayón (1967–1999) in Cuba, to Ben Enwonwu (1917–1994) in Nigeria and Zanzibari painter Fatma Abdullah (1939–1994).

One might ask, why does it seem as though Black figuration has only now become popular or new? Perhaps what is new is the Western gaze on art from Africa

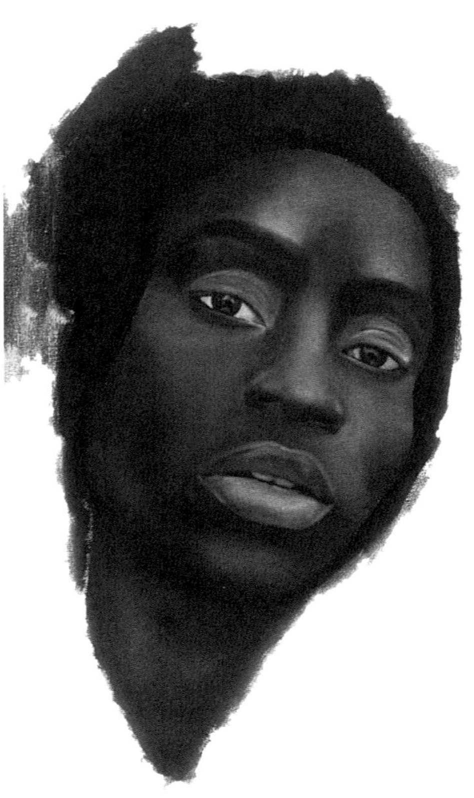

and renewed attention from the art market in this post-pandemic moment. In recent times, countless social-justice movements around the world have resonated with the renewed call of #BlackLivesMatter and been amplified by the murder of George Floyd. Of course, in modern history there has always been a resounding call for Black activism, however, advocacy has been manifested in nuanced forms. What we have seen during the last five years is a continuation of age-old demands for change. At the same time, many Western cultural institutions have been reeling with existential questions around relevance and decolonisation. Also parallel to this has been an increase in right-leaning regimes in the Global North, ones tending towards fascism. The histories, memories and narratives of historically disenfranchised nations, societies and communities urgently needed to come to the fore, and art organizations needed to open up to institutional critique and correction. We continue to learn from thinkers such as Chika Okeke-Agulu, Françoise Vergès, Achille Mbembe, M. NourbeSe Philip and countless others, who have challenged the status quos, prompting different forms of visibility and representation from Africa and its complex diaspora.[2] There is still much work to be done. It is from this backdrop that more attention on Black figurative art has come about.

Additionally, figuration is widely accessible. We all inhabit and express ourselves through our bodies. Therefore, representations of the body are undoubtedly relatable. Perhaps that is one of the reasons why depictions of Blackness, by Black artists working today, have been galvanized to promote discourse around identity, history and race. Of course, there is nothing wrong with this, as long as the agenda is directed at bringing about transformation and not short-lived tokenistic optics.

2.   Seminal texts by these authors include: Enwezor, Okwui and Chika Okeke-Agulu, *Contemporary African Art Since 1980* (Bologna: Damiani, 2009); Vergés, Françoise. "Wandering Souls and Returning Ghosts: Writing the History of the Dispossessed", Yale French Studies, no. 118/119 (2010): 136–54; Mbembe, Achille, "Ways of Seeing: Beyond the New Nativism. Introduction", *African Studies Review* 44, no. 2 (2001), 1–14; Philip, Marlene Nourbese, and Setaey Adamu Boateng, *Zong!* (Middletown, CN: Wesleyan University Press, 2008).

One of the reasons I prefer to write about a renewed attention, or heightened interest, as opposed to a 'rise' in Black figuration, is to remind us that this mode of art was in existence long before the years of recent art-market attention. Consider, for example, Ethiopian religious painting in the 11th-century church, Debre Selam Mikael. Important to note is that Black portraiture in the form of ivory, bronze, terra-cotta and wood can be traced back to the Ile-Ife sculptures of the 14th century, to the 16th-century Nigerian portrait of Idia, Queen Mother, or the 18th-century Chokwe traditions of portraiture in Angola, among many others.

In more recent pictorial history, we might think of the geometric figures in the painting of the Cuban artist Wifredo Lam (1902–1982), composed in the latter half of the 20th century, or the dancing figures created during the 1930s by American artist Clementine Hunter (1887–1988). Consider also the promenading pairs in the rural landscapes of the 1950s by the South African artist Gladys Mgudlandlu (1917–1979), or the seated figures painted by Jamaican artist Osmond Watson (1934–2005) during the 1960s. Black figuration has always been present; however, it simply wasn't seen as having the same value, or as part of the mainstream, in historically white-dominated spaces. Hence, not only does Sungi's practice expand a rich Black and African art canon, it also contributes to continuing dialogue on Black subjectivity and Black consciousness. The works of the above artists are informed by the socio-political contexts in which their creators lived and worked.

In 2007 Senegalese curator N'Goné Fall emphasized the multi-layered entanglements preceding Sungi's generation of artists. In the catalogue of the exhibition *Global Feminisms*, Fall wrote:

> "Colonialism brought in its wake a host of other 'isms': primitivism, exoticism, racism, imperialism, totalitarianism, traumatism. Moving beyond the isms is the challenge that the new generation of female artists is taking up".[3]

Like those that have gone before her, Sungi is not ignorant of these 'isms' but she too has been 'moving beyond' them in order to emphasize other issues. Sungi's work puts less emphasis on struggle and more on merriment. Her canvases are devoid of trauma and toil, which is demonstrated by her dancing, swimming and restful figures. However, this does not mean that her work is apolitical, as her insistence of painting tranquil and joy-filled people is both a form of subversion and a refusal to centralize colonialism.

Though her practice points to more affirmative elements of Africanity and Black subjectivity, Sungi makes an intentional nod towards African feminism. She describes painting as "a way of celebrating the women in [her] life".[4] My broad definition of

3.   Fall, N'Goné, "Providing a Space of Freedom. Women Artists from Africa", in Reilly, Maura, and Linda Nochlin (eds.), *Global Feminisms. New Directions in Contemporary Art at the Brooklyn Museum* (London: Merrell Publishers, 2007).

4.   Owoh, Ugonna-Ora. "Sungi Mlengeya Uses Her Art to Celebrate Tanzanian and Ugandan Women". *OkayAfrica*. Last modified June 15, 2022. https://www.okayafrica.com/sungi-Sungi-interview/.

feminism in this context is drawn from thinkers such as Shereen Essof, Bell Hooks, and Chimamanda Ngozi Adiche, who collectively point to very particular Black and Afro-centric feminist manifestations. Collectively, they write about forms of feminism that are complicated by race, religion and culture. Adding her voice to this Black feminist chorus, Fall reminds us that the issues affecting Africans post-liberation were indeed complex and very particular. She proposes that while white women were burning their bras overseas, "women had too much to do in modern Africa than to listen to their Western 'sisters'".[5] And, regarding the generation of African women post-1990, she goes on to make the observation:

> "This committed generation raised questions about male versus female, submission versus power control, tradition versus modernity, and the local versus the global. They took on the challenge of questioning their society – how they fit into it as women, and how they relate to the world as Africans".[6]

As a result, I like to think of Sungi, born in the 1990s, as part of another historical continuum, one of women artists from Africa. By depicting her subjects in repose, at leisure or elatedly in movement, she emphasizes understated narratives that stem from joy. She hopes that women can see multiple aspects of themselves reflected in her work. This does not mean that her figures never exude vulnerability, for Sungi believes that "vulnerability can be celebrated" and is an empowering characteristic.[7] Sungi may not display the same militancy and provocativeness as her predecessors Tracey Rose (1974–), Bernie Searle (1964–), Bill Kouélany (1965–) and other artists discussed in Fall's text, however, like them, she employs the body as her means to expand on the narratives of the women in her world.

The body is evidently a vital medium to Sungi. It is the only element in her work given tone and colour. Yet, instead of reiterating that the woman's body has been a site of oppression, she stresses the fact that the body can simply be. It can take up space without having to carry the burden of protest or be forced to channel a societal agenda. Frustrated by the limited portrayals of local women she saw all around her, when Sungi started painting, she wanted to discard the tired image of the burdened Black woman and portray her in multifaceted alternative forms. That is why many of her figures are undaunted, bold and calm. She depicts different body types and gestures. We see long arms thrust into the air, fingers clicking, fingers lightly resting on shoulders, hands squeezed, heels kicking up and lunging thighs. Serene faces boldly stare back at us from white canvases. However, some look away, or at each other, largely unbothered by our gaze. In contrast to the subjects in European Renaissance paintings, Sungi's women are neither passive nor decorative. They are not painted in postures of servitude.

5.   Fall, p. 1.

6.   Fall, p. 2.

7.   This is taken from an online conversation the author had with Sungi on 3 October 2024.

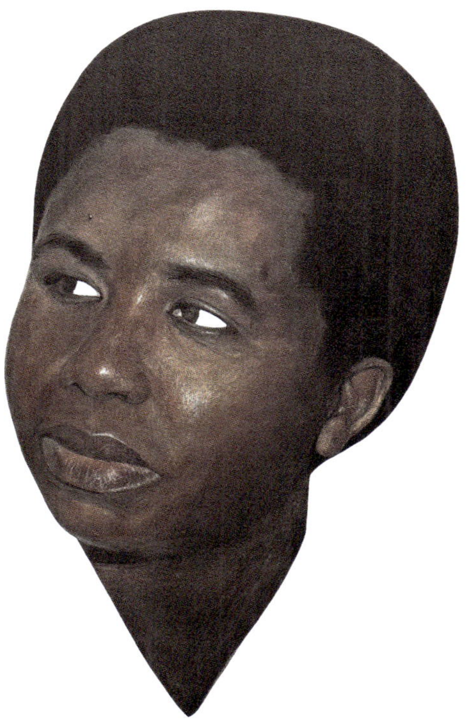

Similarly, unlike so many ancestors captured by the colonial photographers of the 1800s, her subjects have power, they subvert objectification and exoticism. Sungi's portraits mirror the more honest and aspirational aspects of daily life.

Her muses are drawn from such places as Arusha, Dar es Salaam and Kampala, all cities she has once called home. Some of these are women who had gifted her with "the most comforting, fondest memories" and painting is a way of immortalizing them. Today her works are produced from images of her personal circle, acquaintances, performance collaborators and family photographs. Thus, each painting is simultaneously an ode to a woman in her local society, an extension of herself, and a documentation of an essence captured at a specific moment.

Sungi's figures are formed by enchanting tones of deep mahogany and ebony. When in front of one of her paintings, you might notice that though the skin of her figures is often painted dark, there is always depth and volume. Her paintings are neither matte nor flat, they serve to glorify Blackness. Sungi delicately portrays skin with warmth and exuberance, giving her figures a subtle glow. This is evident in the manner in which soft light bounces off a clavicle or the rounded part of a nose is reflected in the curves of a smiling cheek or tilted forehead. Light emerges sensitively through the skin or on its surface, it even appears in the folds of a raised under-arm.

However, some may wonder what painting Black skin so dark does for Black representation. Could this be a method of making Blackness hyper visible? In 1998, when the artist Kerry James Marshall (1955–) was asked a similar question about his deep black figures, he replied:

8.   Rowell, Charles H., and Kerry James Marshall, "An Interview with Kerry James Marshall", *Callaloo* 21, no. 1 (1998): 263–72.

9.   I worked closely with Koyo Kouoh at the Zeitz MOCAA. Together we curated a travelling exhibition titled *When We See Us: A Century of Black Figuration in Painting*, which featured Sungi. As a result of the extensive research we did on Black figuration, we had numerous conversations about parallel aesthetics, simultaneity of practice and the Kerry James Marshall effect. Kouoh gave many public presentations and interviews on Black figuration in which she elaborated on this subject.

10. Ibid.

11. Ibid.

"The reason why I painted them as black as they are was so that they operate as rhetorical figures. They are literally and rhetorically black in the same way that we describe ourselves as black people in America; we use that extreme position to designate ourselves in contrast to a white power structure of the country or the white mainstream".[8]

In a similar way, Sungi's use of dark tones also places emphasis on Blackness. However, unlike Marshall, doing so is not a direct response to white oppression. Even though racial politics is not at the forefront of Sungi's practice, because of the time we live in, I like to read into it a determination to make visible a form of Africanness that is conceptually informed by nuanced narratives from Tanzania and Uganda. I like to think of it as a push back against colourism which still plagues women in many Black communities today.

In speaking about Black figuration, Cameroonian curator Koyo Kouoh has often used the term 'Kerry James Marshall Effect' to discuss the influence that Marshall has had on other artists.[9] Younger painters around the world have directly and indirectly referenced Marshall's 'extreme position' of using very dark melanin to create figures engaged in everyday activities. Kouoh thus draws connections between the work of Marshall and Sungi alongside artists such as Zandile Tshabalala (1999–) and Spephelo Mnguni (1990–), both from South Africa, Raphael Adjetey Mayne (1983–) from Ghana, Elladj Lincy Deloumeaux (1995–) from Guadeloupe and Marc Padeu (1990–) from Cameroon, to name only a few.[10]

With reference to similarities of style, composition and subject matter amongst artists around the world who may or may not have been aware of each other, Kouoh also talks of simultaneity of practice and parallel aesthetics in 20th- and 21st-century Black figuration.[11] Are there comparable aesthetics between Sungi and the works of Barkley Hendricks (1945–2007)? Sungi marvels at the fact that her work is regularly compared to Hendricks'. As someone who started out in the world of banking, and having never attended an art academy, Sungi speaks of how she never knew of Hendricks until her own painting practice had become established and people began to mention him. Ironically, though she and Hendricks were born four decades apart and have come to prominence in different eras and geographies, they do indeed employ similar techniques. Both have represented spirited, self-possessed figures whose postures radiate confidence. Both have composed groupings of two to five figures from the same viewpoint. Sometimes the figures are the same person in different poses. They have both used an arresting solo figure who occupies the centre of the canvas from top to bottom. In most cases the figures in both artists' works have a performative presence, in that they all seem aware of being watched. They often pose, sit or move with un-flinching agency in spite of the viewer's presence. There are also technical parallels in the blending and glazing methods used by both artists. Similarities even exist in the coloration between certain works. Hendricks' predominant use of white in *October's Gone…Goodnight* (1973), *Slick* (1977), *What's Going On?* (1974) and *Lagos Ladies (Gbemi, Bisi, Niki, Christy)* (1978) is echoed in Sungi's practice. I see this as a beautiful coincidence and confirmation that though the Black experience has local specificities, when it comes to art, there is also a perpetual multi-generational, trans-continental metaphorical call and response.

For Sungi, using the empty white background was initially a curious happenstance that she immediately decided to build on. She states:

> "I wanted to make a painting with a perfect background, and I had no clue on what the background would be. So, I started painting the face first and, when I was done, I really loved how it looked. There was a contrast of the dark skin against the white background and that was beautiful".[12]

The stark, contrasting whiteness of everything that is not flesh makes her figures timeless, since our attention is directed solely at their skin. The absence of adornment and other contextual information prevents us from making fixed assumptions about time, space and distance, with the result that the depicted bodies are fully emancipated; it also allows for both local and universal readings. Even when Sungi's figures appear in water, there is still a sense of physical and metaphorical weightlessness. For Sungi, water represents "expansiveness, tranquillity and beauty".[13]

At the height of his career in the 1990s, Mozambican-Zimbabwean painter Luis Meque (1966–1998) famously said, "I am Black, I think Black, I paint Black".[14] It was important for him to make work that mirrored his own experience. In the same way, it was natural for the little girl in NoViolet Bulawayo's story to insist on an African 'normal' Christ that resembled the people around her. Like Meque, Bulawayo's little girl, and generations of others, Sungi draws on who she is and what is around her. In my view, she documents personal and collective aspects of womanhood from a particular East African positionality. Her meditations are embodied in floating dark hues against a bare background. Just as light is reflected on all of Sungi's figures, her desire is that each one of us may somehow see our ambitions and the more affirming aspects of our experiences reflected in her paintings.

12. Conversation between the author and Sungi on 2 November 2024.

13. Ibid.

14. Huggins, Derek, *Luis Meque 1966-1998*, exhibition leaflet, 28 March 2017 (Harare: Gallery Delta, 2017).

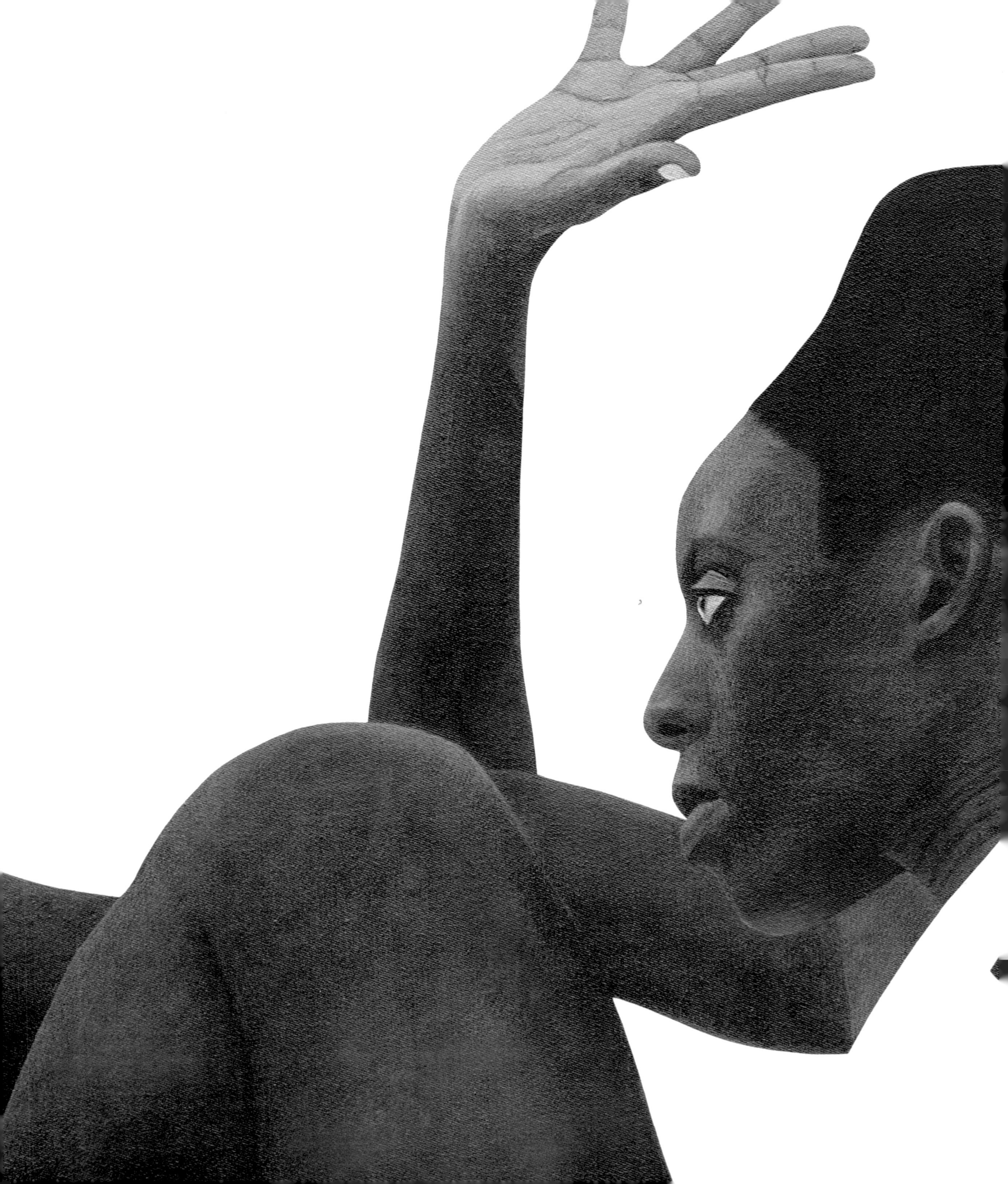

WORKS

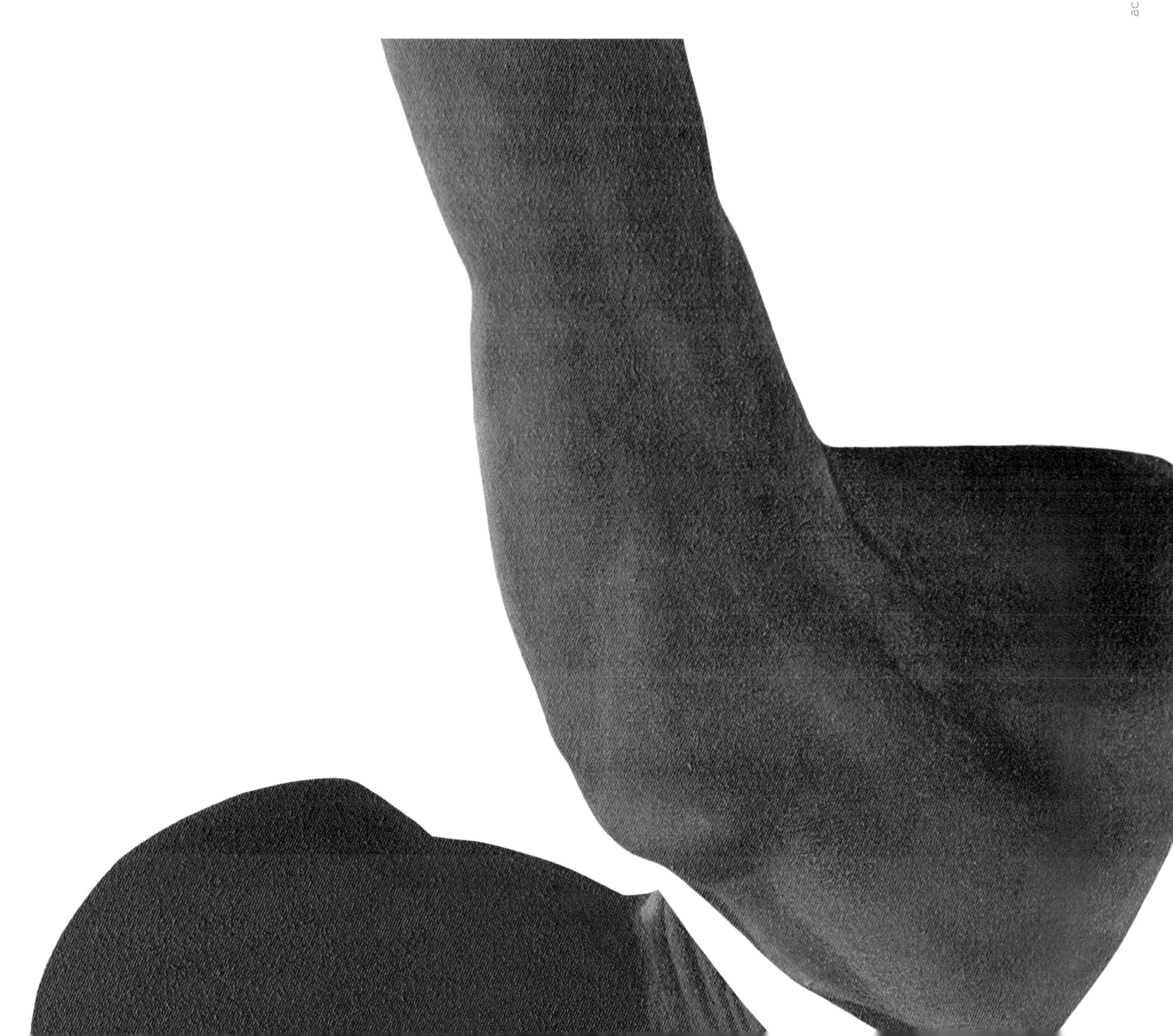

Crossroads
(detail), 2022
acrylic on canvas
150 × 200 cm

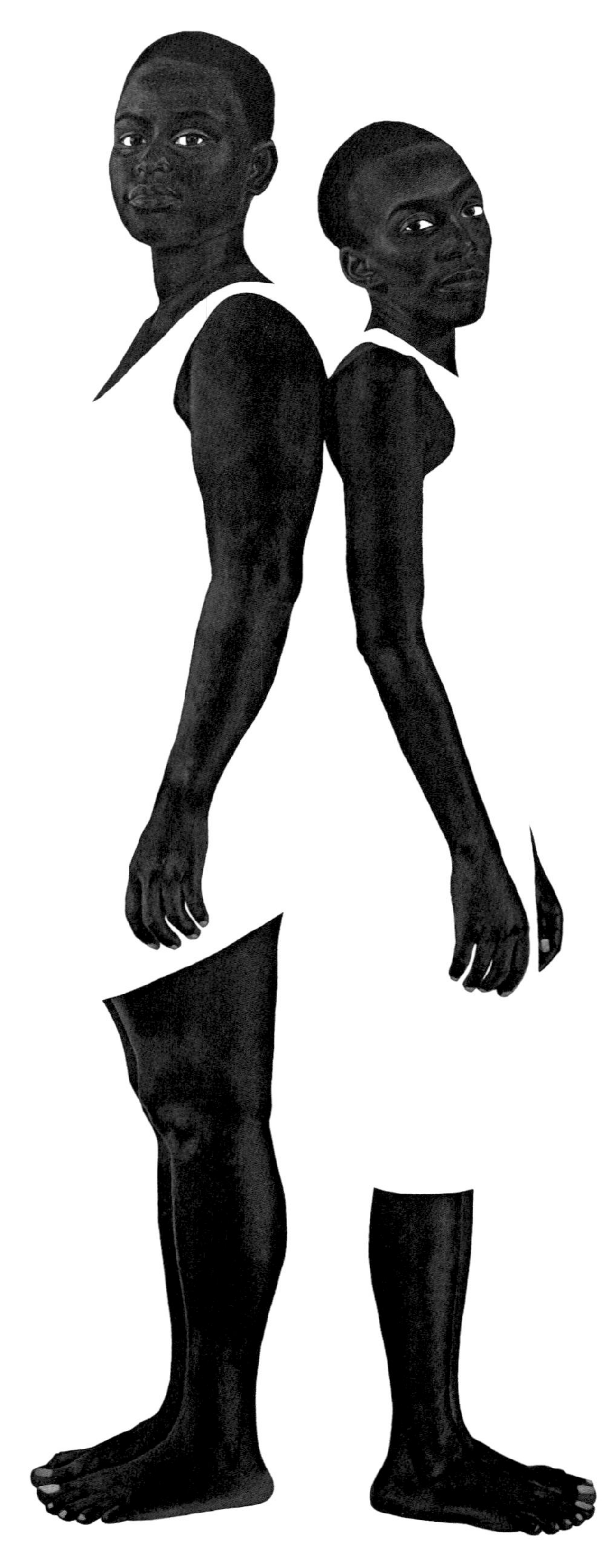

Back, 2019
acrylic on canvas
150 × 110 cm

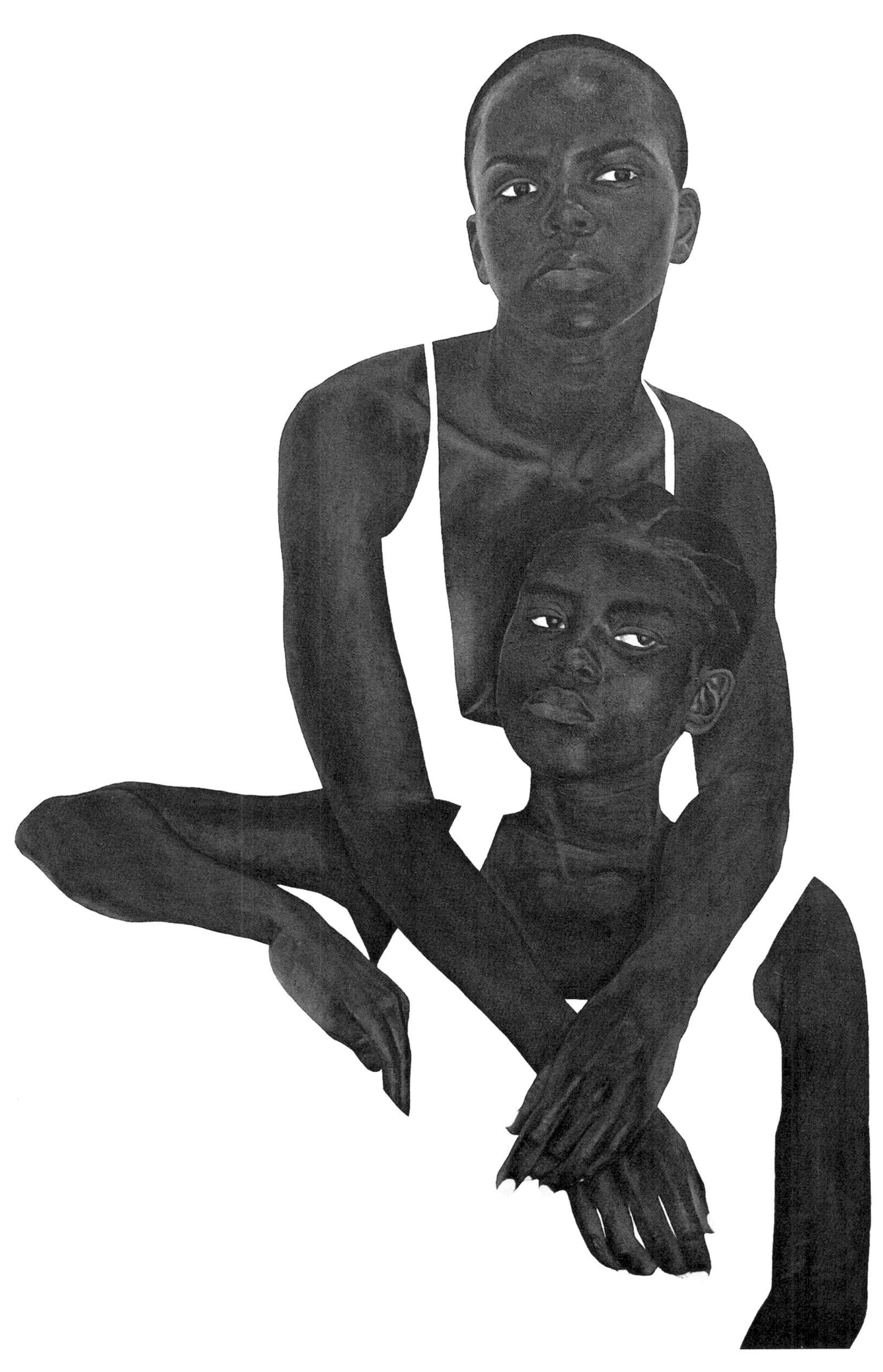

Constant III, 2019
acrylic on canvas
140 × 140 cm

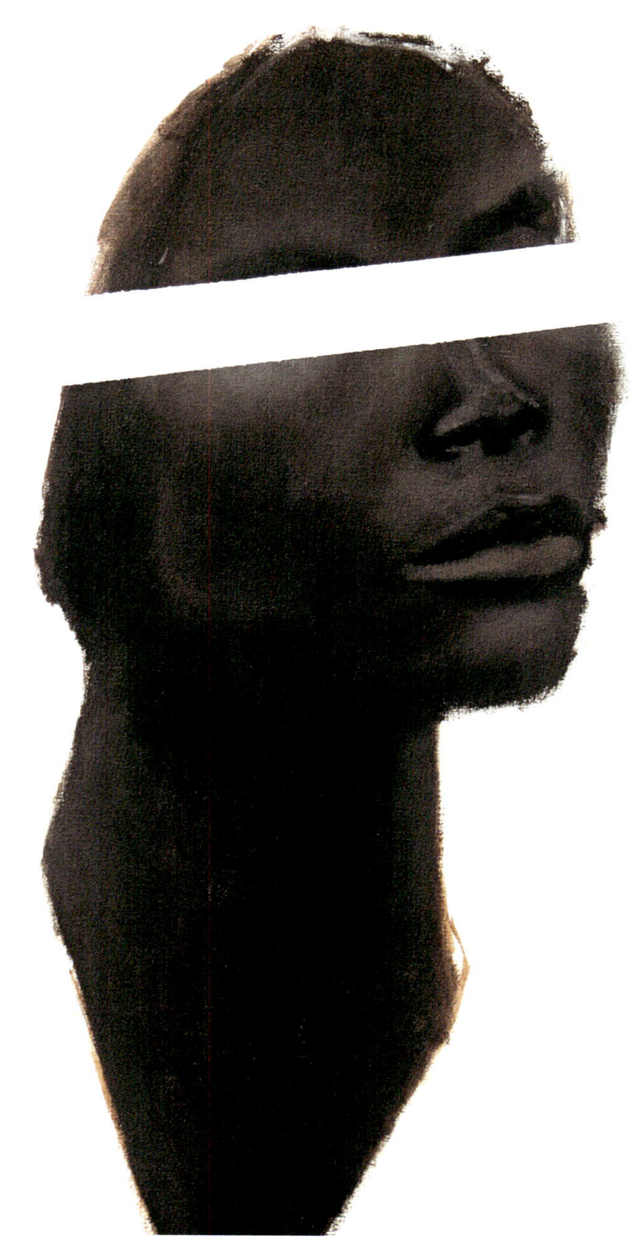

Blind, 2019
acrylic on canvas
90 × 60 cm

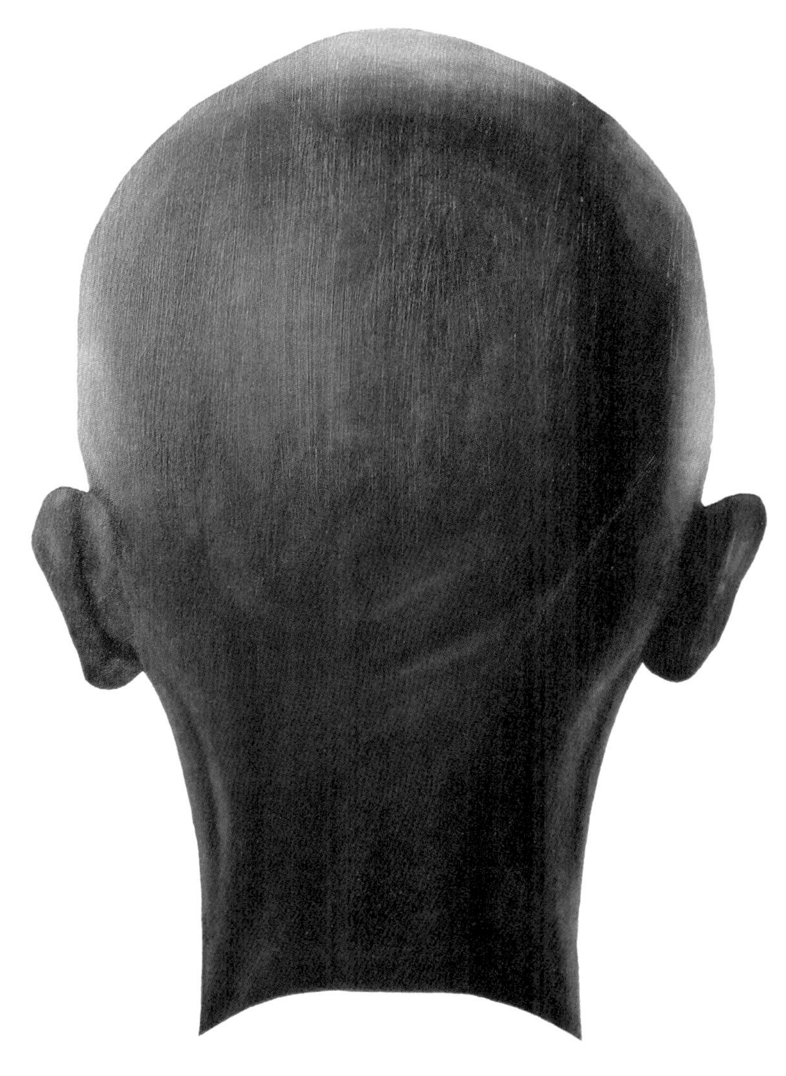

Breathless, 2019
acrylic on canvas
86 × 61 cm

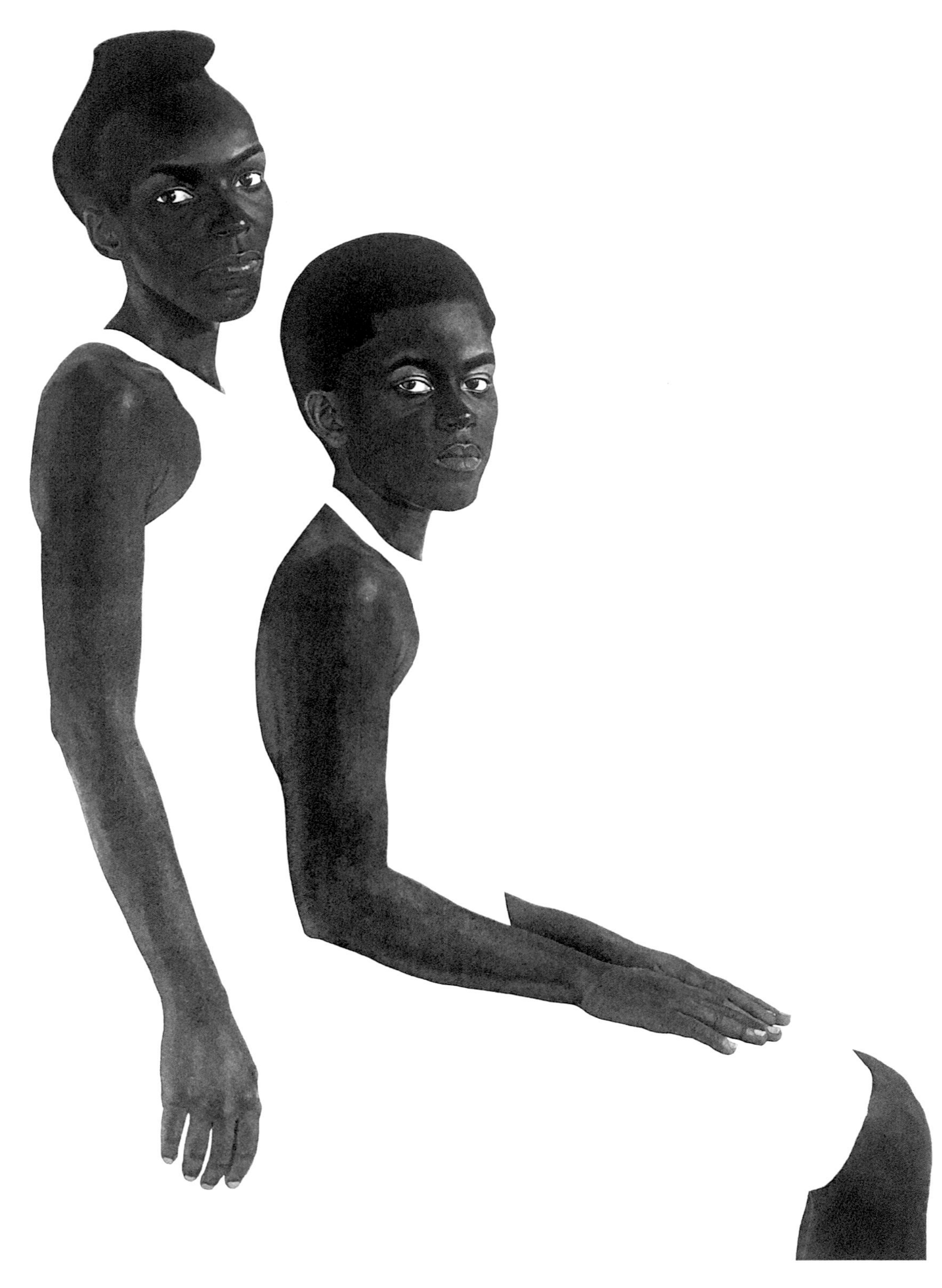

The Hems of Our Skirts, 2020
acrylic on canvas
140 × 130 cm

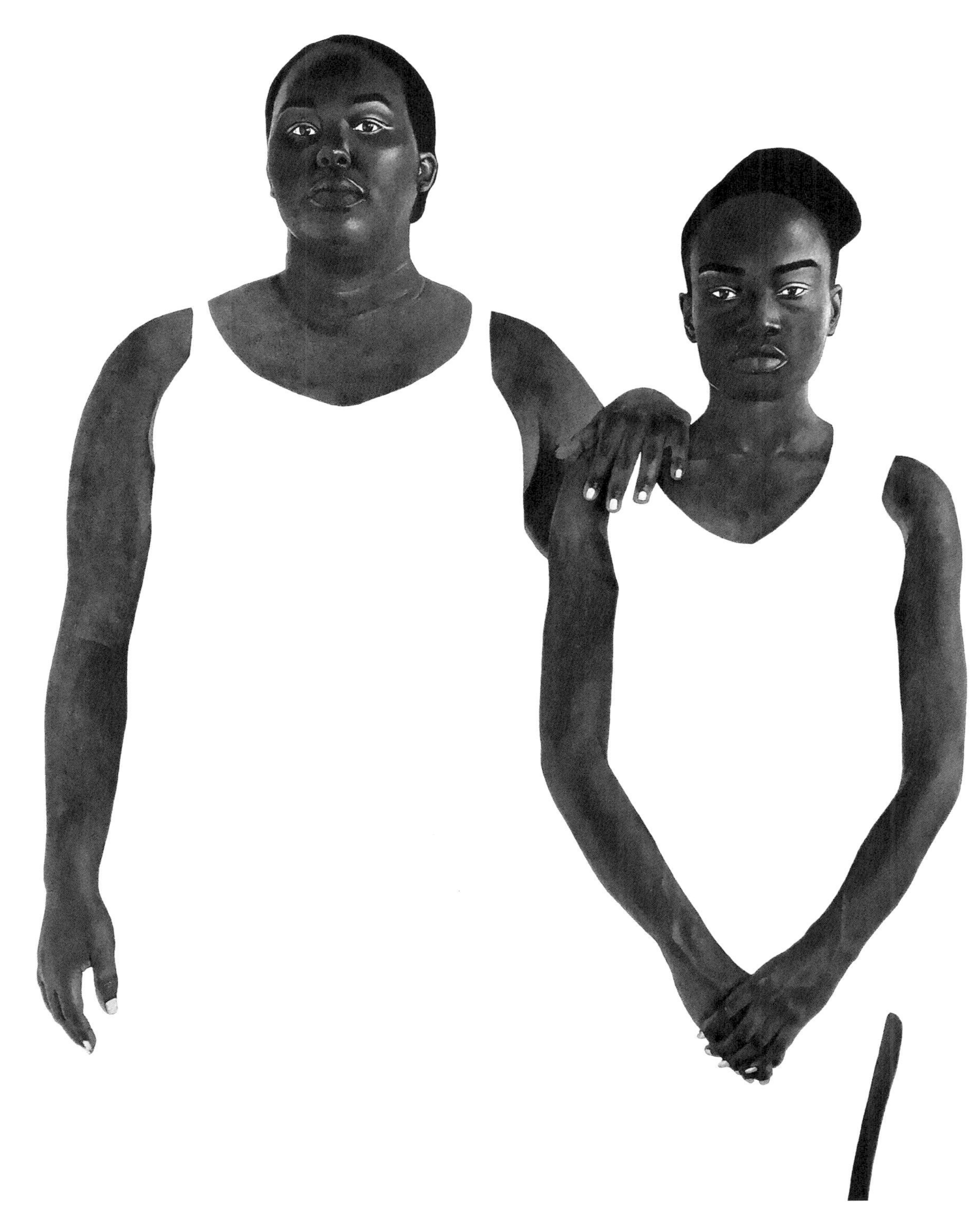

At Heart I, 2020
acrylic on canvas
140 × 130 cm

At Heart II, 2020
acrylic on canvas
140 × 130 cm

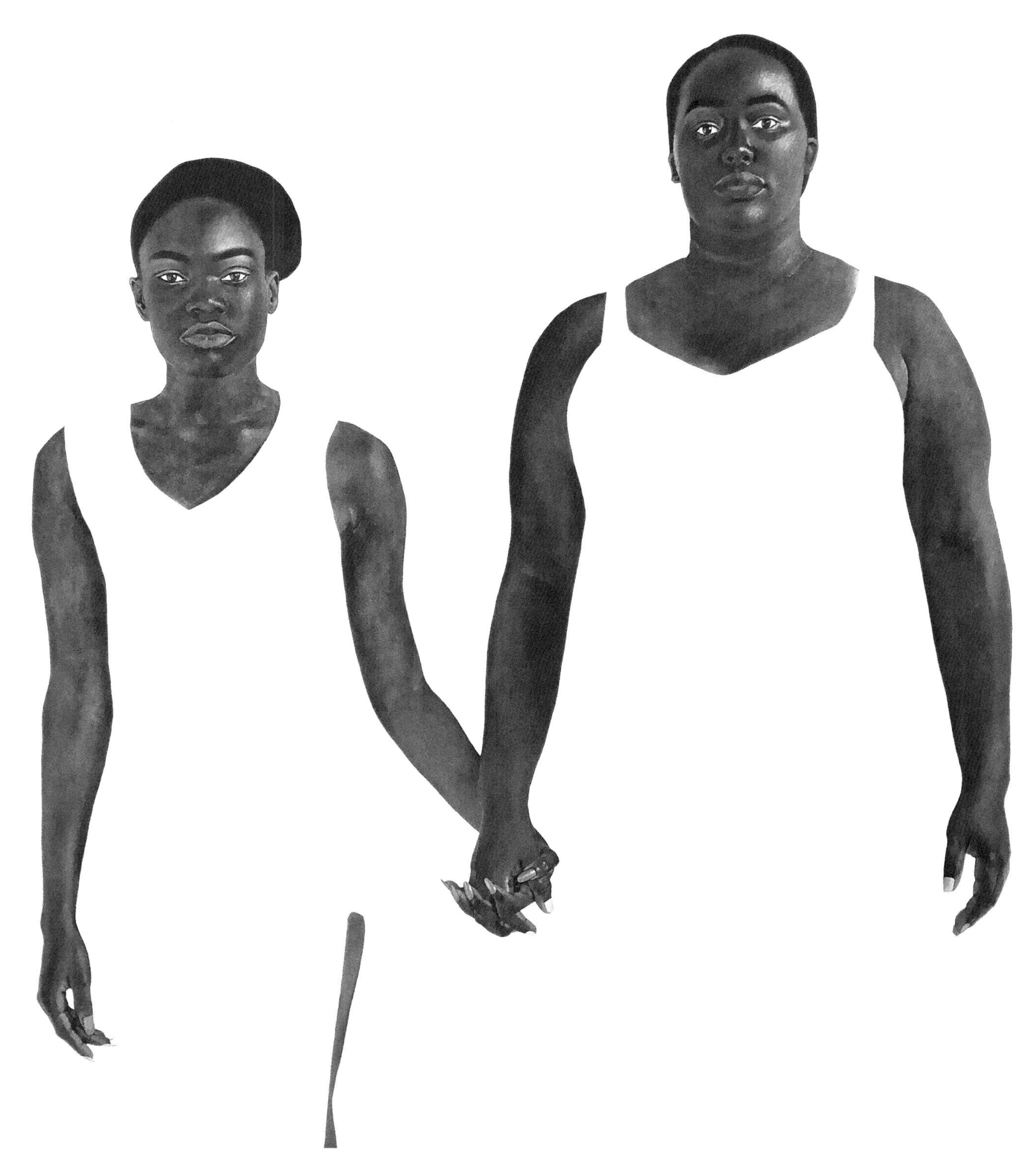

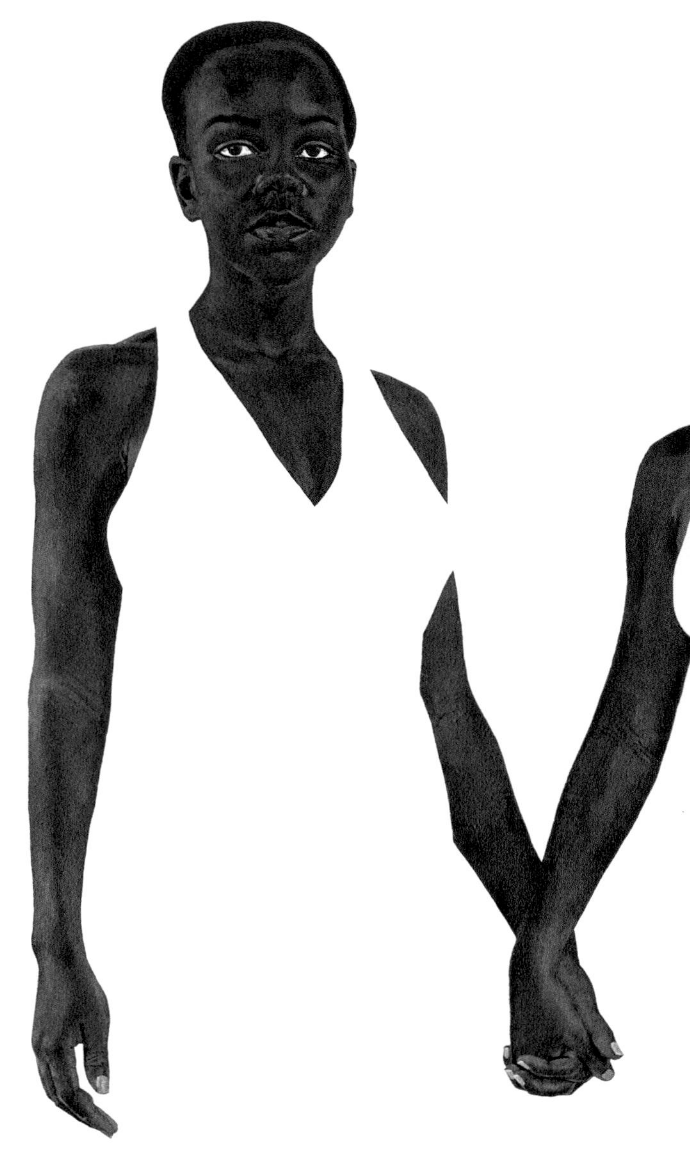
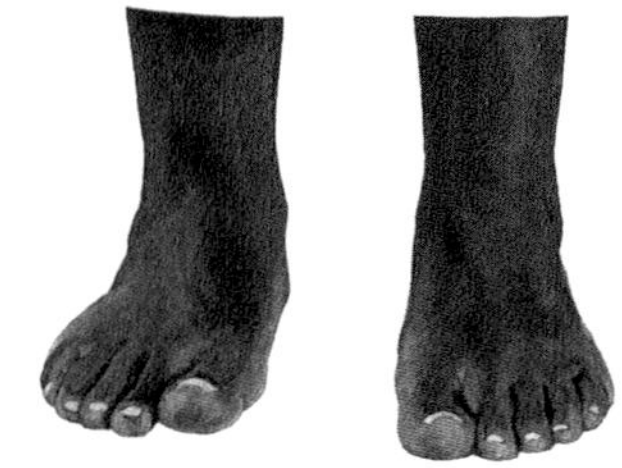

Across, 2020
acrylic on canvas
140 × 200 cm

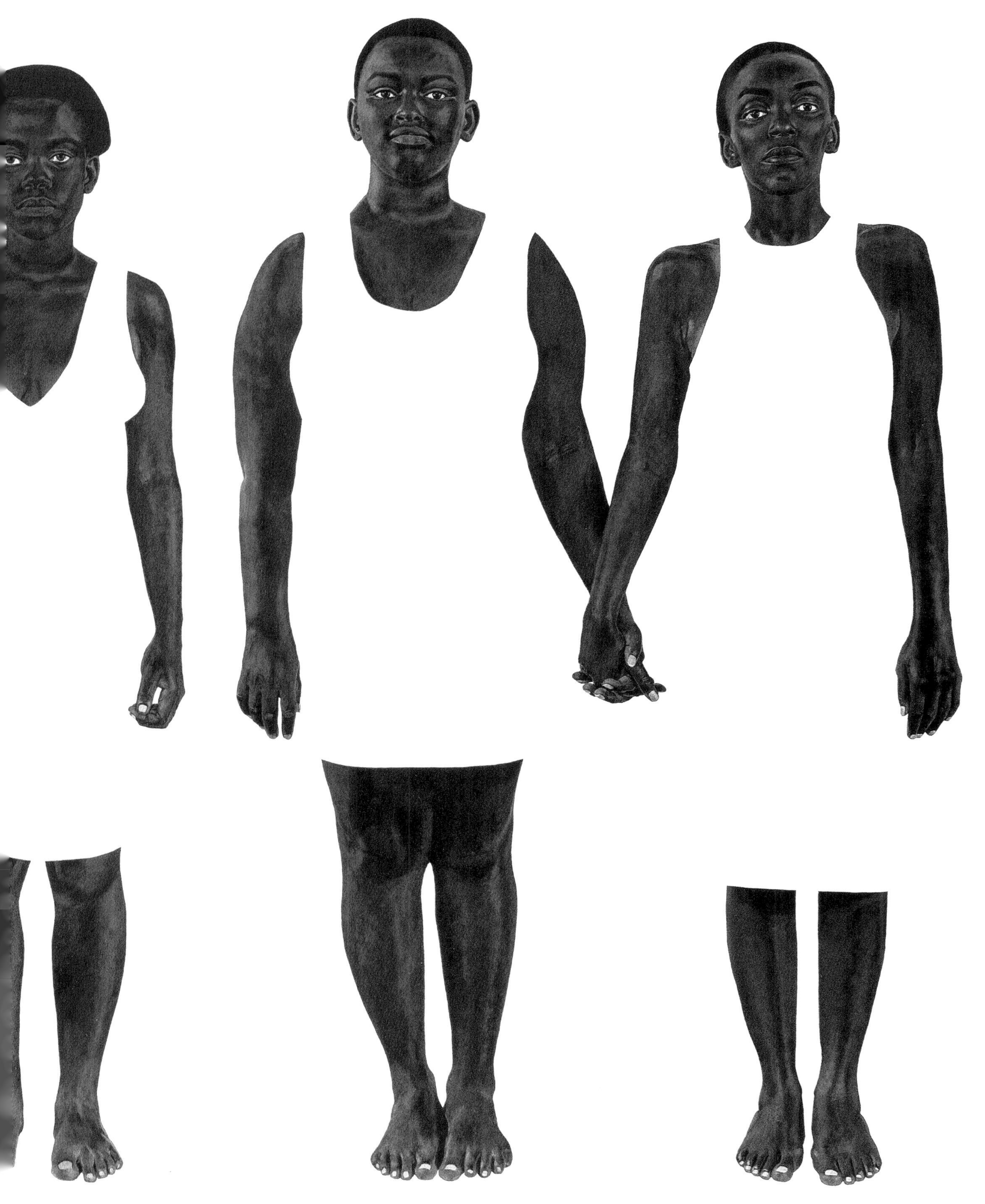

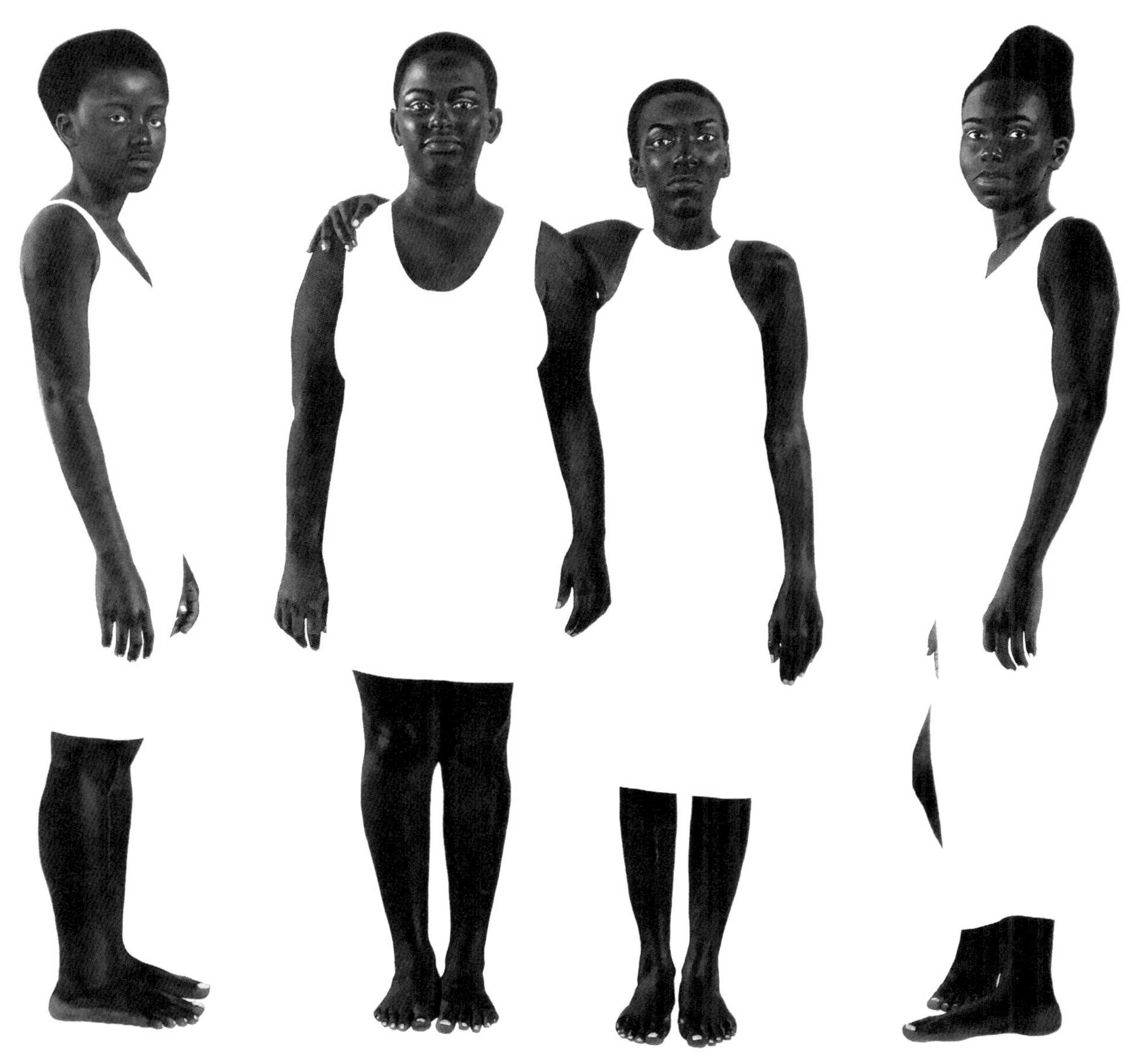

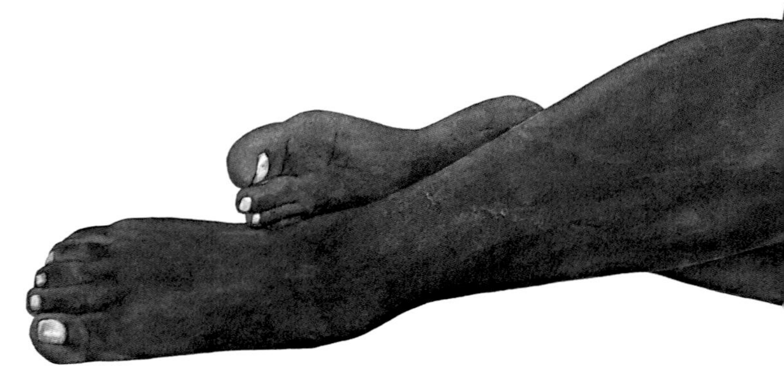

Unclench, 2020
acrylic on canvas
140 × 200 cm

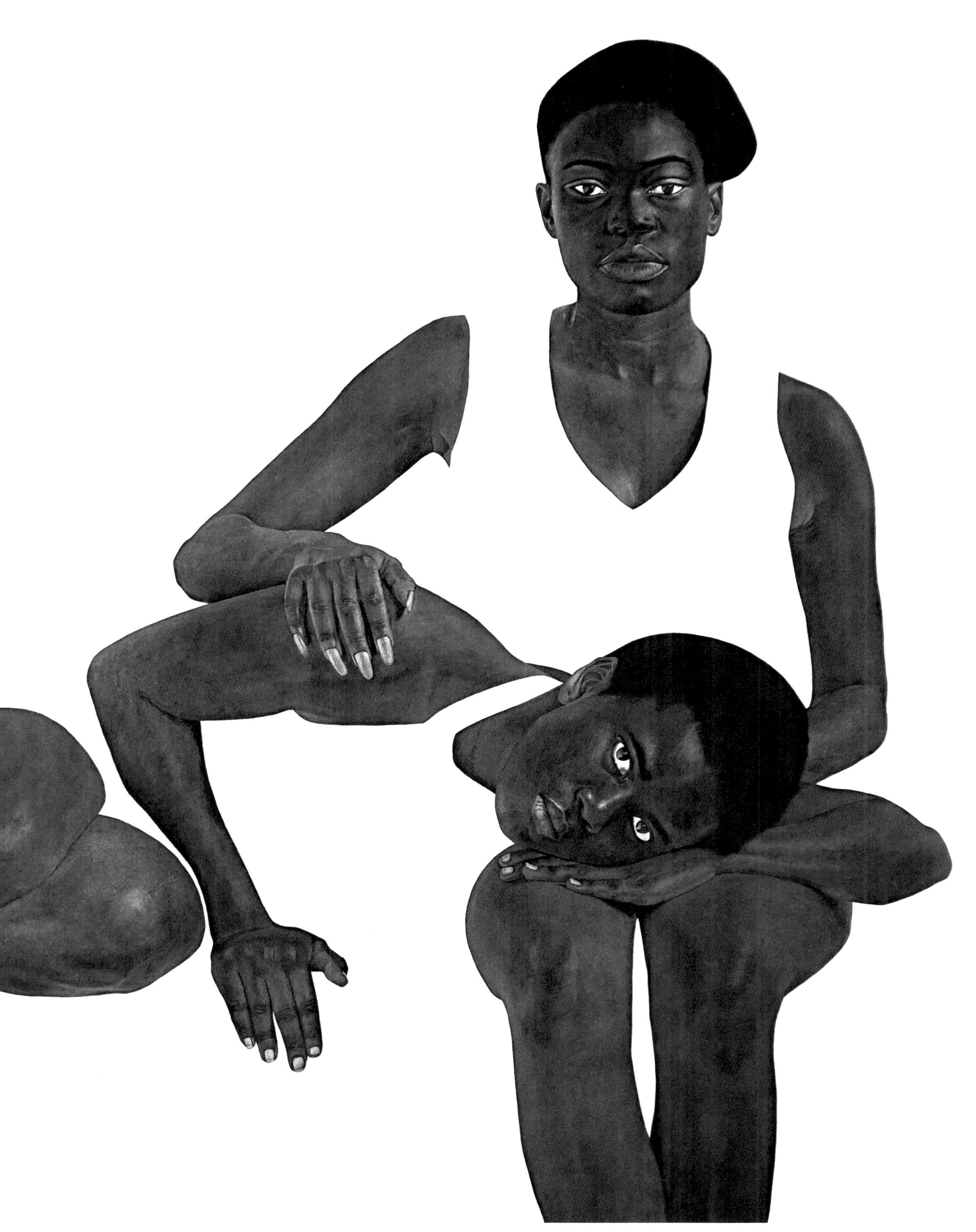

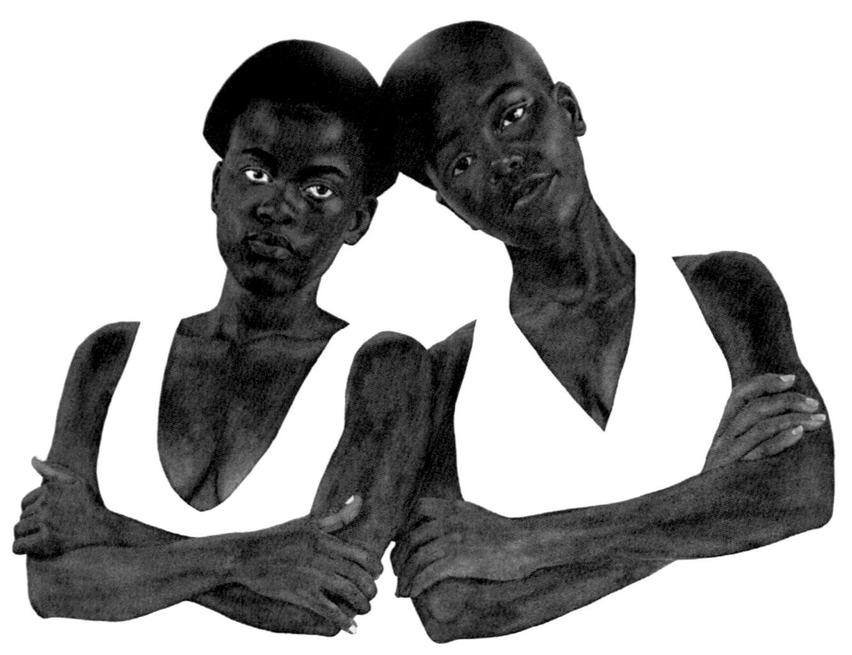

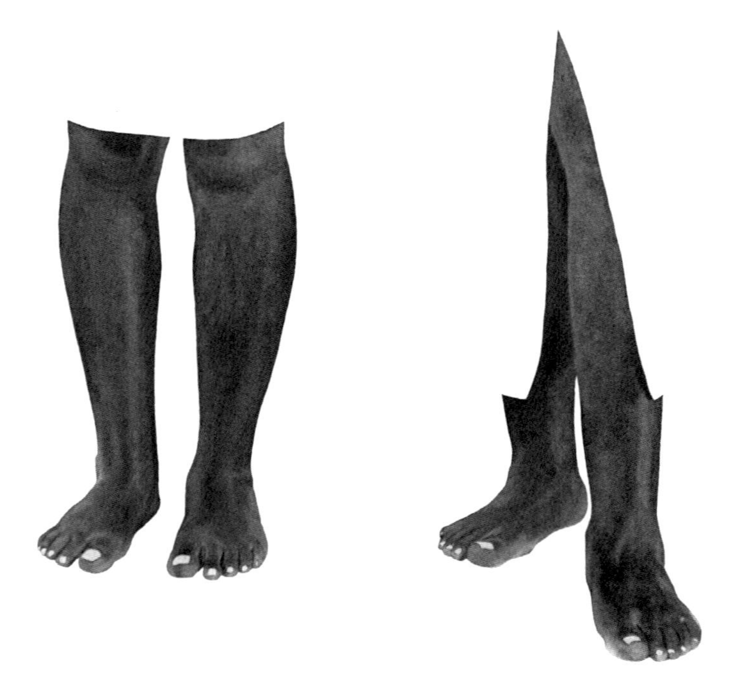

In Our Long Dress, 2020
acrylic on canvas
150 × 110 cm

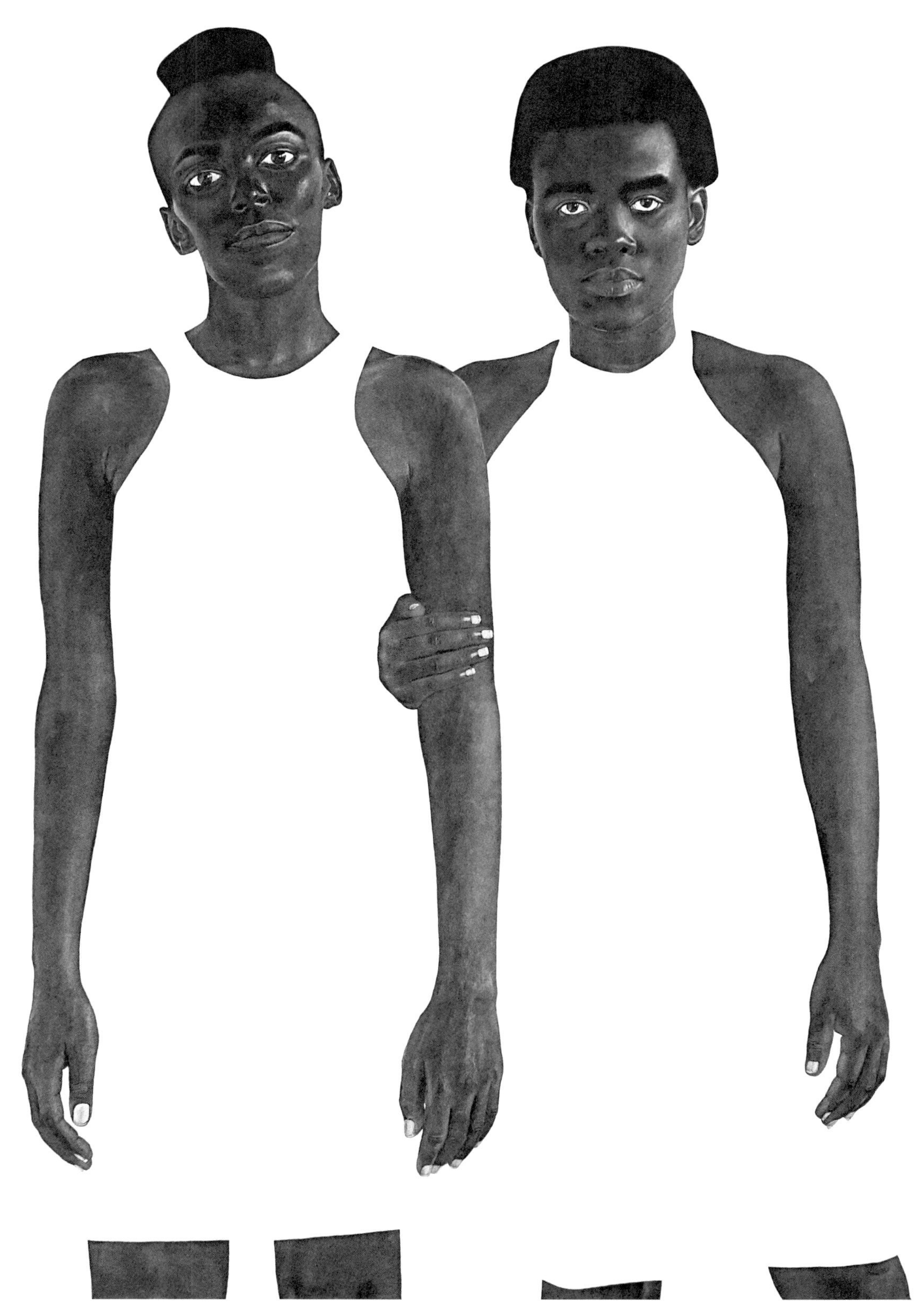

The Secrets in Our Hems, 2020
acrylic on canvas
140 × 130 cm

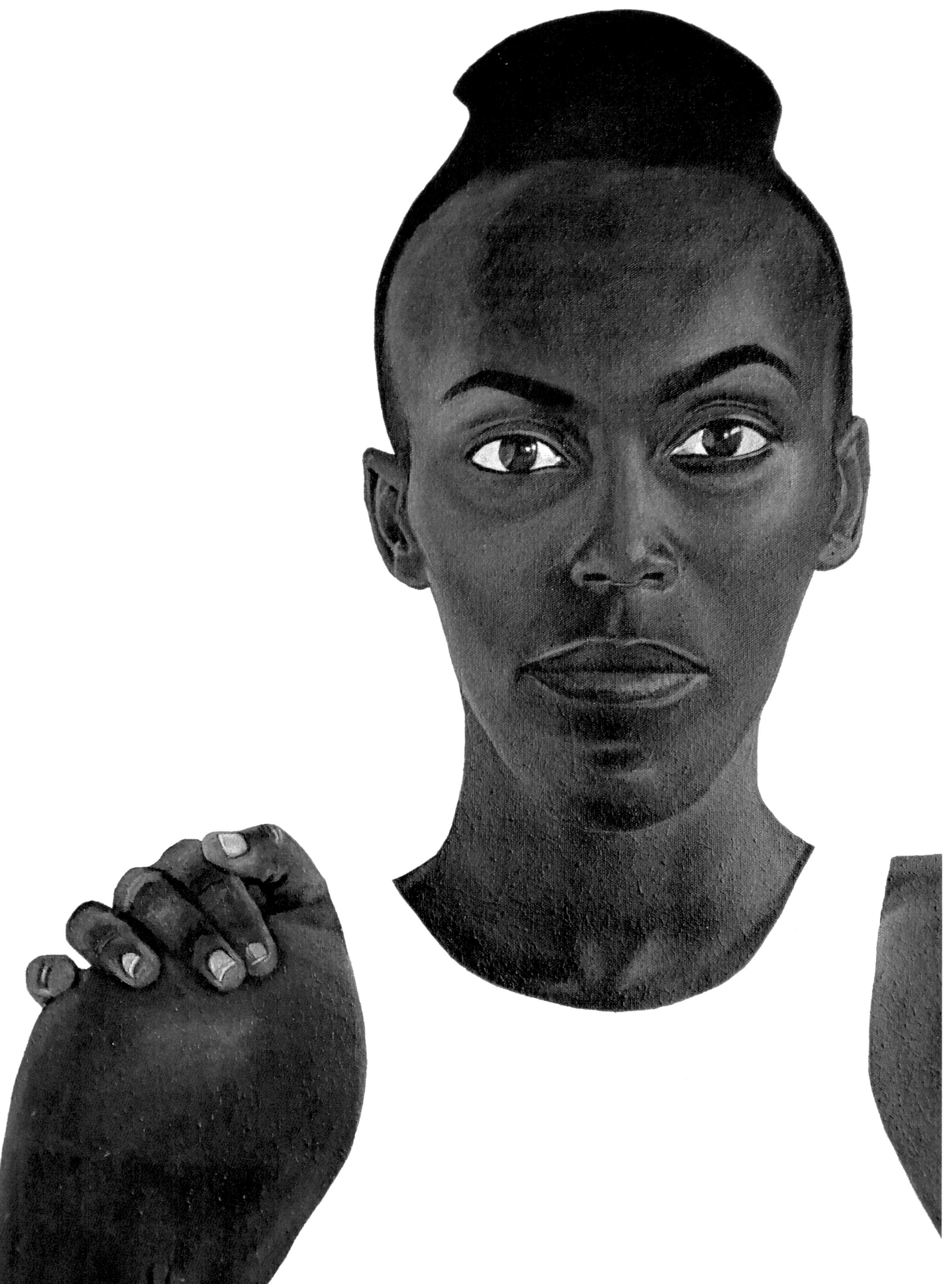

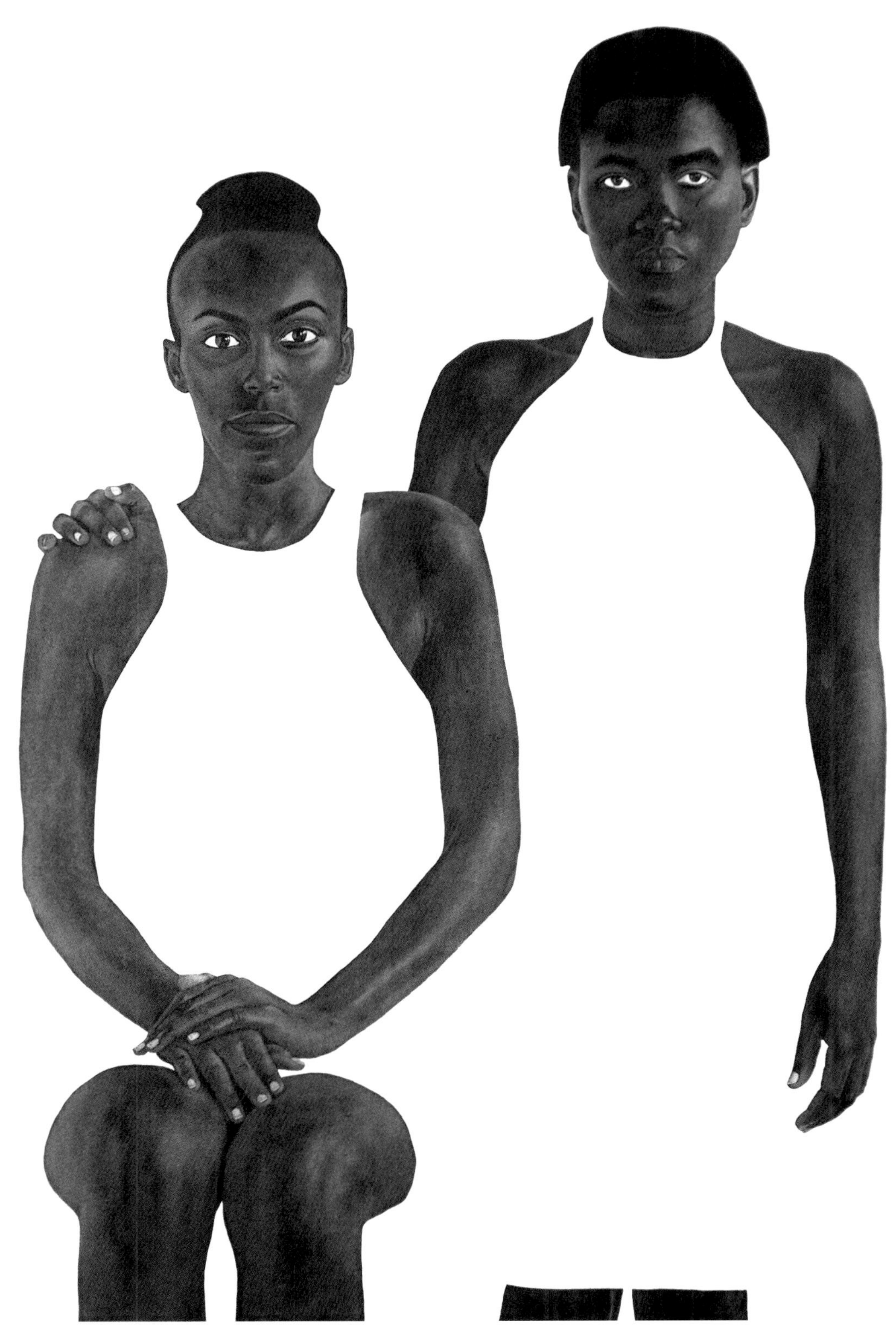

Still (detail), 2020
acrylic on canvas
140 × 130 cm

Still, 2020
acrylic on canvas
140 × 130 cm

Kyomu, 2020
acrylic on canvas
86 × 60 cm

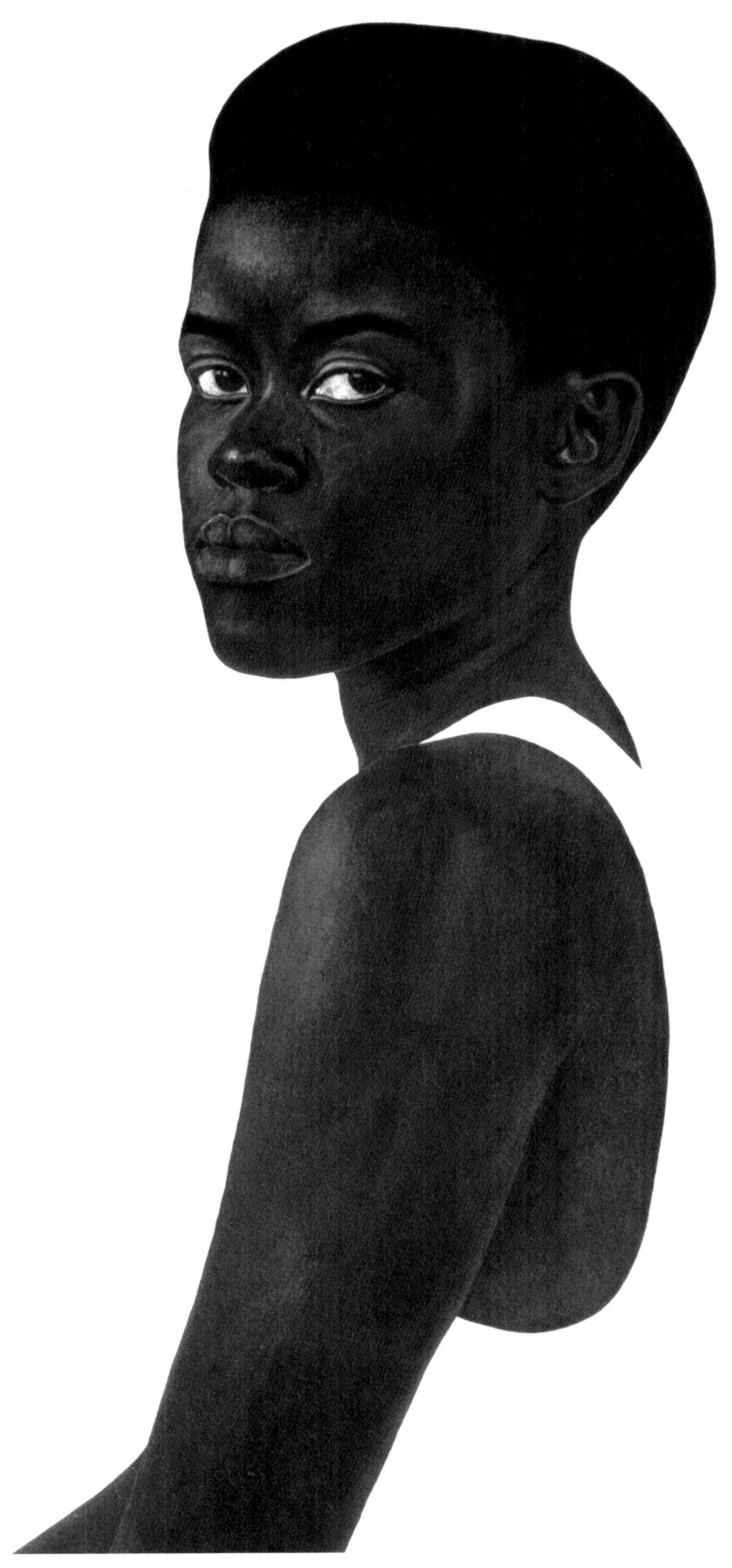

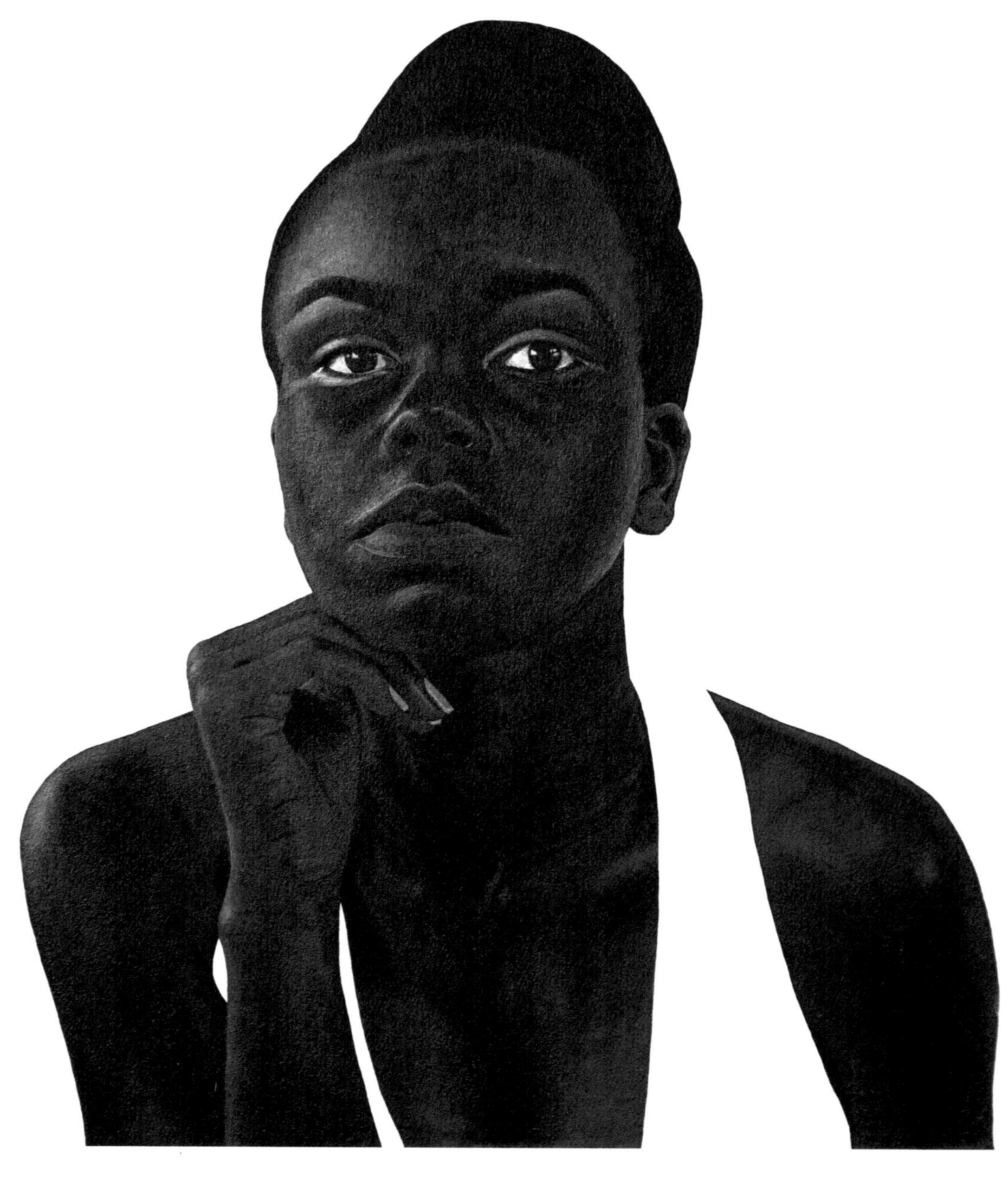

Liirwa II, 2020
acrylic on canvas
60 × 75 cm

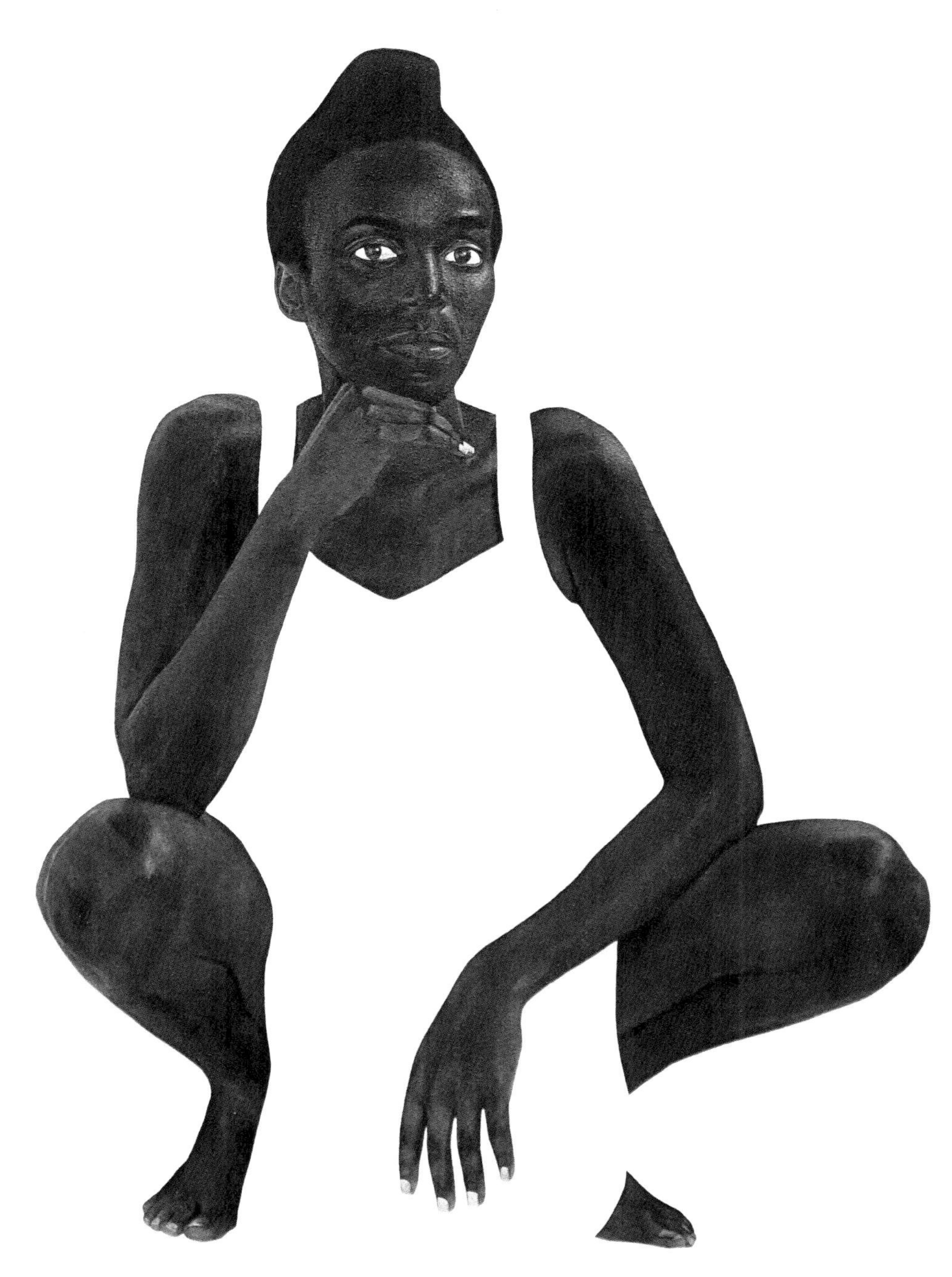

Ahueni, 2020
acrylic on canvas
150 × 140 cm

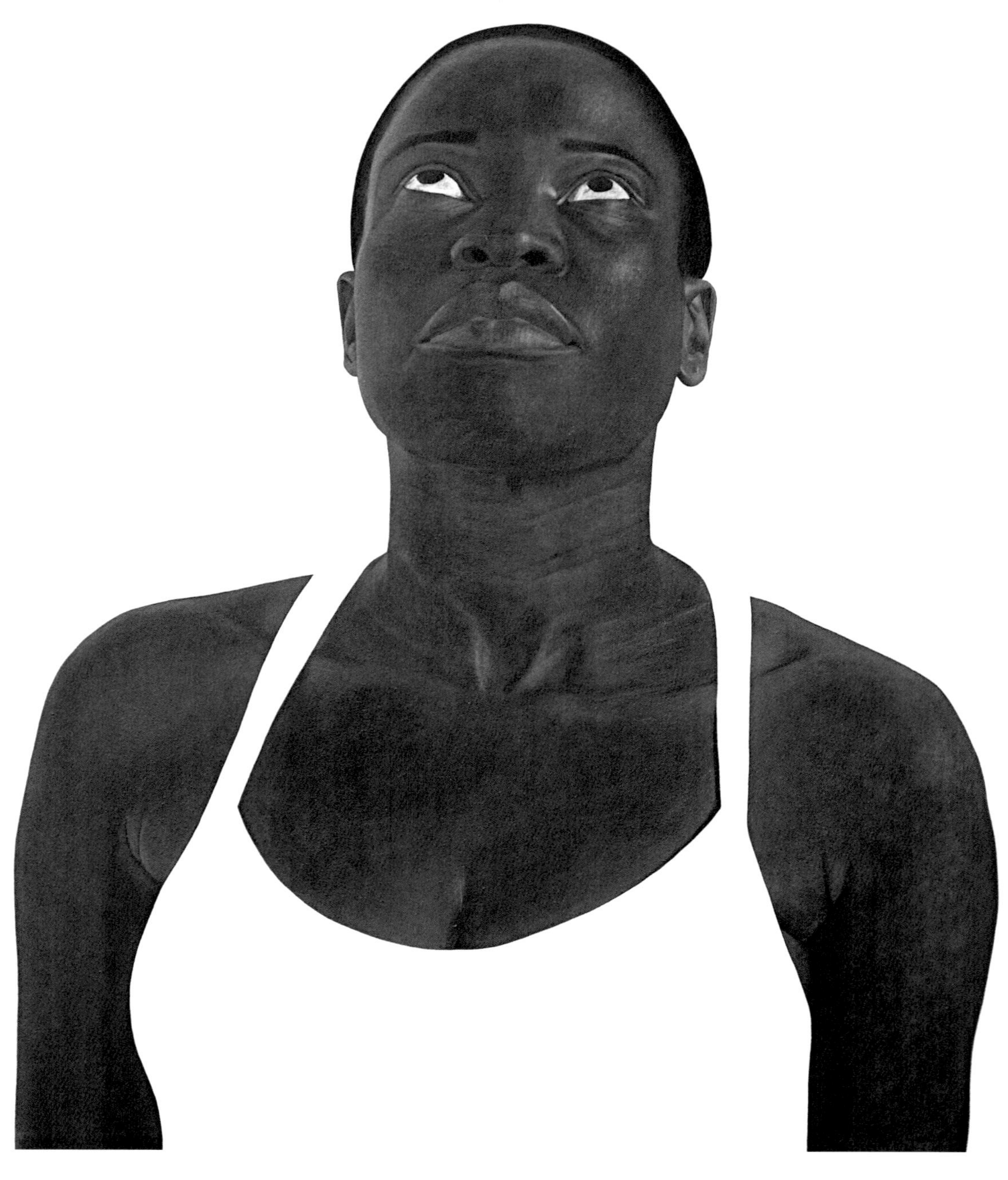

Up, 2020
acrylic on canvas
140 × 130 cm

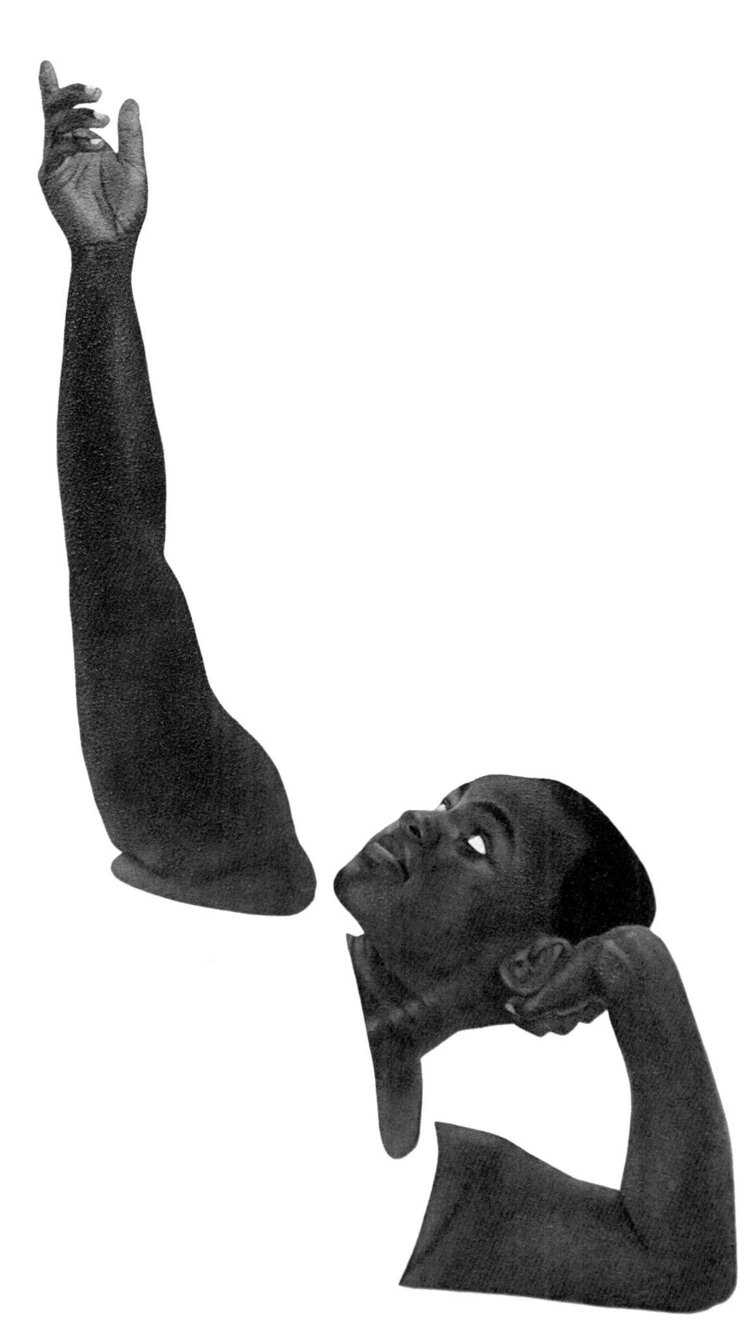
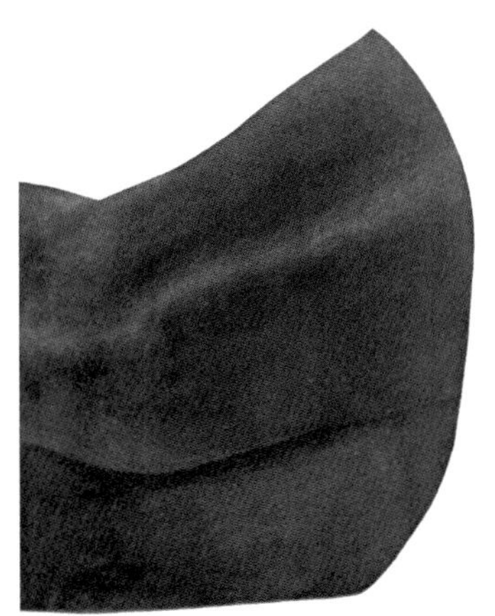

Ascend, 2020
acrylic on canvas
150 × 140 cm

Kaa, 2020
acrylic on canvas
140 × 130 cm

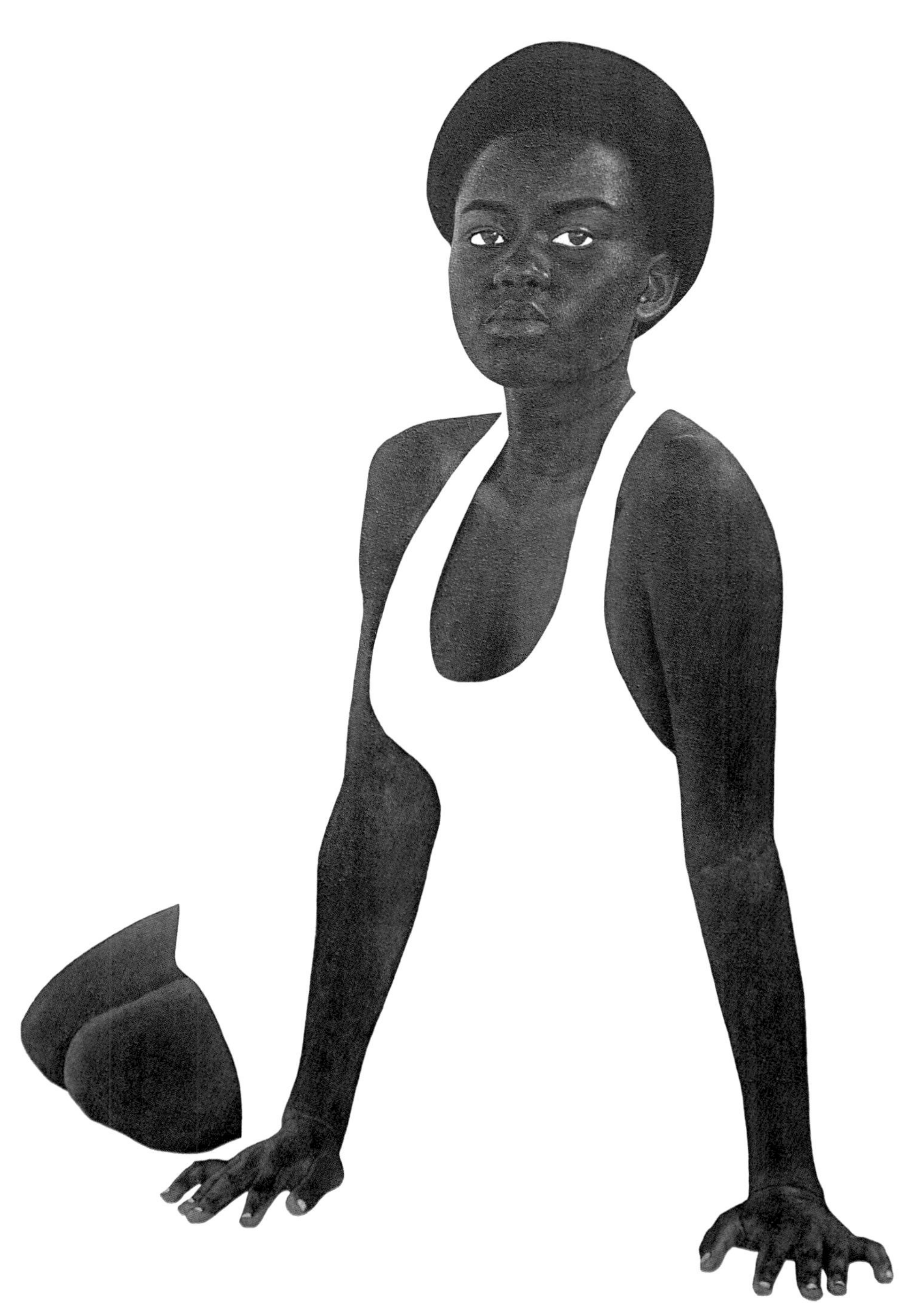

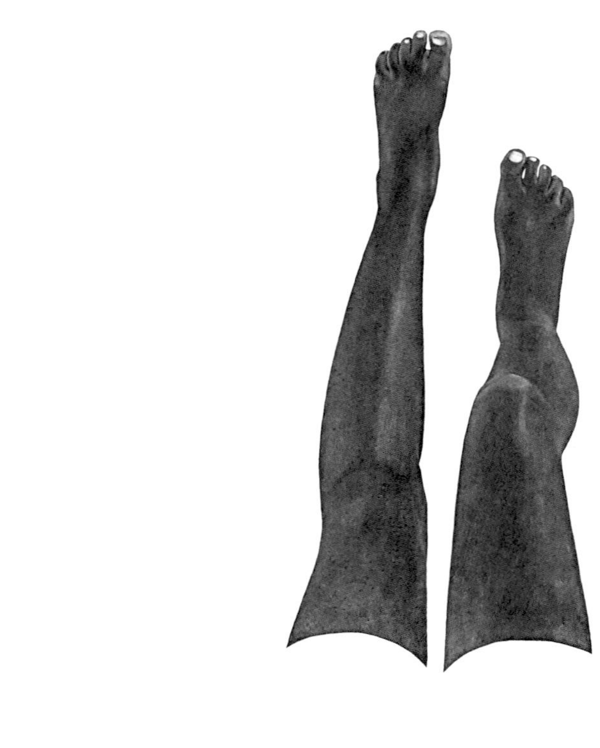
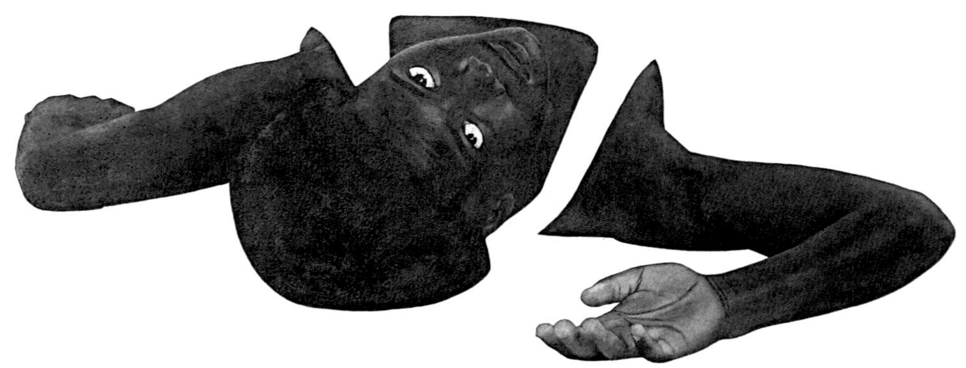

Molten, 2020
acrylic on canvas
150 × 140 cm

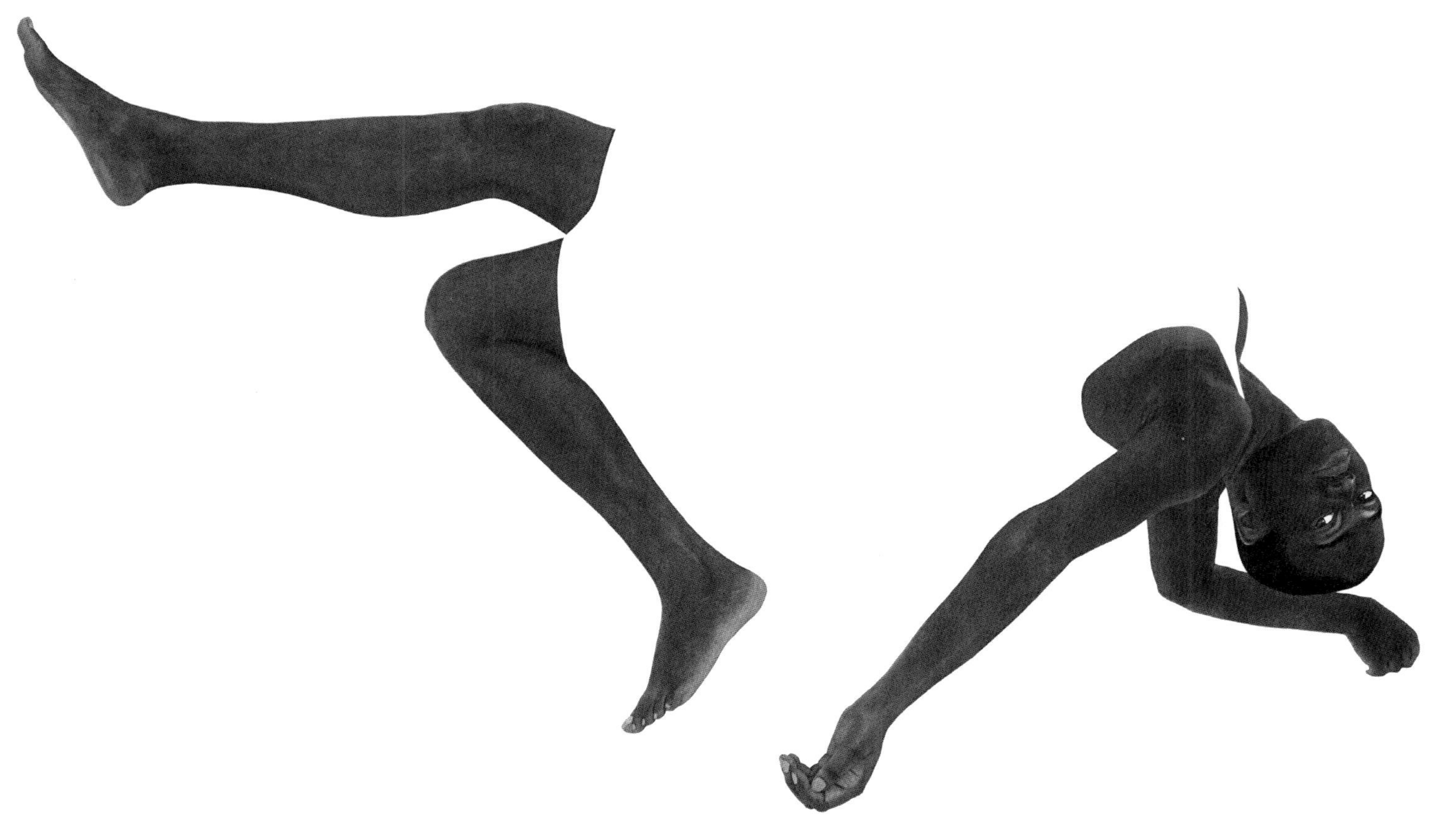

Precontemplation, 2020
acrylic on canvas
140 × 200 cm

Sungi Mlengeya's painting *Ruka* is an ideal work for an academic
museum. Not only is it an exercise in the art of painting through its
capture of the subtleties of skin tone and refined engagement of
negative space, it also evokes the field of dance. How does an artist
depict movement in a still medium like painting? The stark contrast
between the positive space of the dancer's body and the negative space
of her clothing, melded seamlessly into the background, creates
a visual vibration and bounces the viewers' eyes across the canvas.
In 2020, former professors Sara Guyer and Scott Straus inspired
the Chazen Museum of Art, University of Wisconsin–Madison to form
a collection of contemporary art – the "Contemporary African Art
Initiative" – to promote the relationship between the university and the
African continent and to stimulate growth in the arts on campus.
Acquisitions were primarily funded through the generosity of the Straus
Family Foundation and supplemented by the Chazen's Seefried
Horsfall Endowment Fund. In consultation with the director, Amy Gilman,
I selected works by artists of different ages and educational
backgrounds from across Africa. In forming the collection, we sought to
demonstrate the breadth of African creativity in multiple mediums
during the last decade. Many of the works we acquired speak not just
of specific African stories but also of universal narratives to which
our students may relate. Mlengeya often uses friends and family as her
models. This particular painting not only captures the palpable sense
of 'dance', it also documents her personal lived experience and vibrant
circle of support.
Margaret Nagawa, a Ugandan artist and curator currently based in
Atlanta, Georgia, curated an exhibition at the Chazen in fall 2023.
She placed *Ruka* right at the start, a fitting place for a promising artist in
the field of contemporary painting.

Katherine Alcauskas, Chief Curator
Chazen Museum of Art, University of Wisconsin–Madison

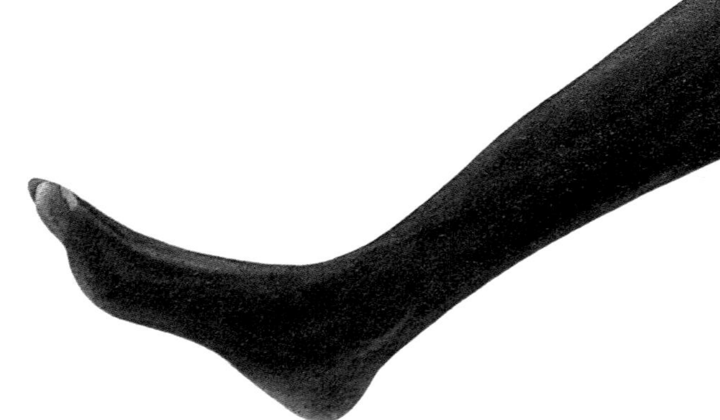

Ruka, 2021
acrylic on canvas
140 × 200 cm

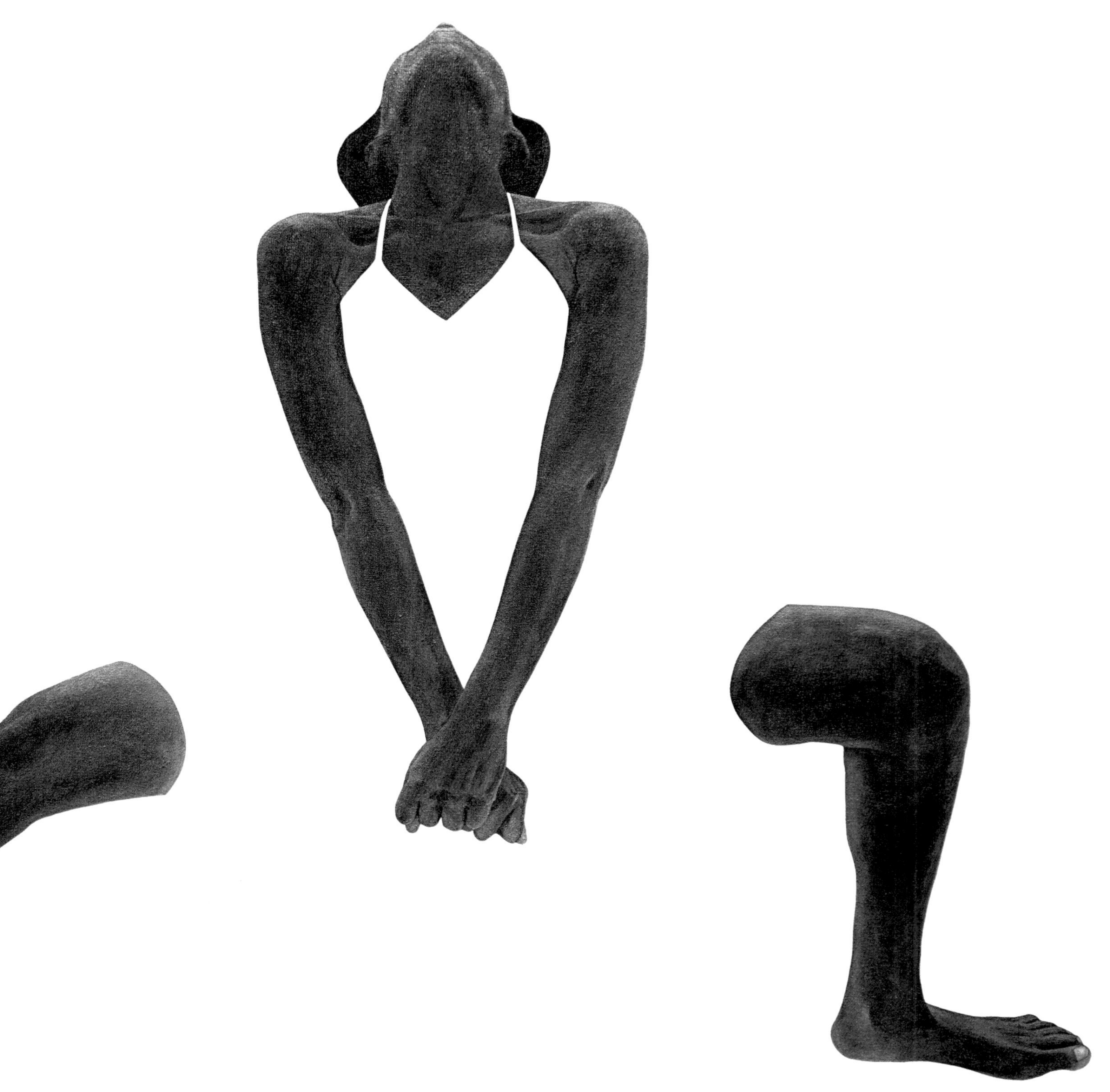

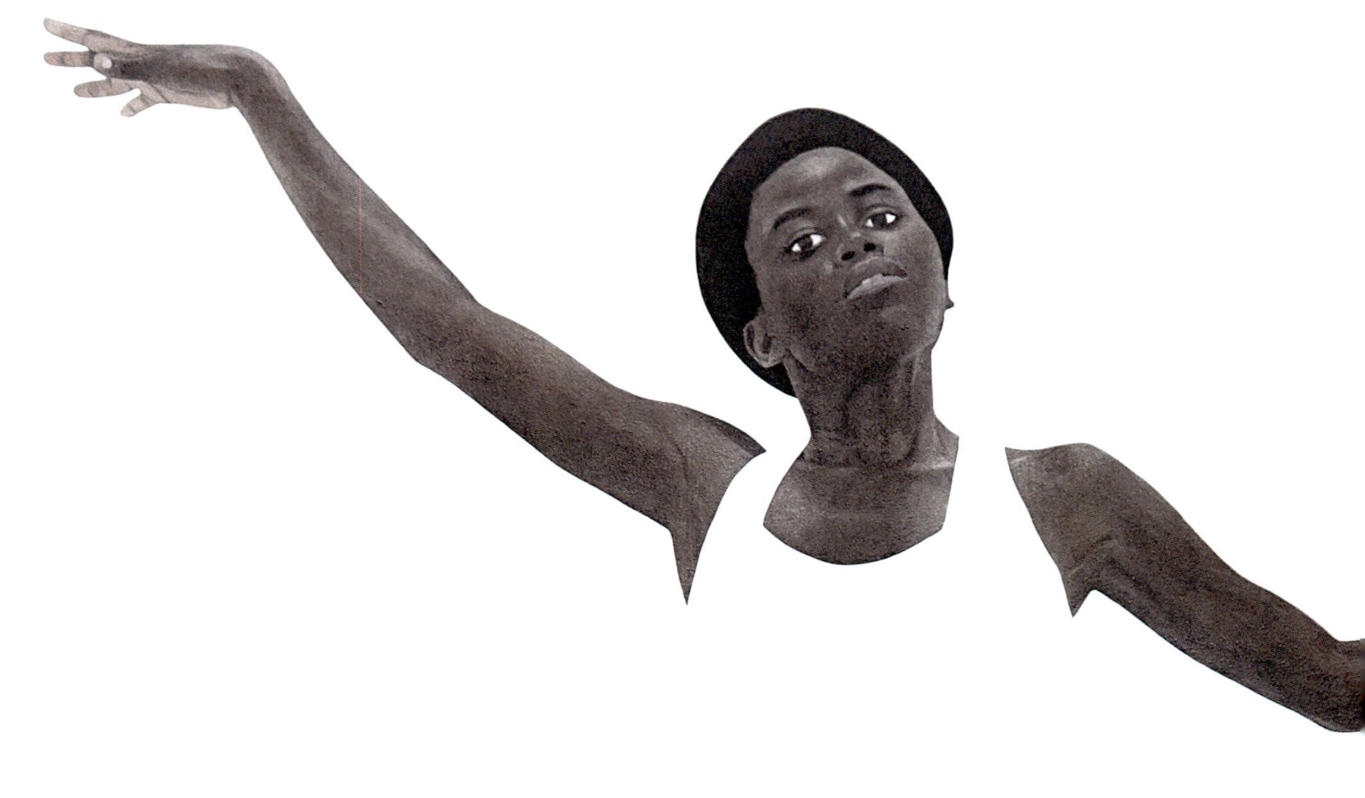
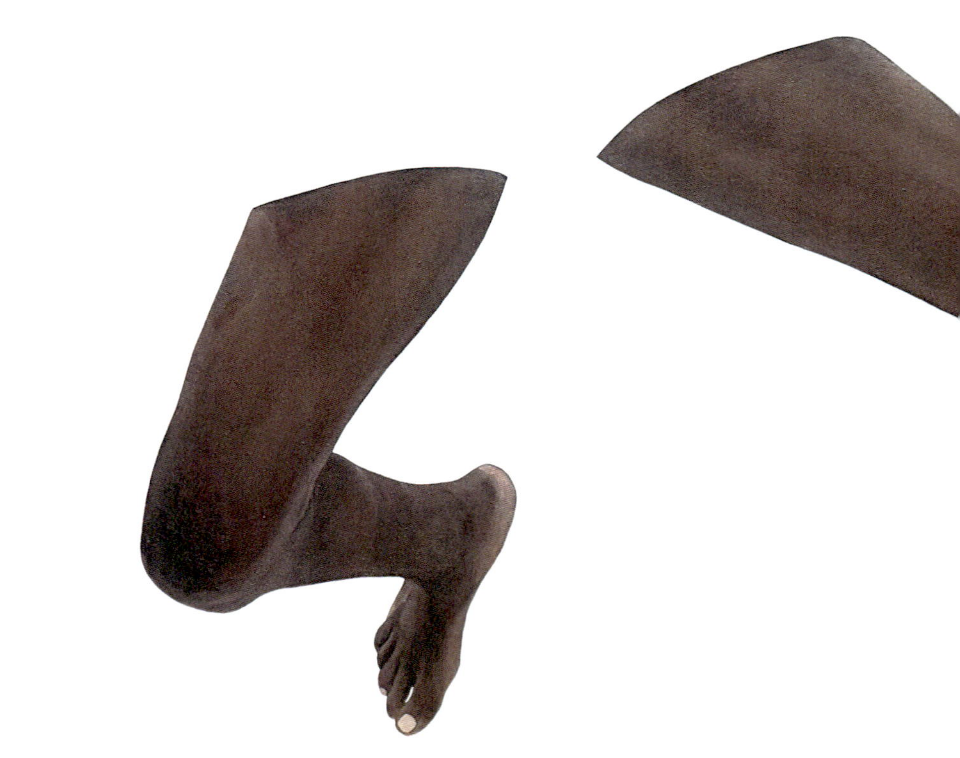

Huru, 2021
acrylic on canvas
150 × 200 cm

Dance, 2021
acrylic on canvas
150 × 140 cm

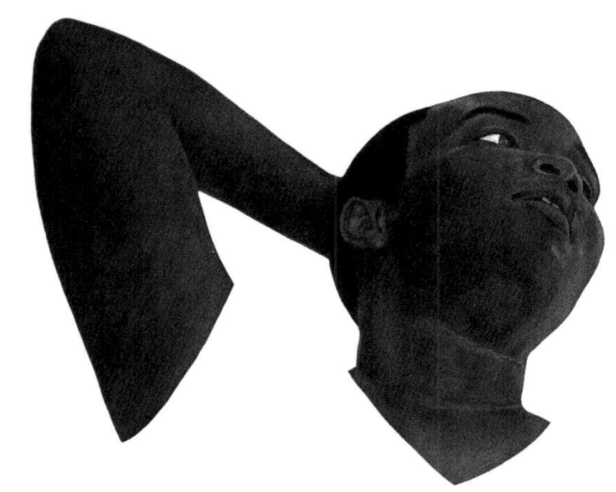

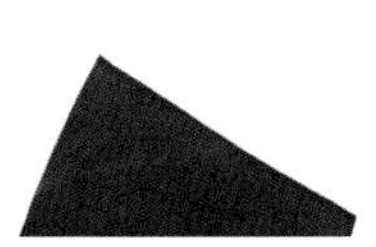

Mafeelings, 2021
acrylic on canvas
150 × 140 cm

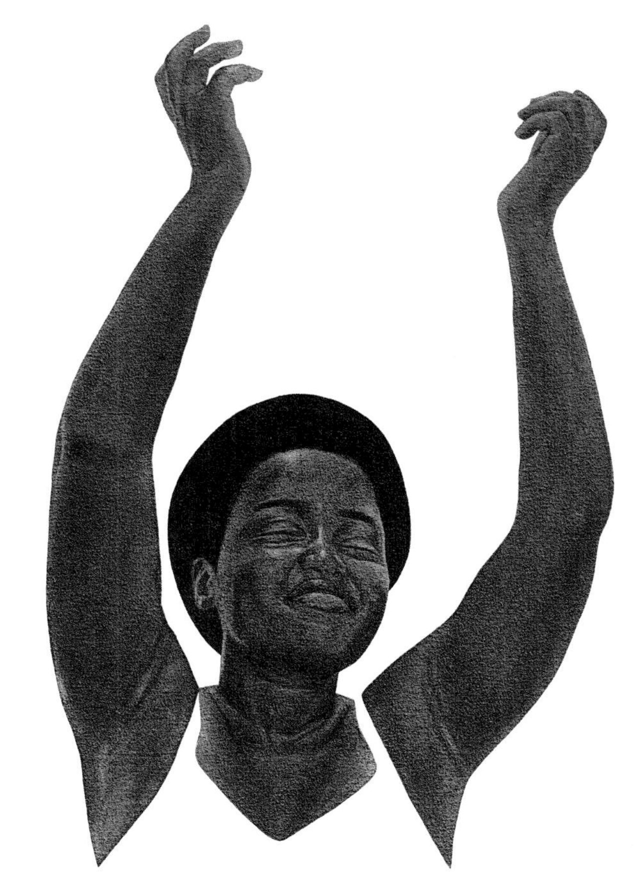

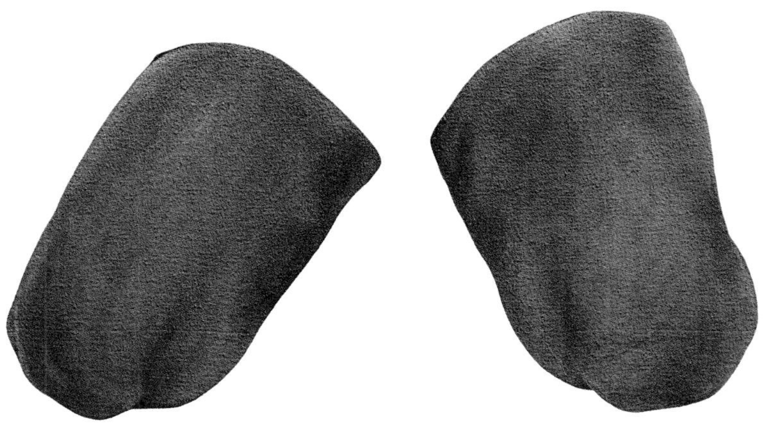

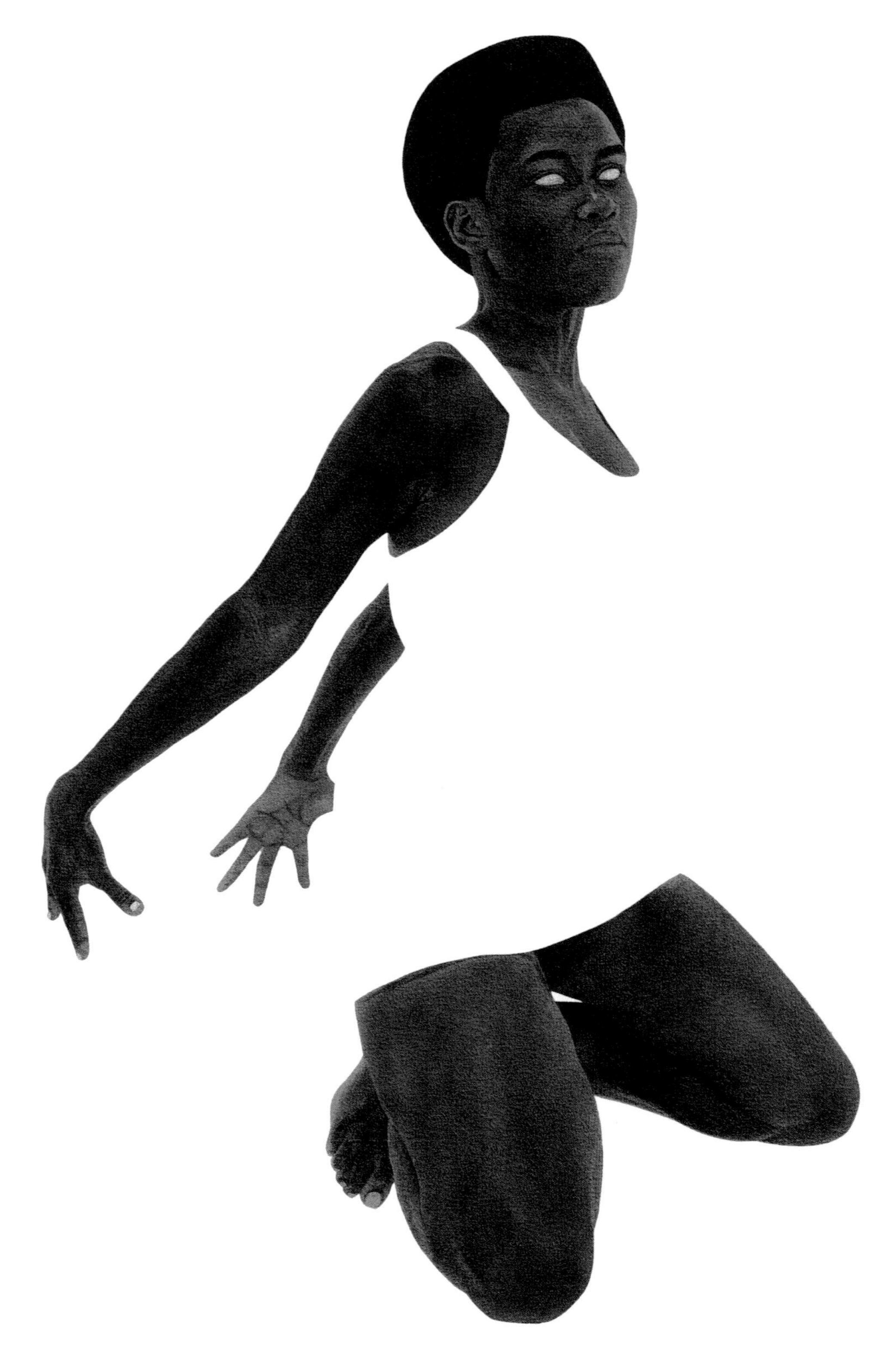

Ngoma, 2021
acrylic on canvas
150 × 200 cm

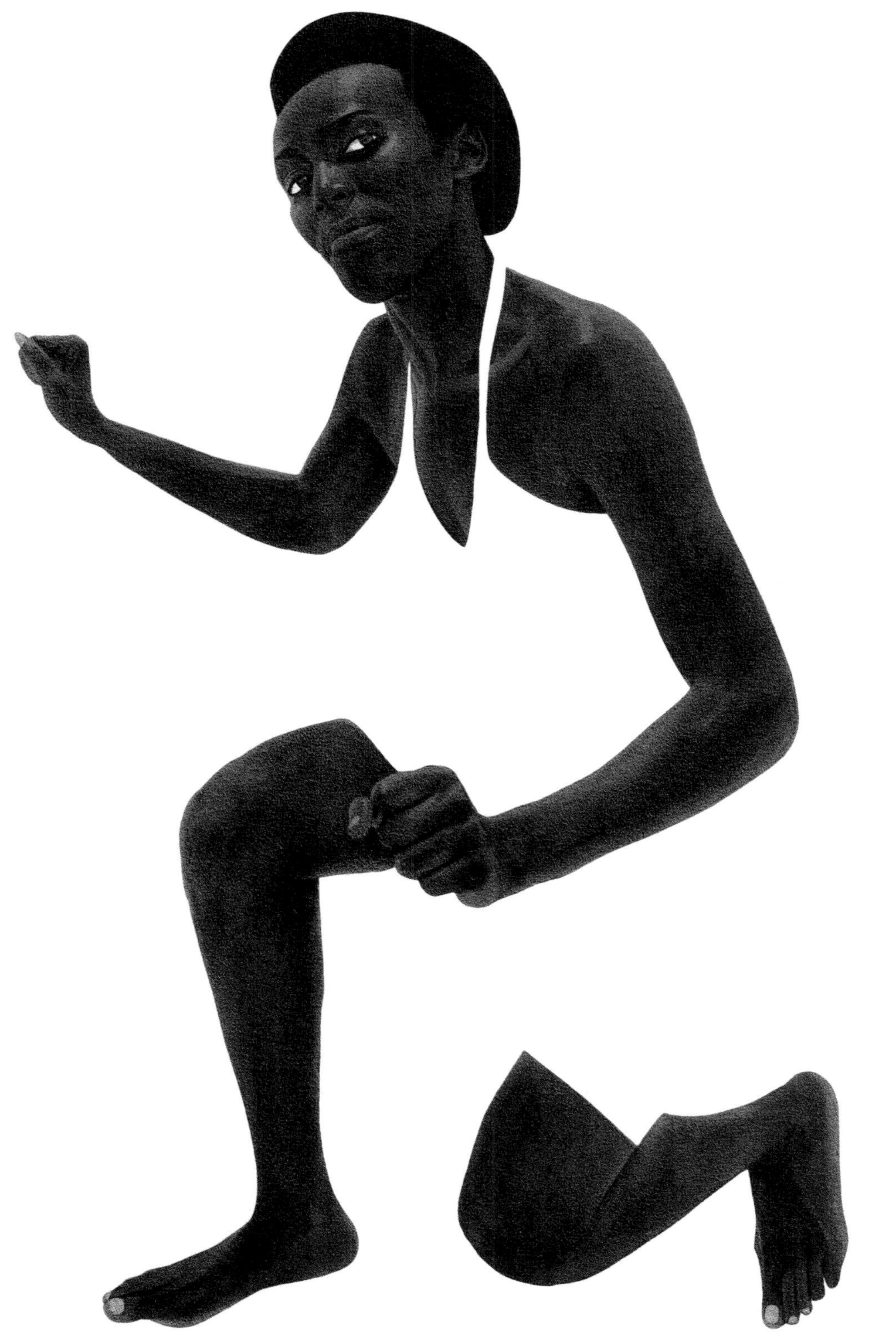

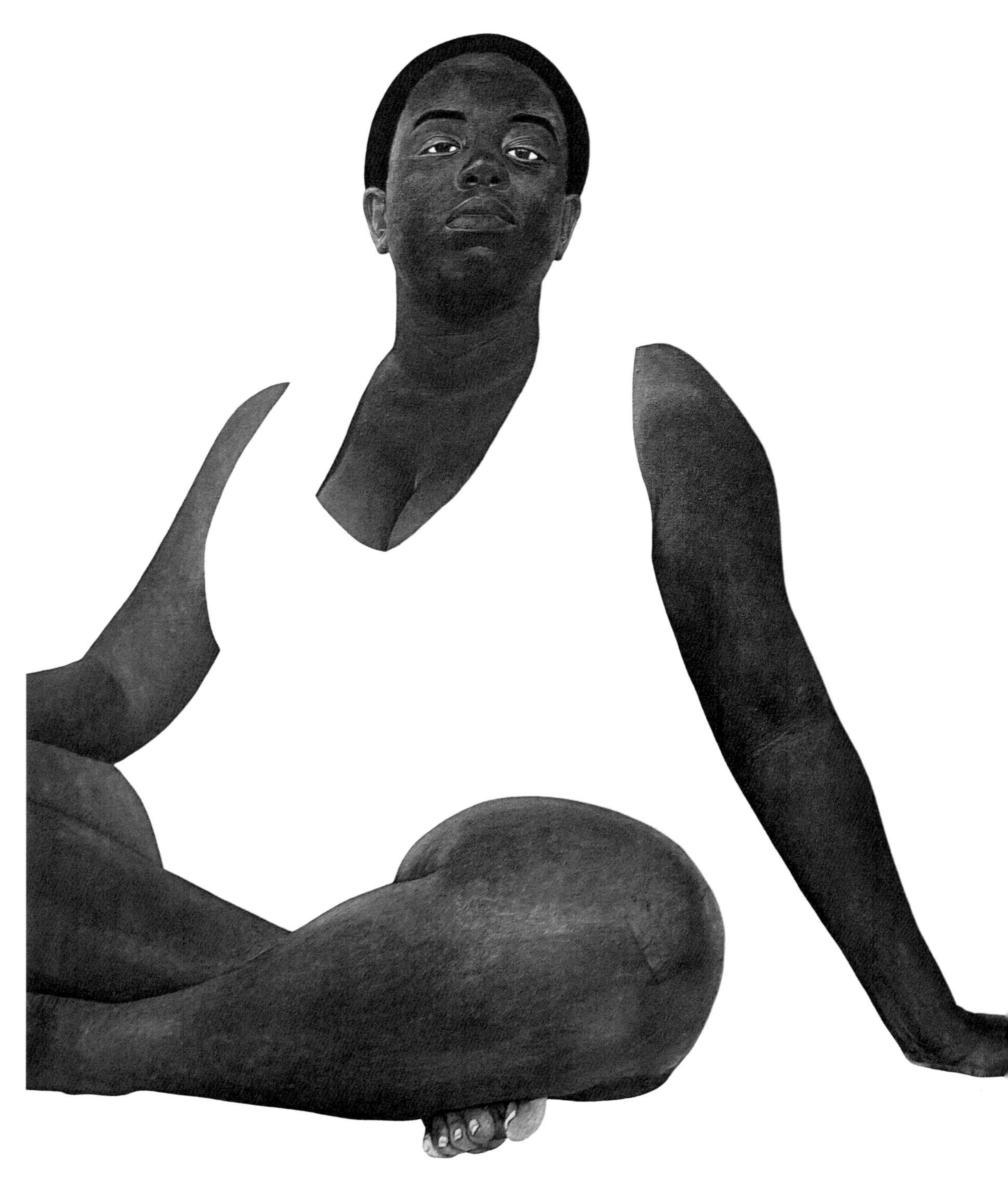

Continuity, 2021
acrylic on canvas
140 × 200 cm

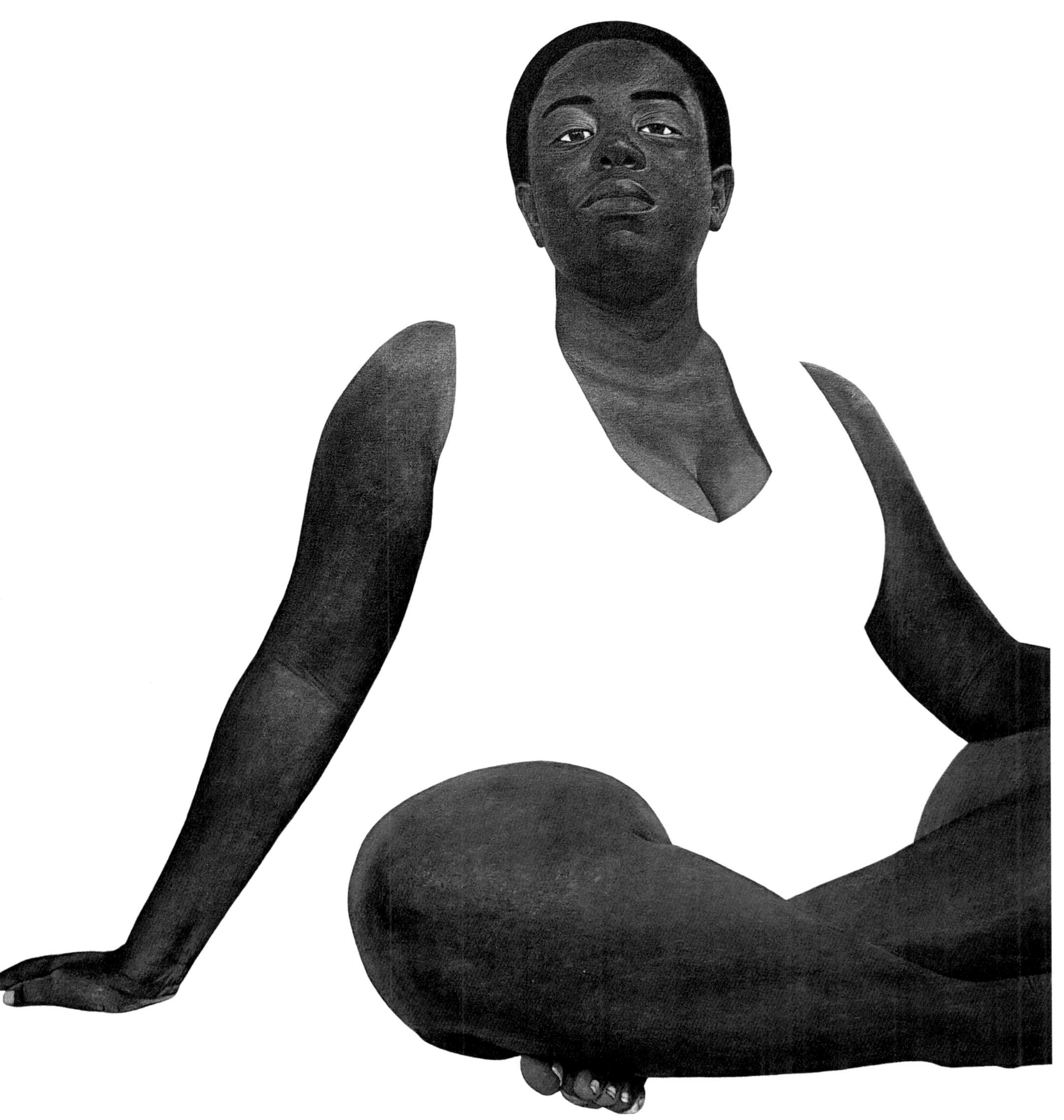

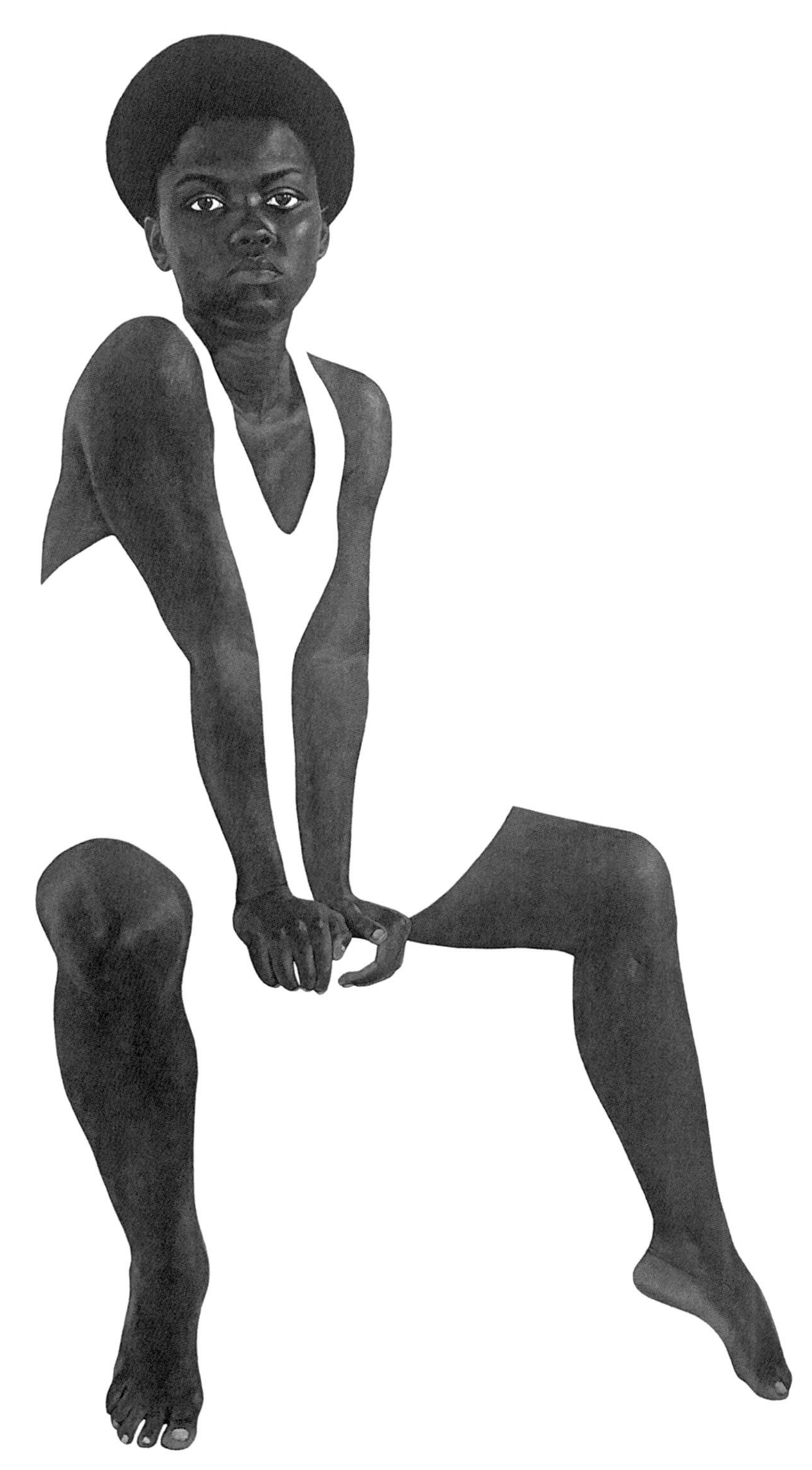

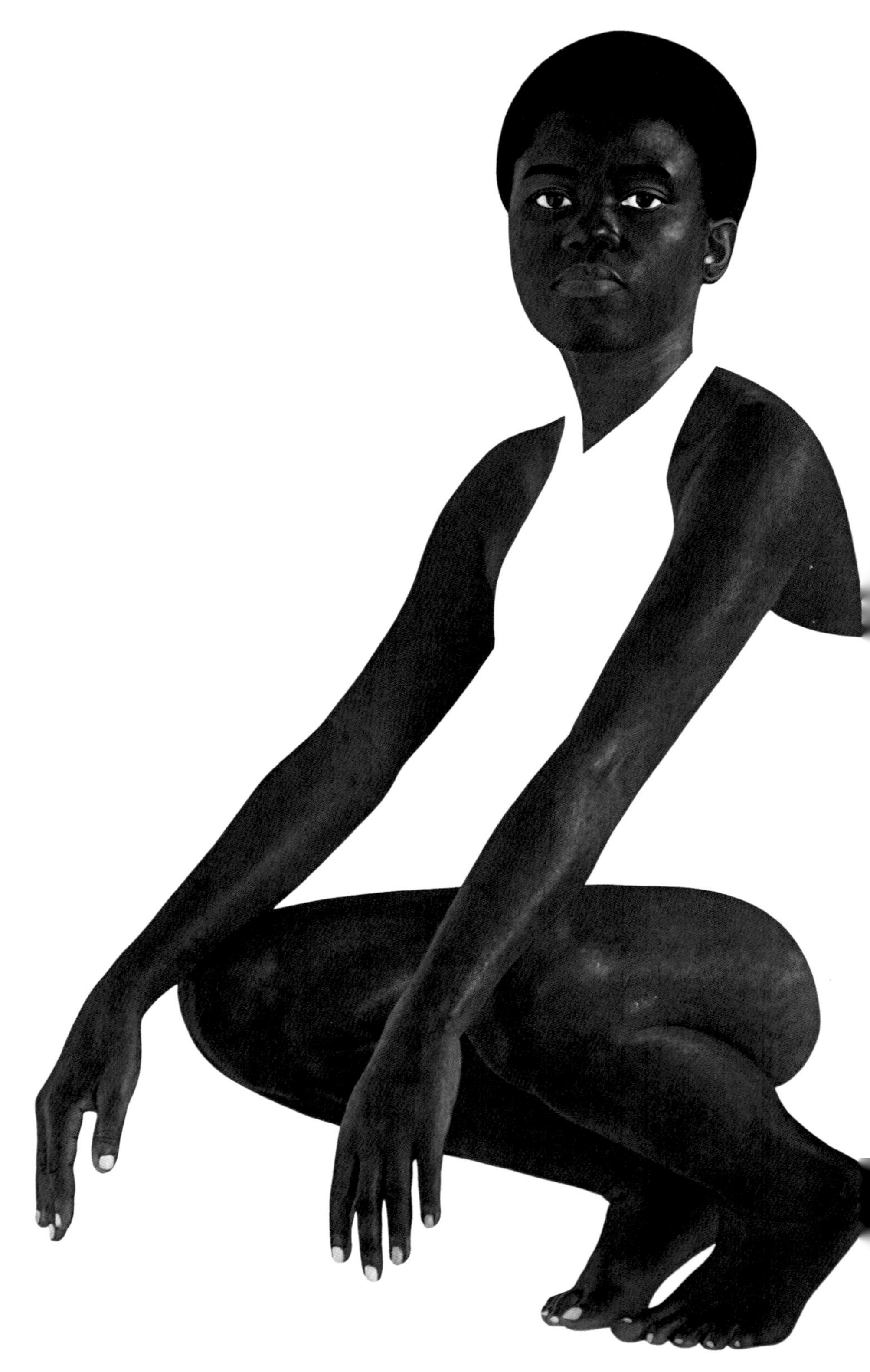

Influence, 2021
acrylic on canvas
140 × 200 cm

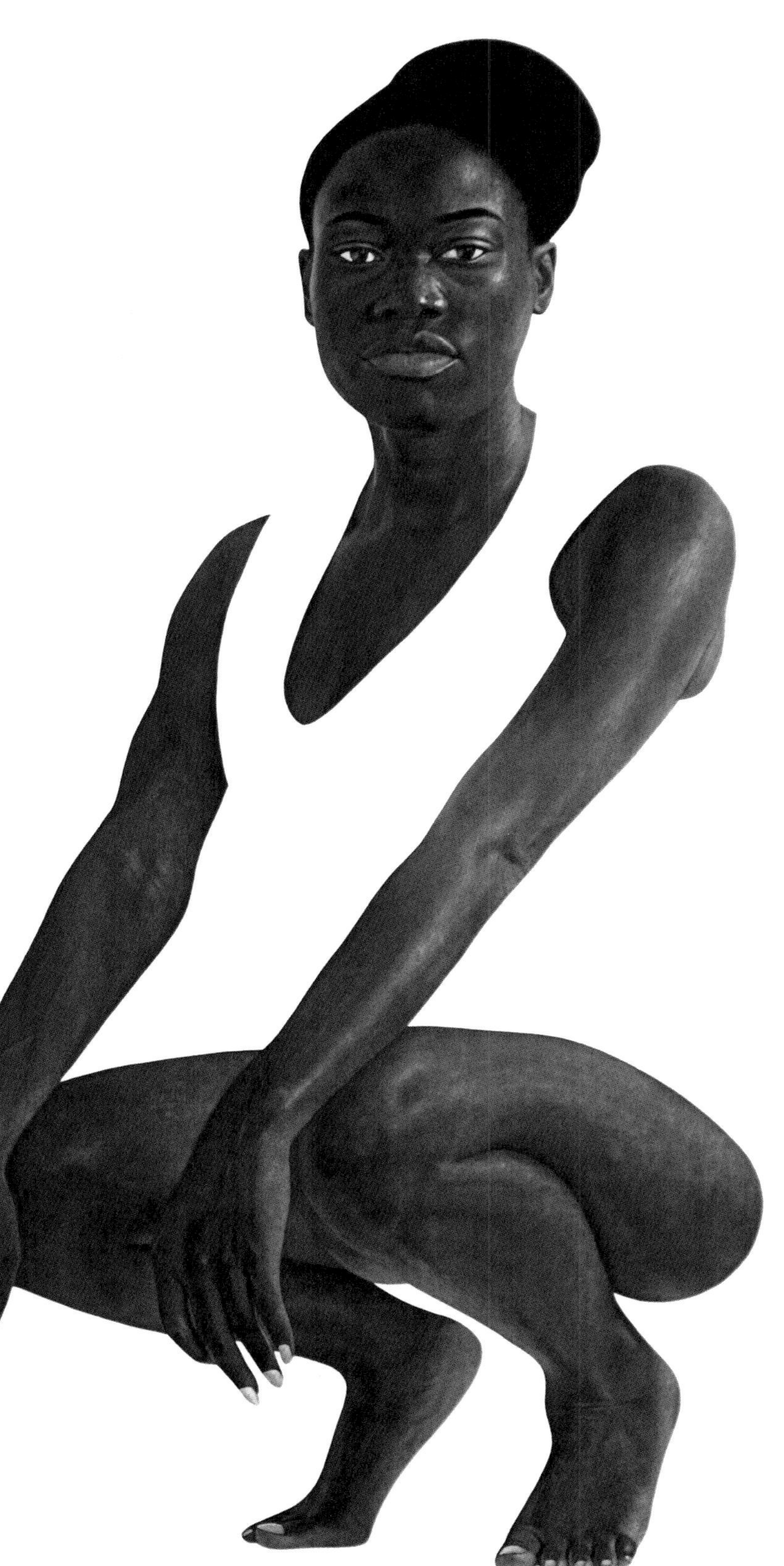

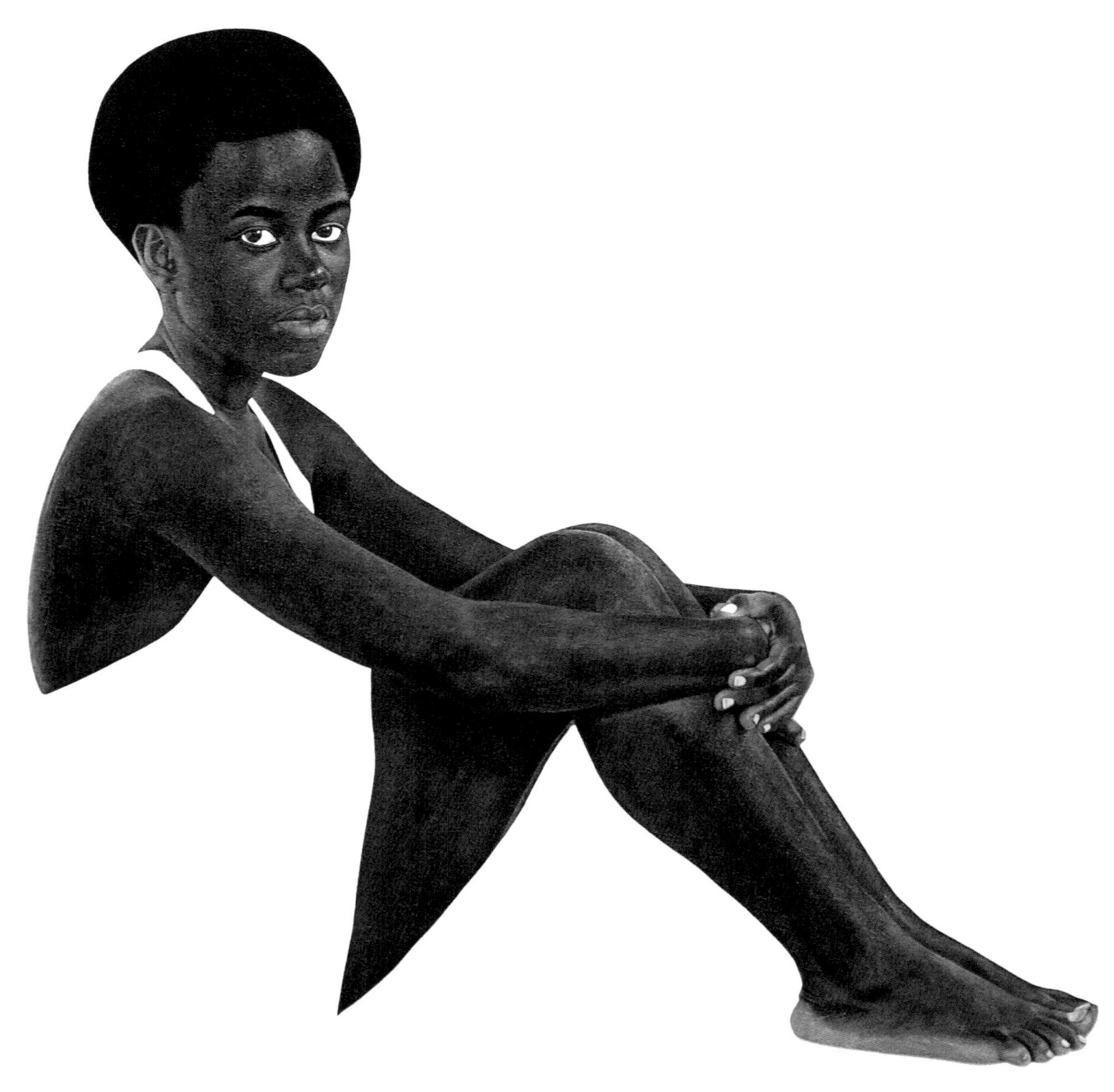

Naked Eye, 2021
acrylic on canvas
150 × 140 cm

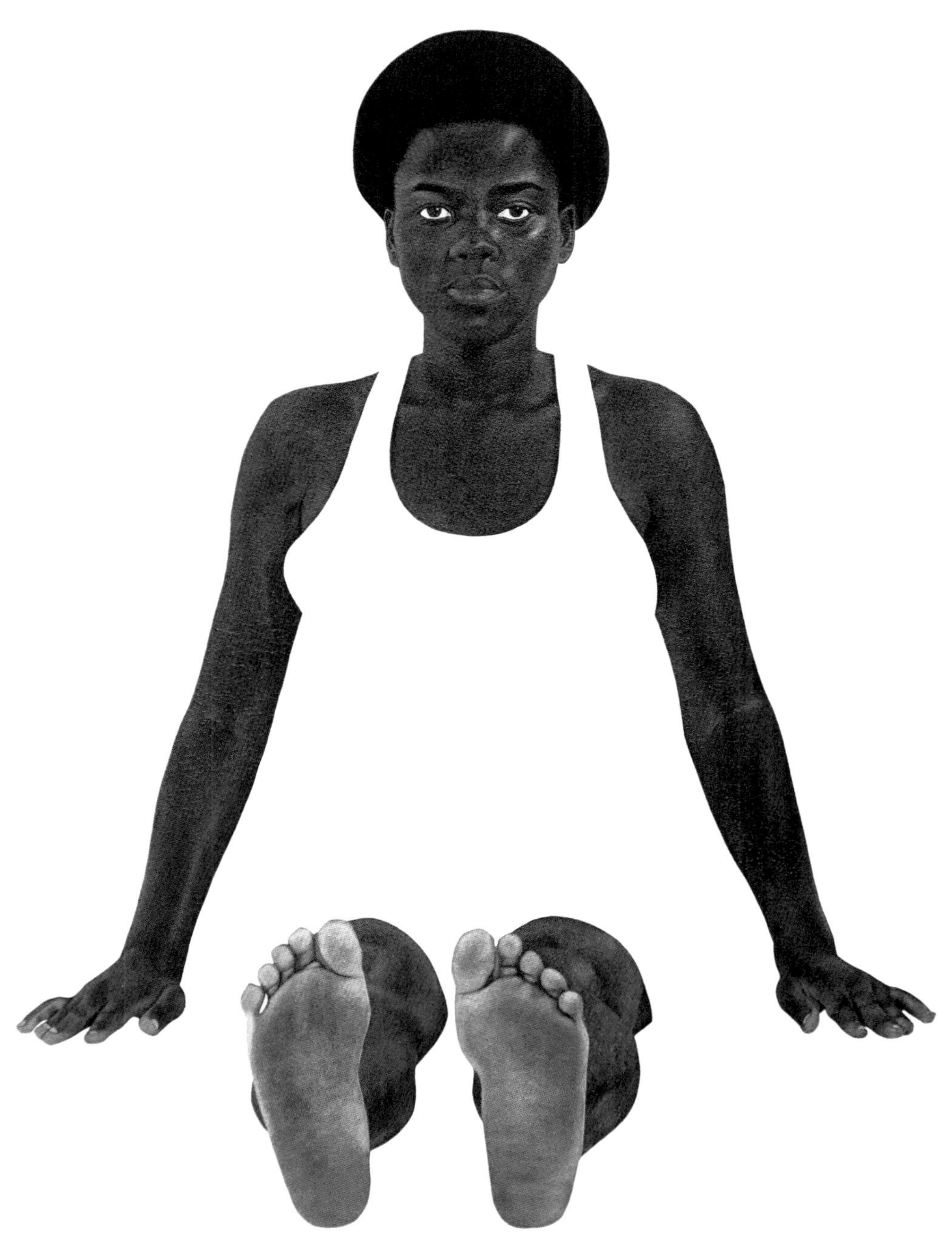

Chaotic Disposition, 2021
acrylic on canvas
140 × 130 cm

Outcome, 2021
acrylic on canvas
200 × 140 cm

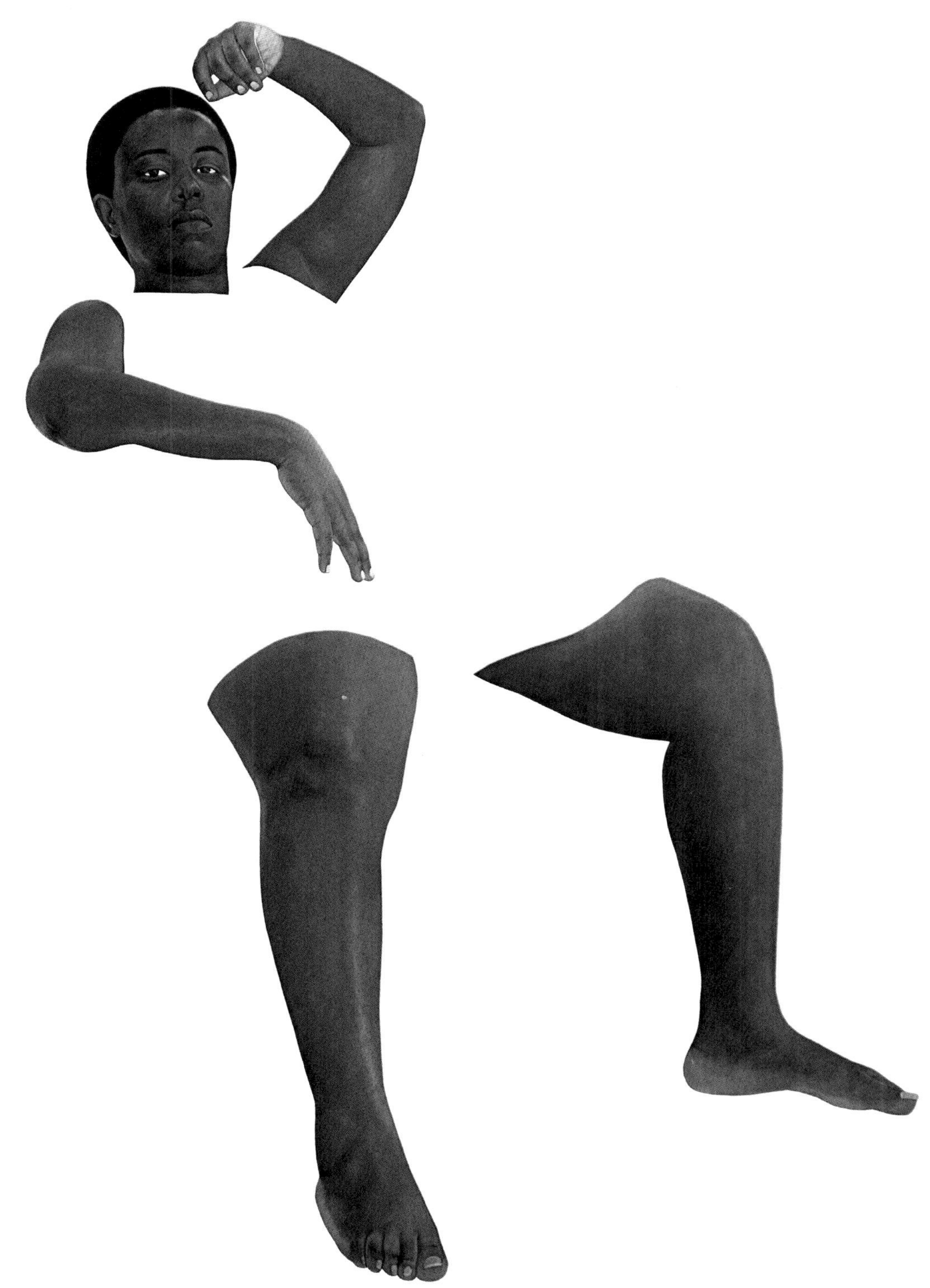

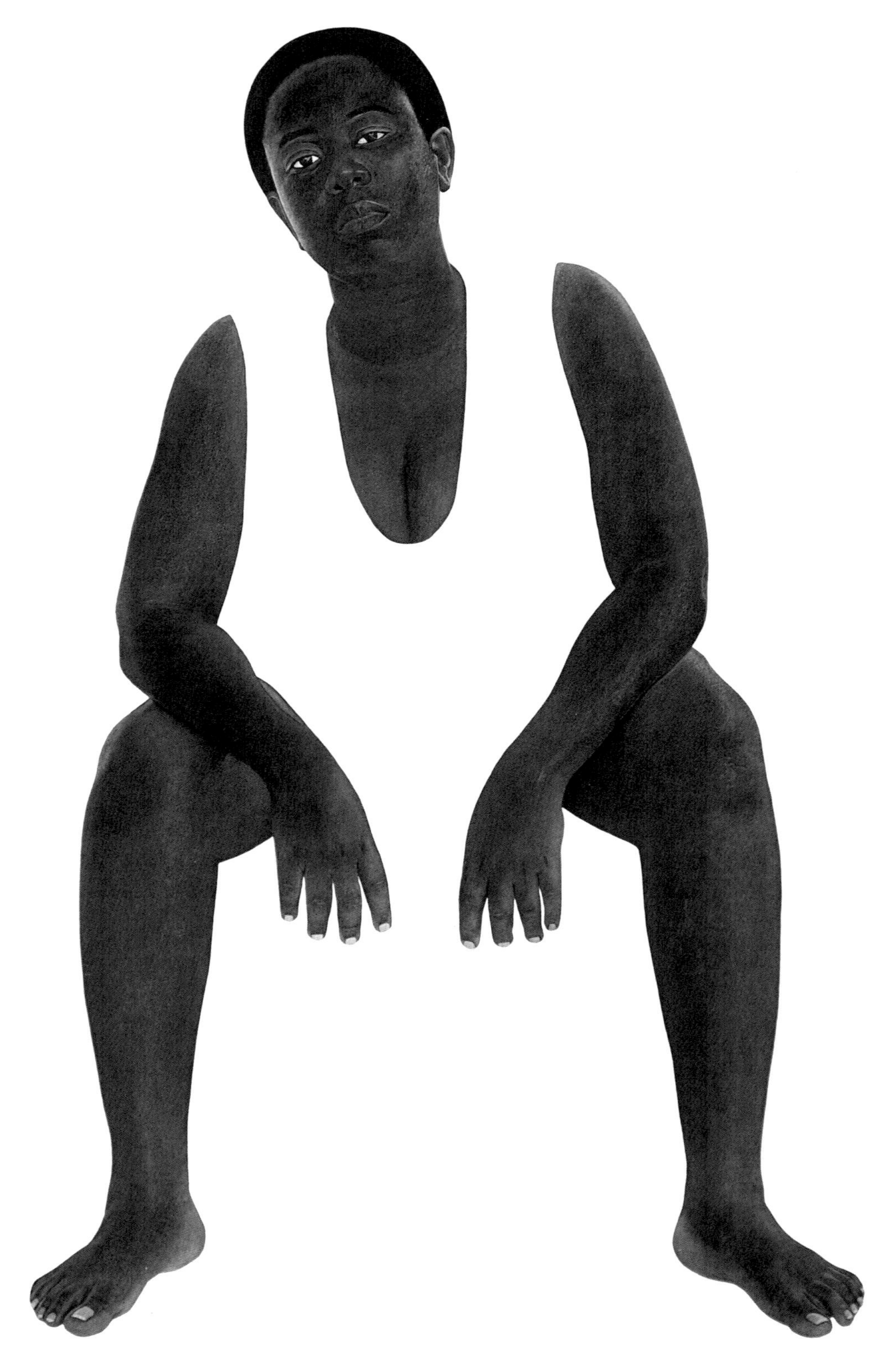

Prepared, 2021
acrylic on canvas
150 × 140 cm

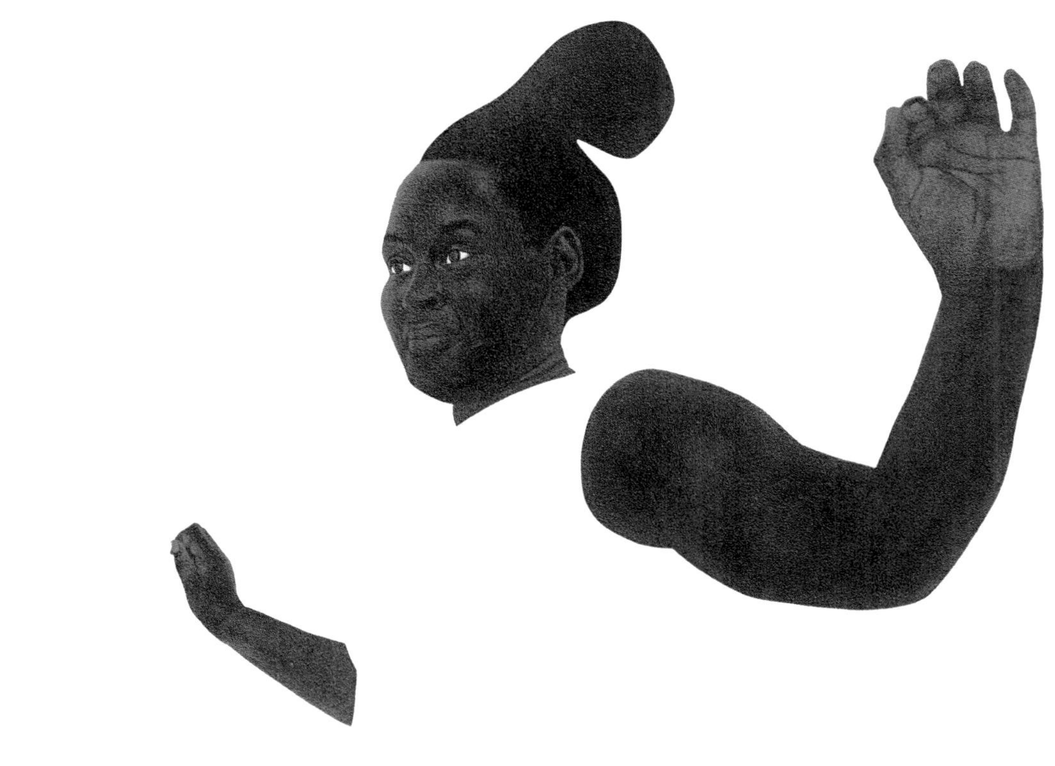
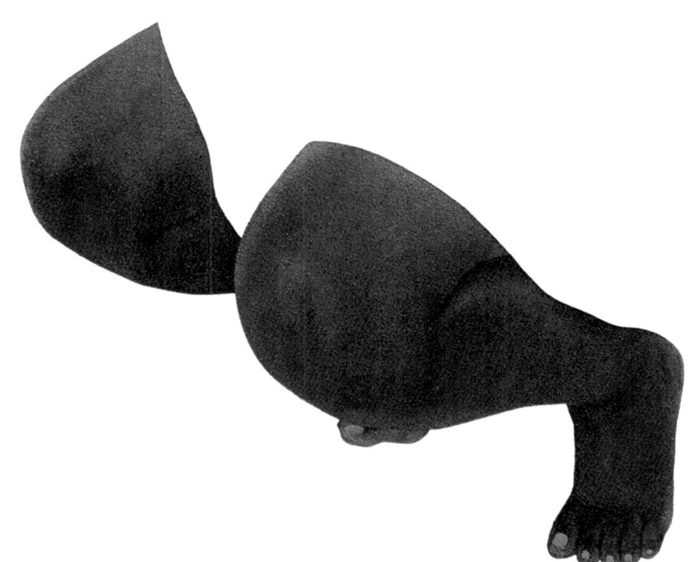

Play, 2021
acrylic on canvas
150 × 140 cm

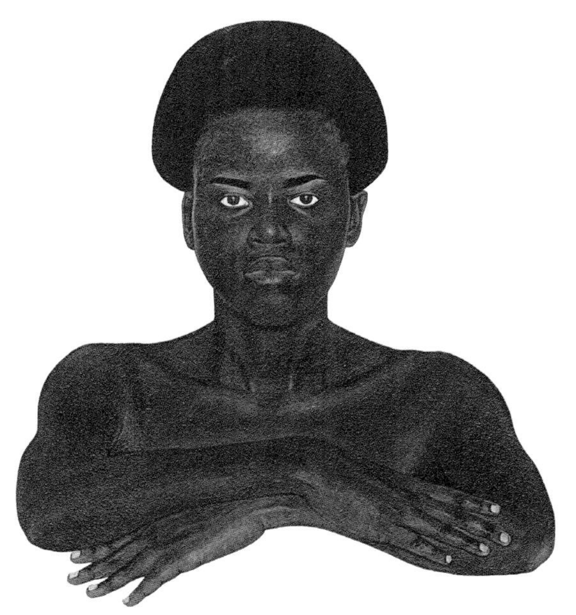

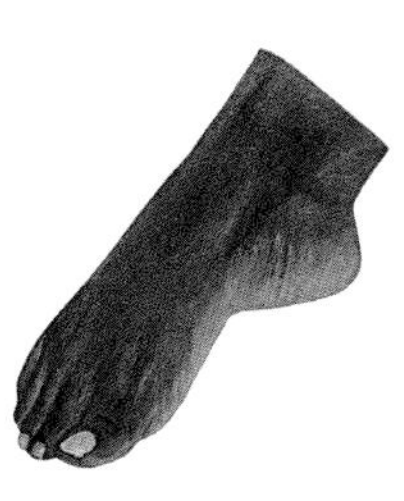

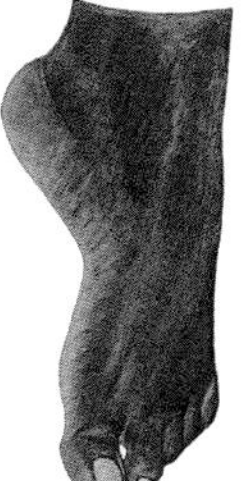

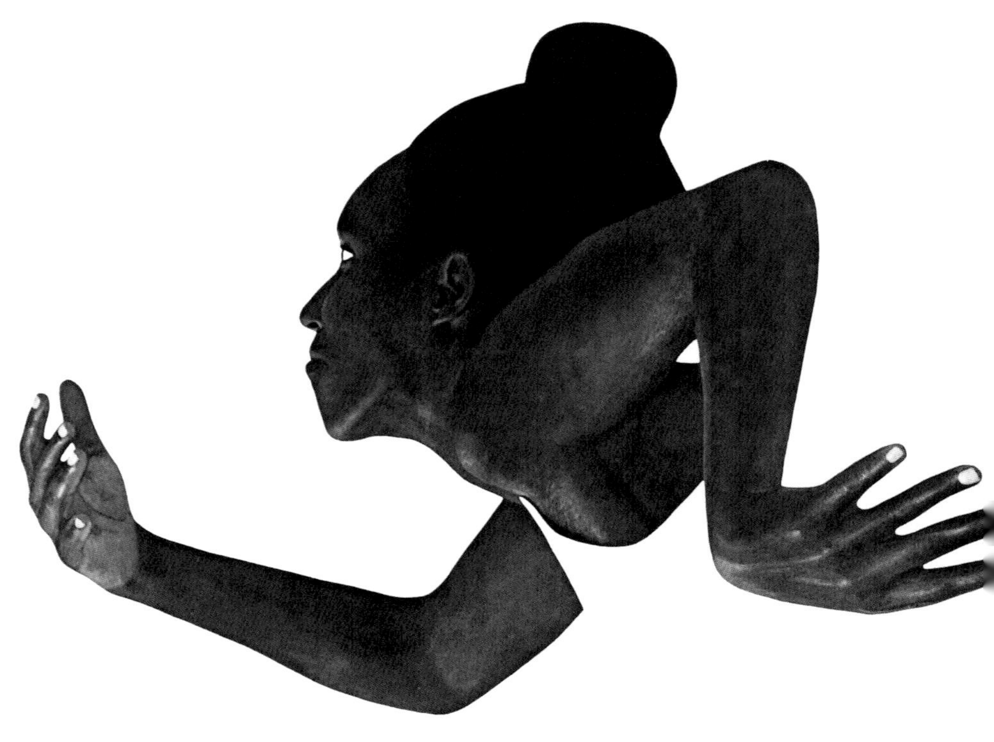

Contemplation, 2021
acrylic on canvas
140 × 200 cm

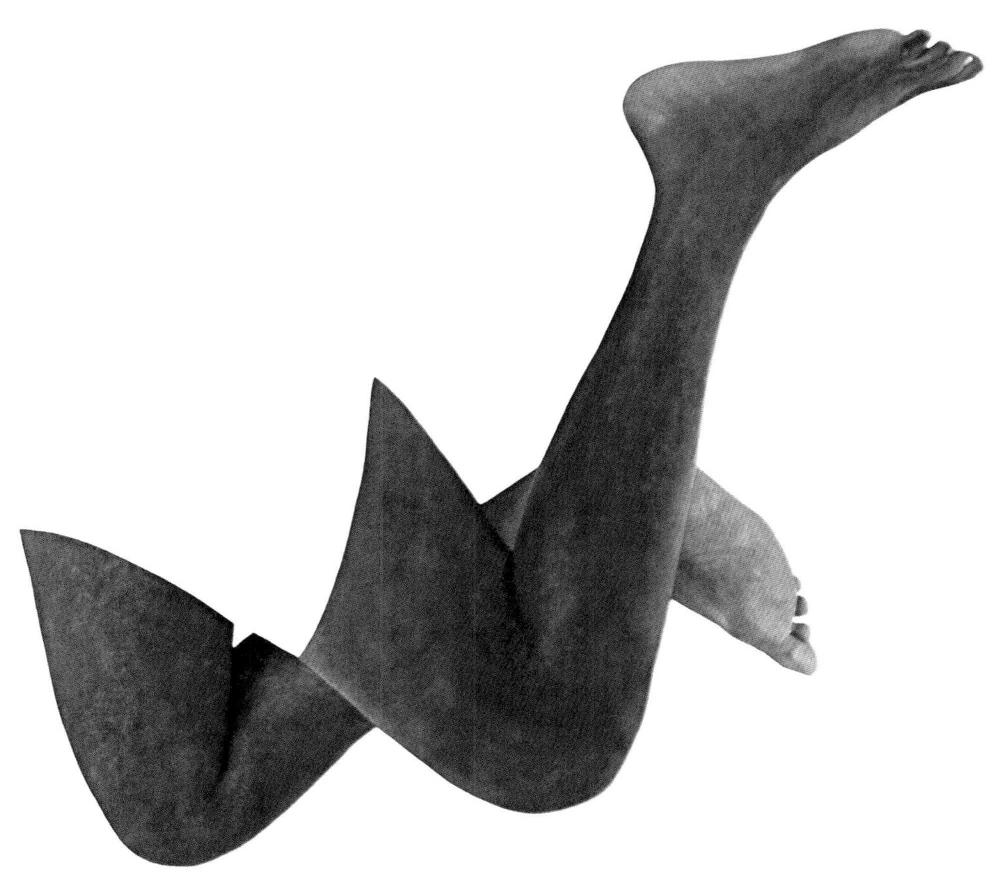

All Ways, 2022
acrylic on canvas
200 × 150 cm

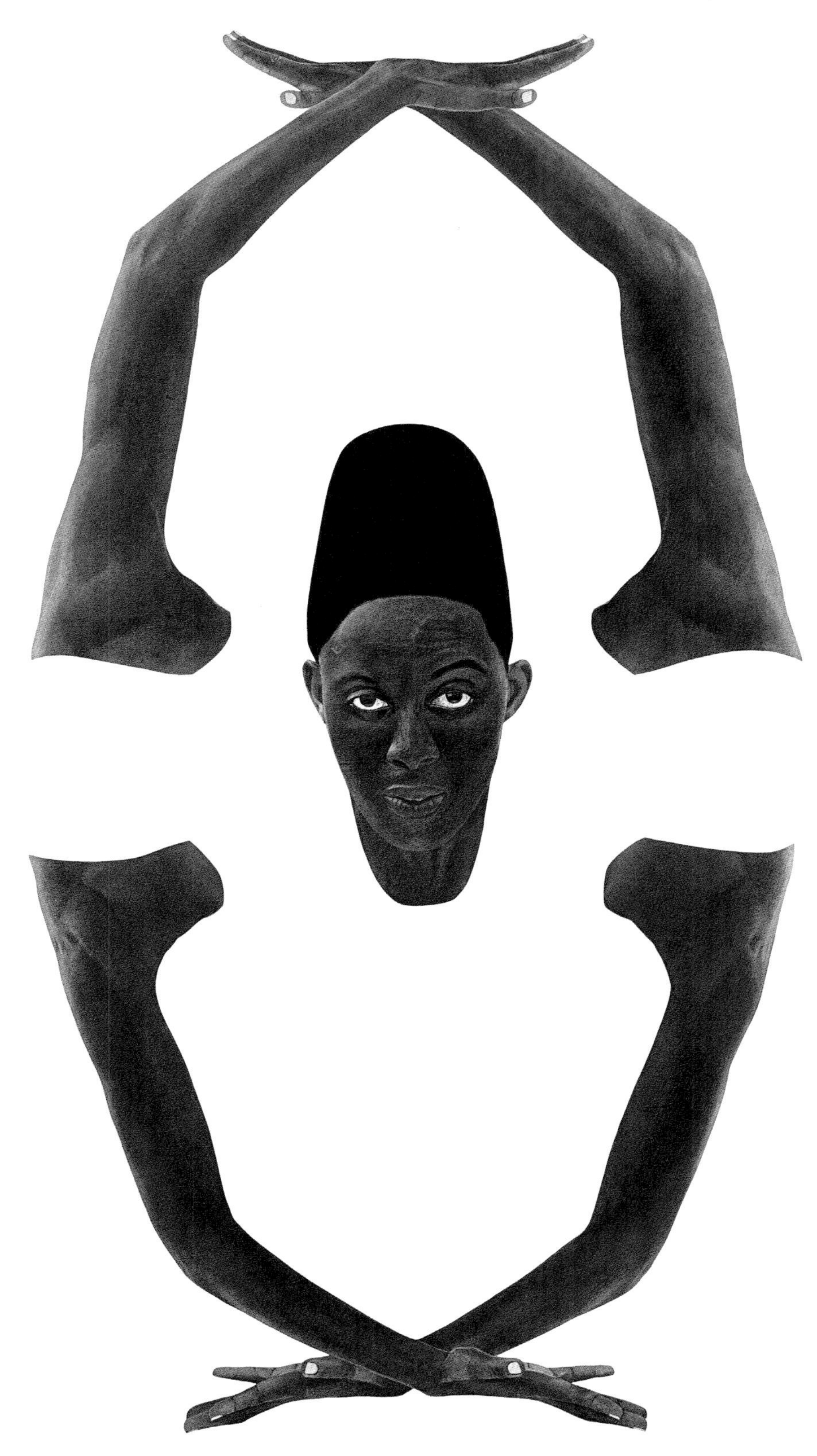

Dust Rising, 2022
acrylic on canvas
200 × 140 cm

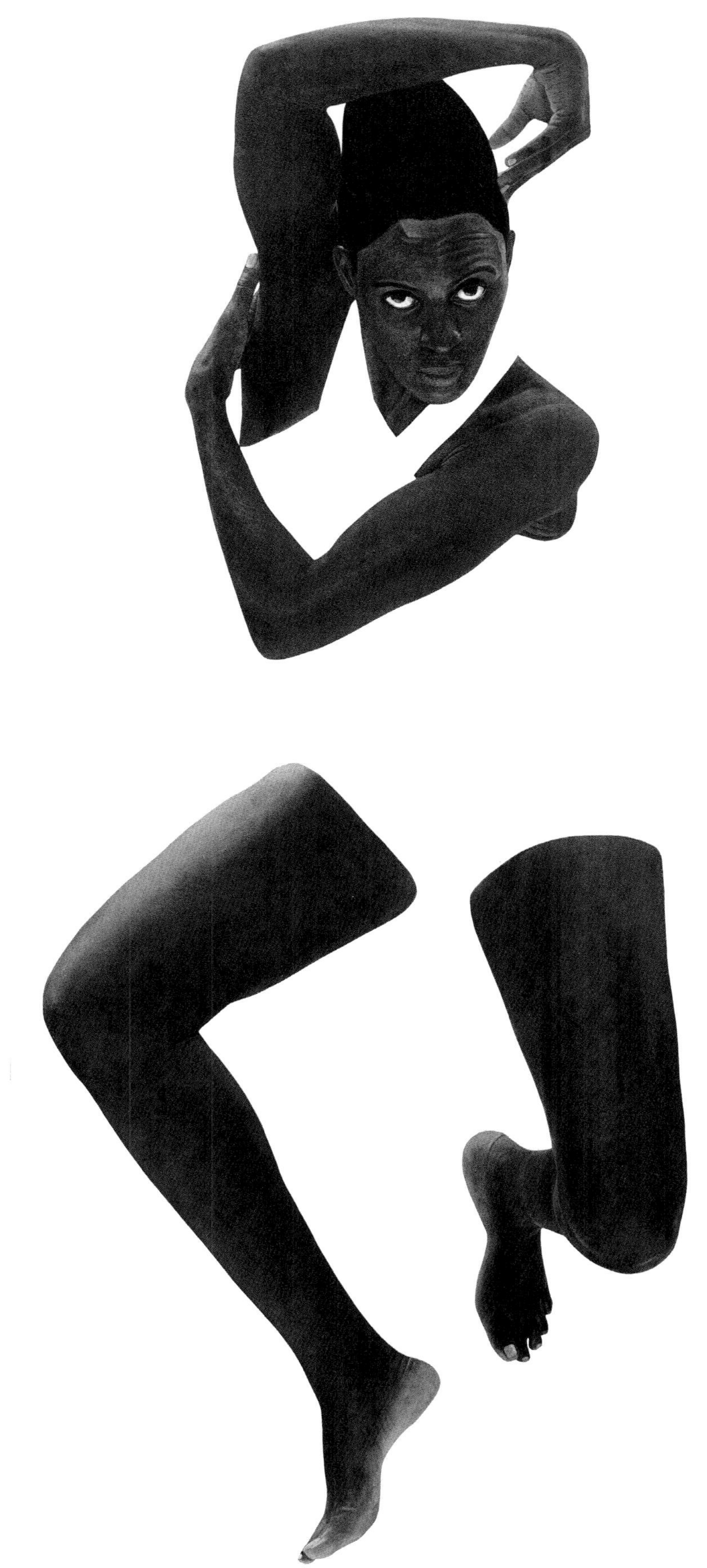

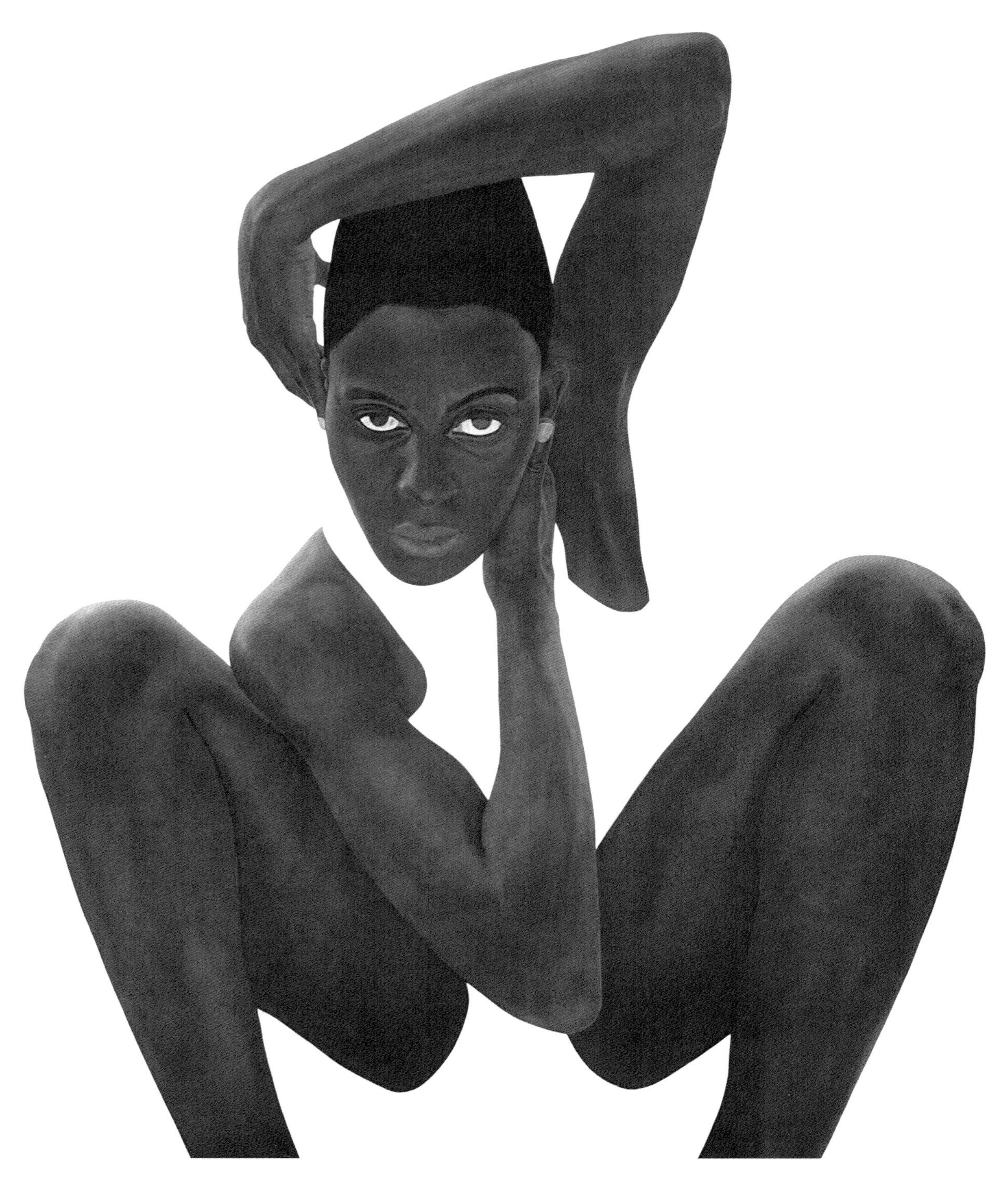

Wallow, 2022
acrylic on canvas
150 × 140 cm

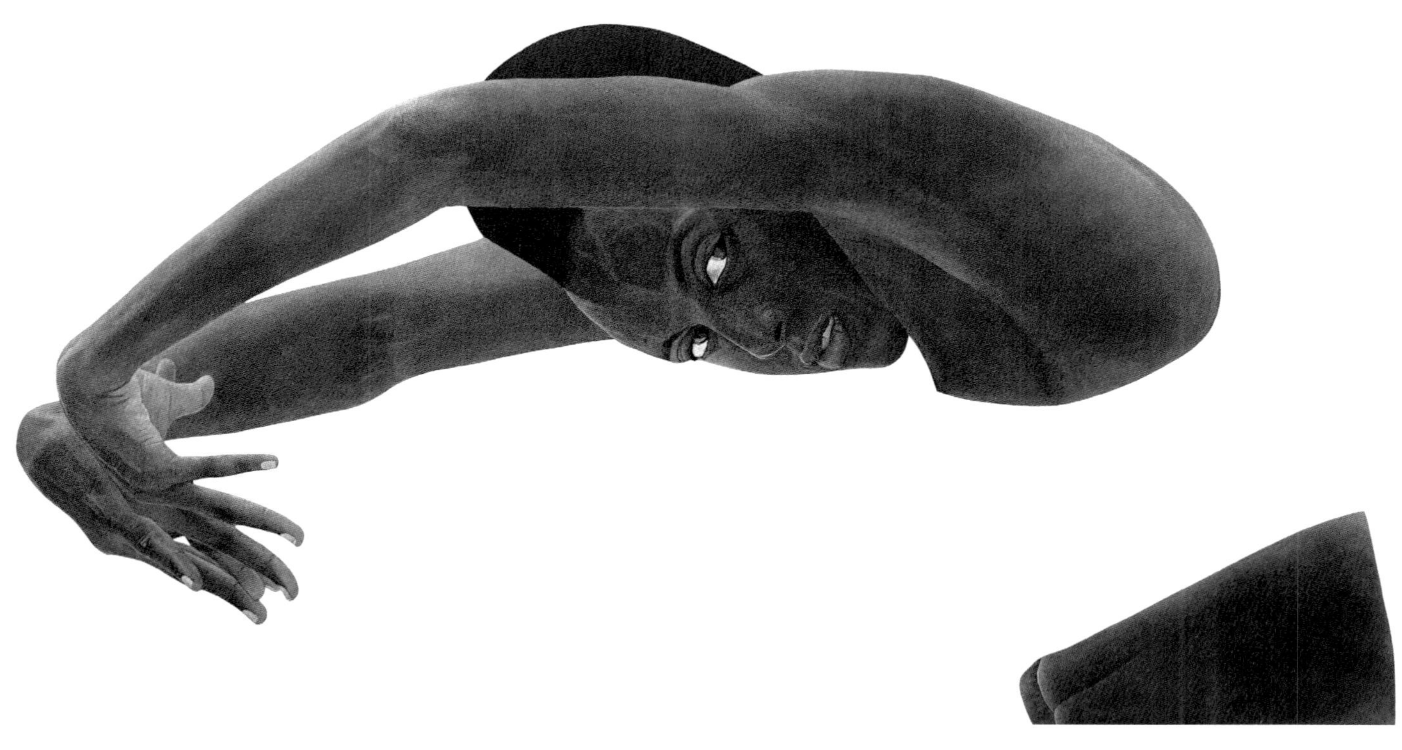

Wear Down, 2022
acrylic on canvas
140 × 150 cm

Years ago, at Frieze London, I was looking for new artists for my foundation and my personal collection when one of my friends referred me to a "new female artist", whom she found very interesting. Sungi Mlengeya's work moved me from the first moment. Her minimalist paintings of black women on a white background, where parts are left undefined, captivated me emotionally. The visible body parts dialogue with the negative space surrounding them, creating a strong tension and sense of empowerment. Sungi's art tells us stories of contemporary African womanhood, self-determination and freedom through movement.

I started to read about her in detail and reached out to her through her gallery. I wanted to show Sungi's works in a solo exhibition at my foundation B.LA, whose mission is female empowerment in order to support and grow future women leaders. Our exhibition in Vienna *Don't Try. Don't Not Try* was a true success. Two of her works – *Spring* and *Wallow* – were later exhibited in the Albertina Modern in Vienna.

I wish her the very best for her future journey.

Birgit Lauda, Philanthropist
Birgit Lauda Art Foundation (B.LA)

Spring, 2022
acrylic on canvas
140 × 150 cm

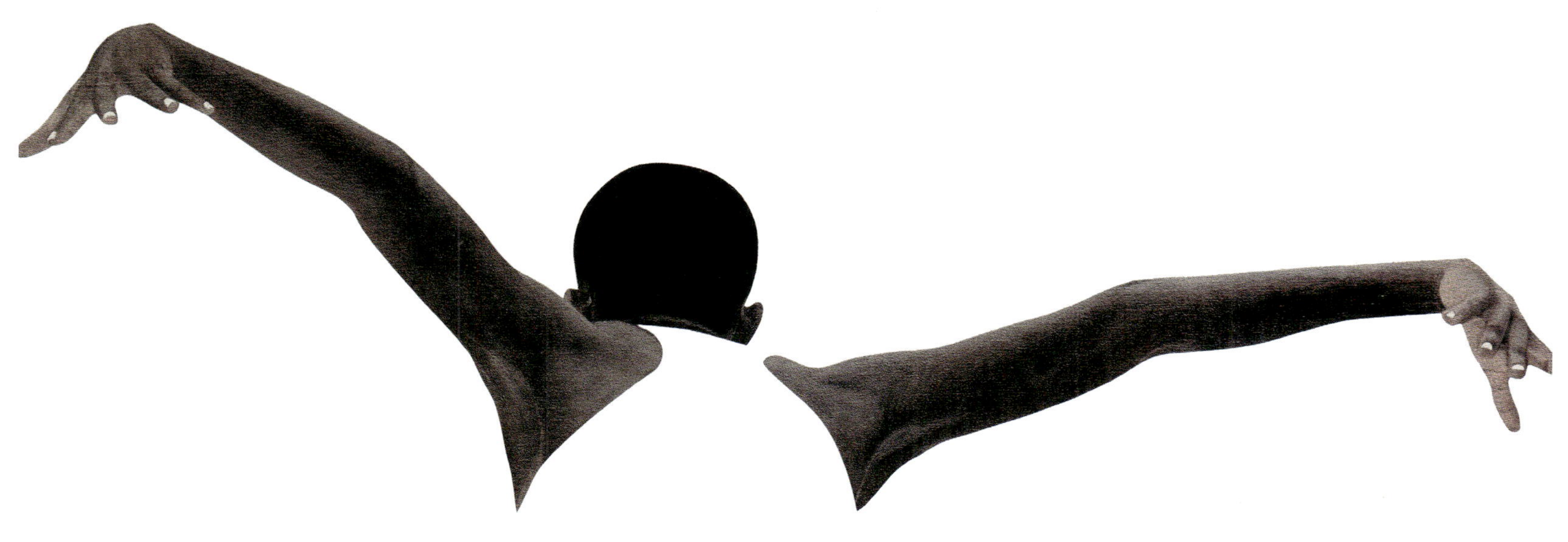
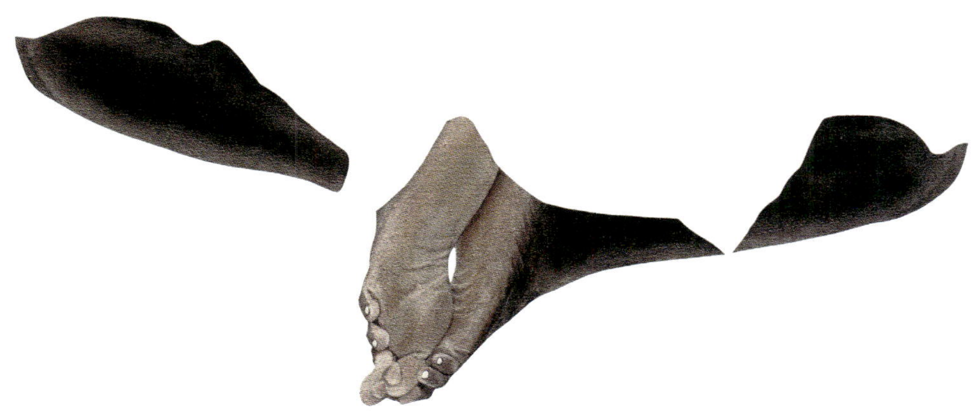

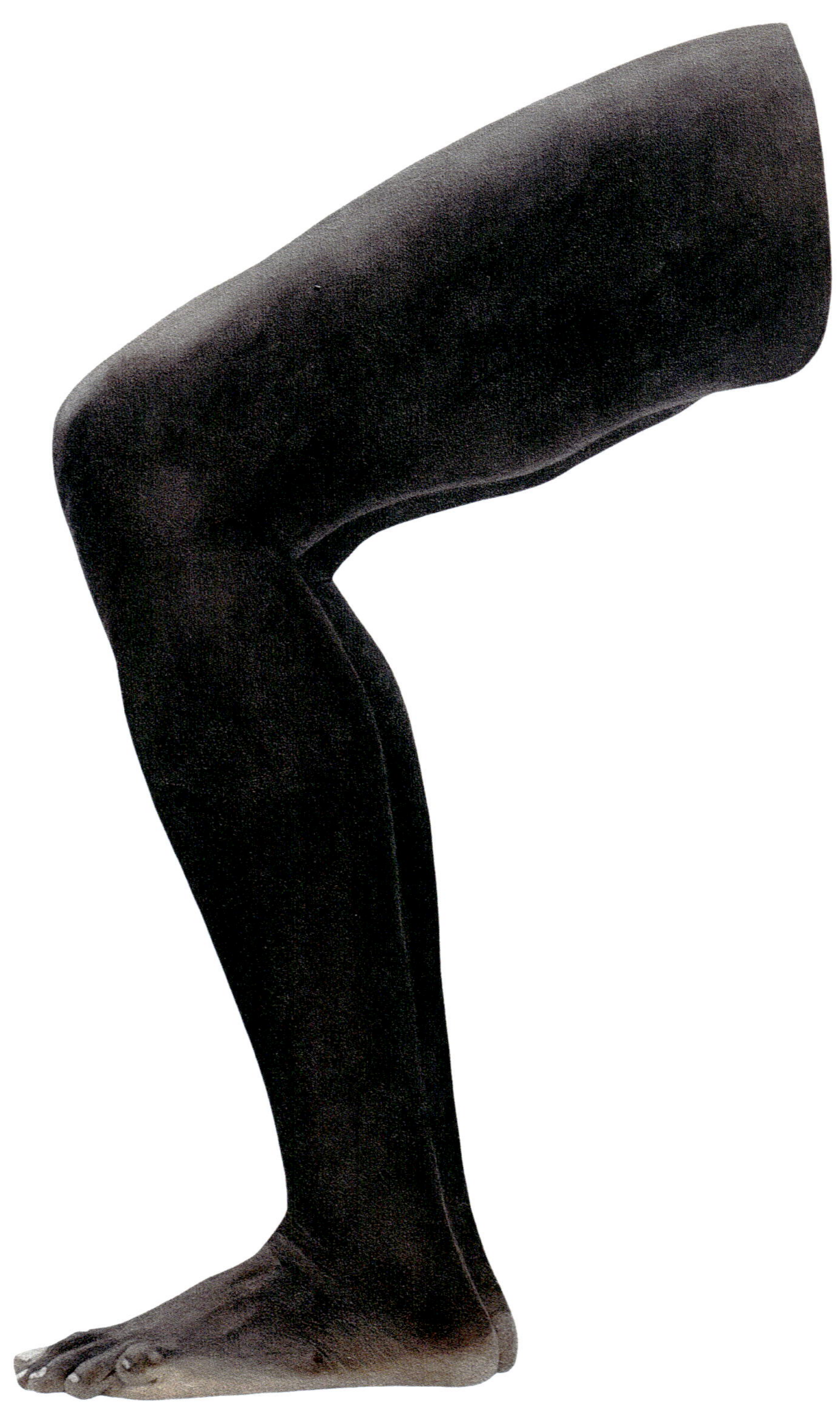

Eye-Side Down, 2022
acrylic on canvas
150 × 200 cm

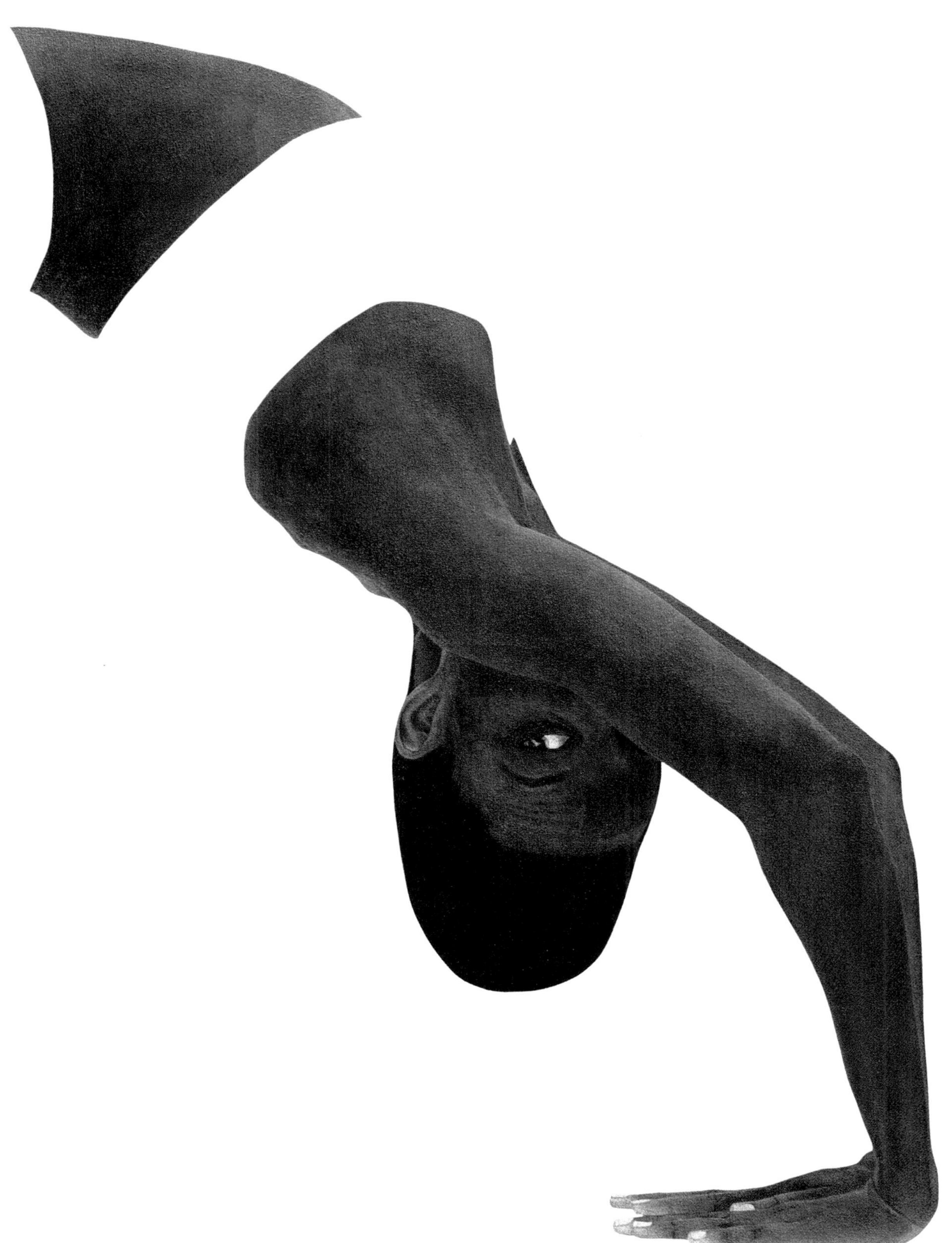

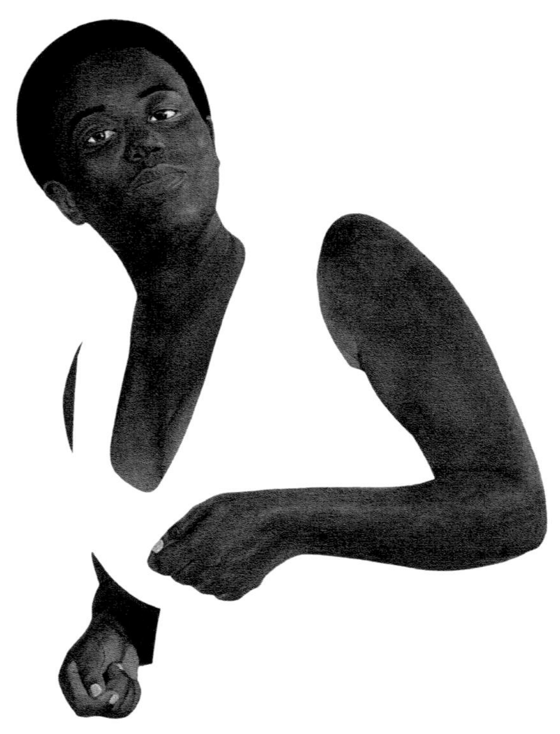

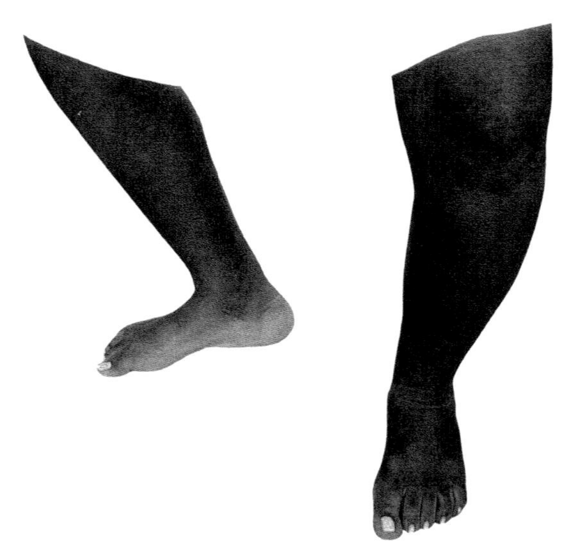

Kidada, 2022
acrylic on canvas
200 × 140 cm

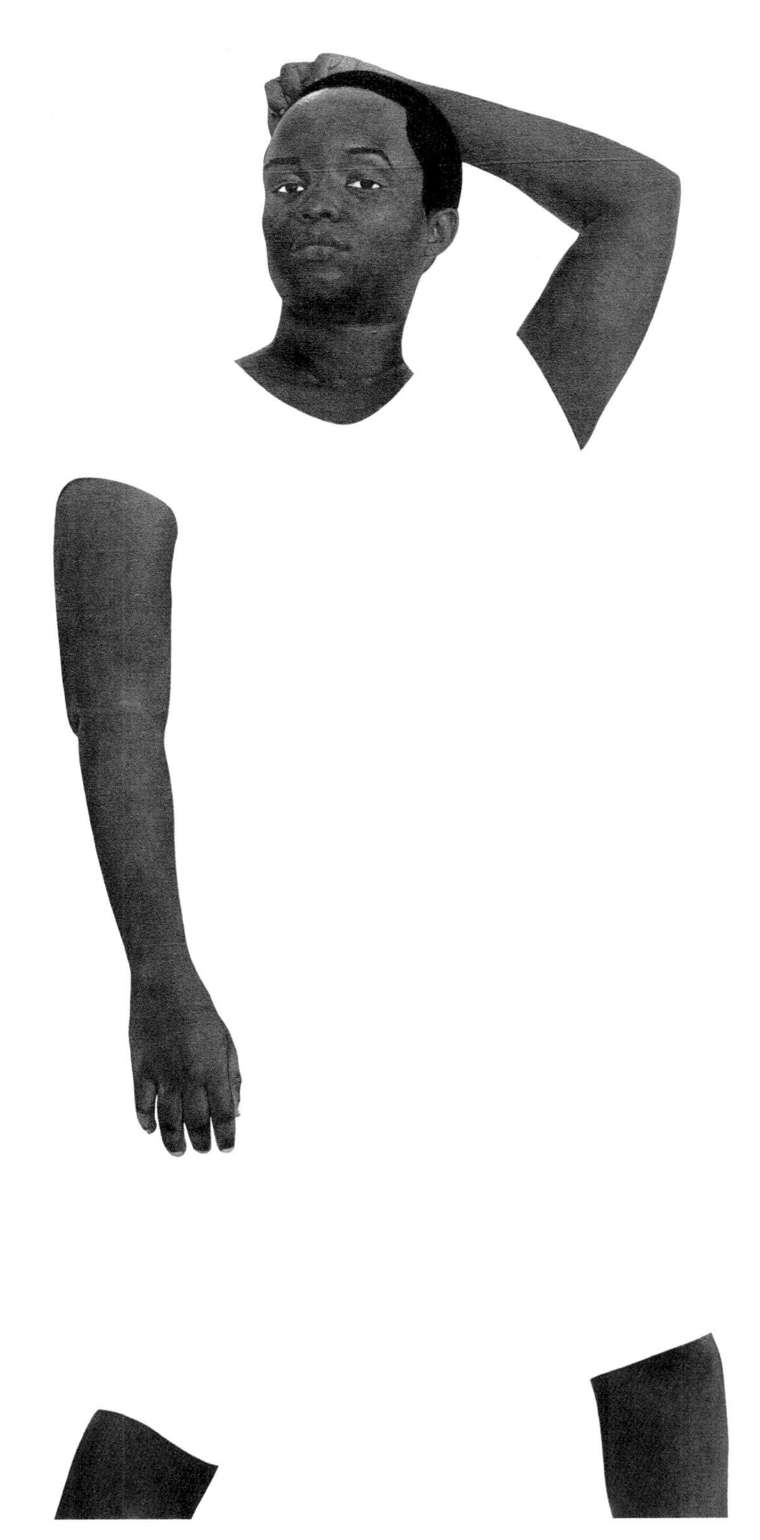

Still, 2022
acrylic on canvas
140 × 130 cm

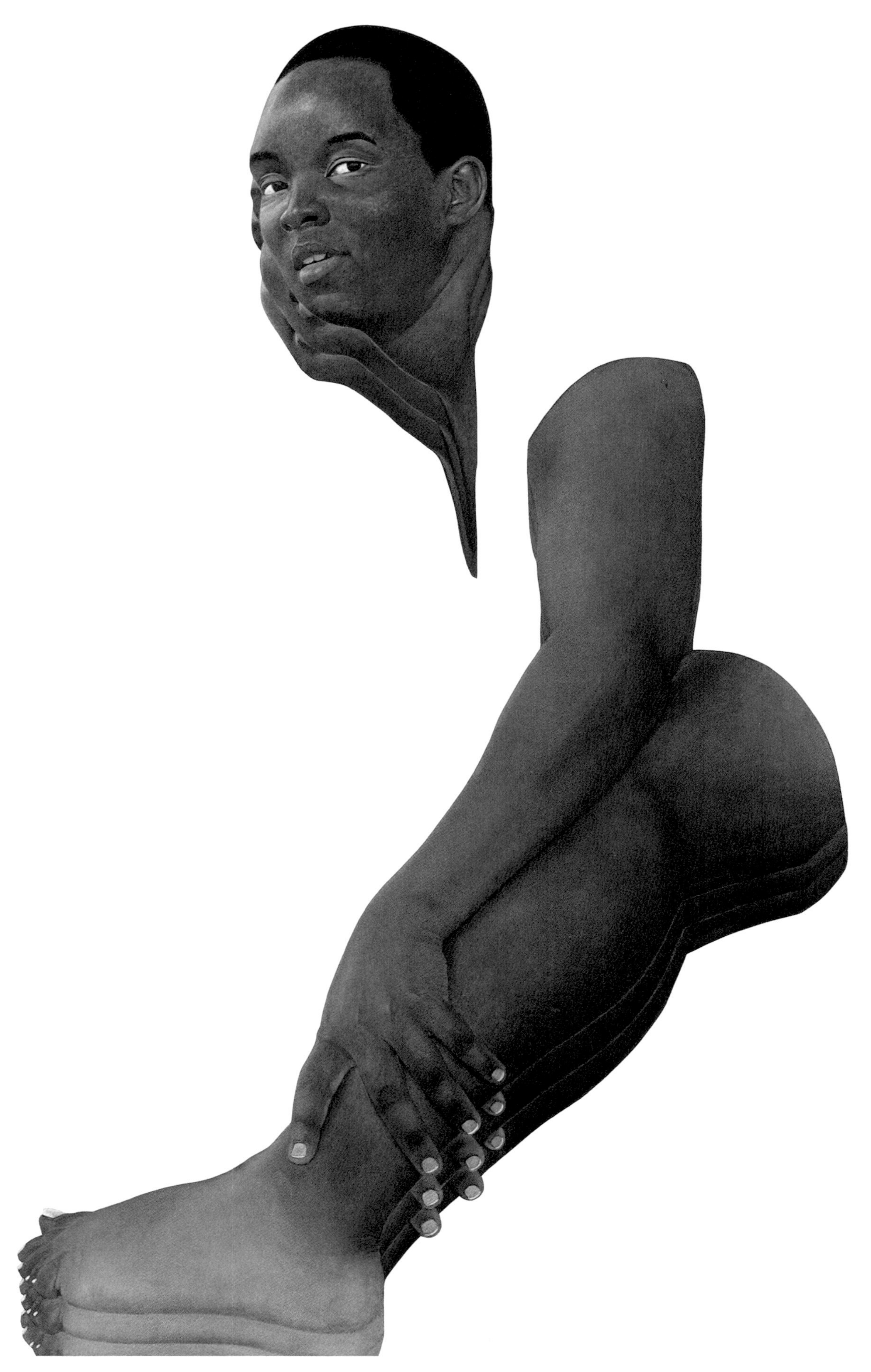

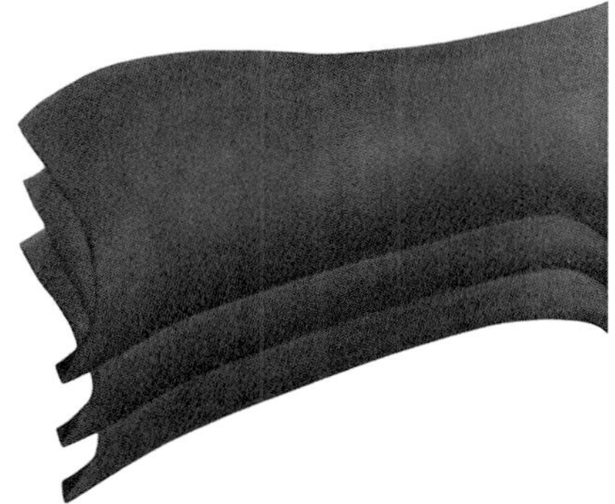

Vibration, 2022
acrylic on canvas
150 × 200 cm

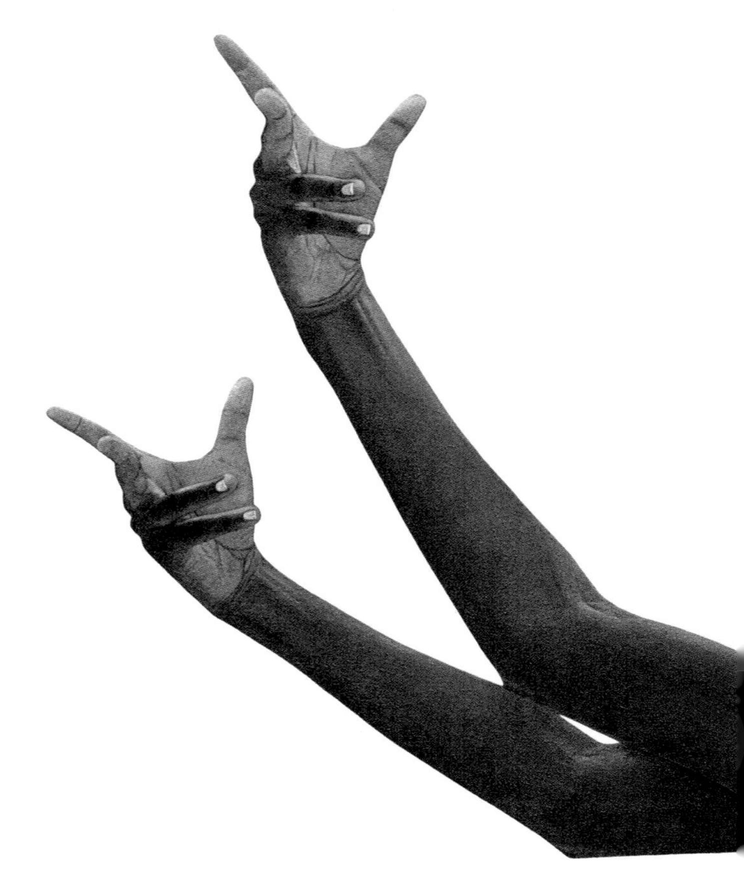

Transcendence, 2022
acrylic on canvas
150 × 200 cm

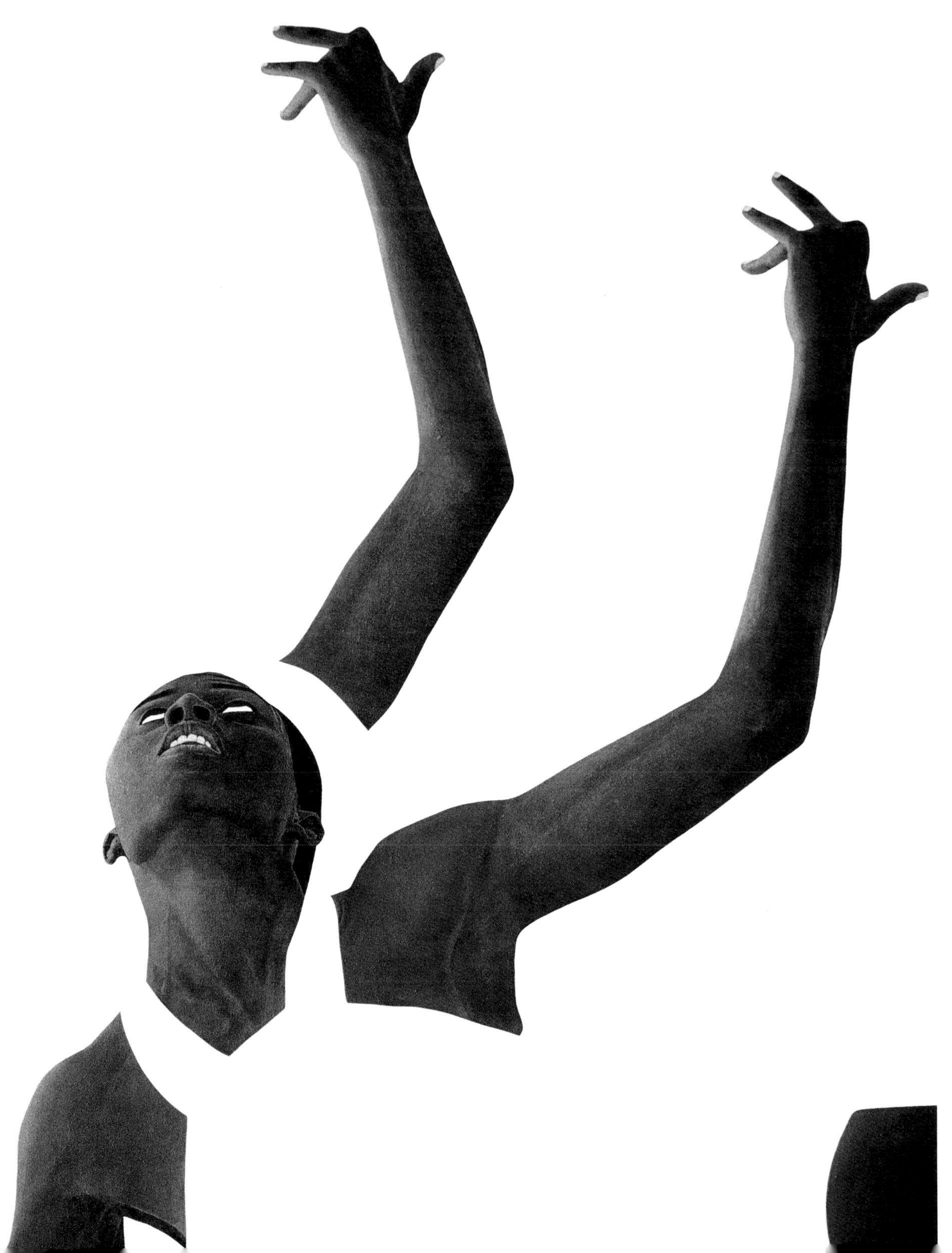

Njia Tatu, 2022
acrylic on canvas
200 × 150 cm

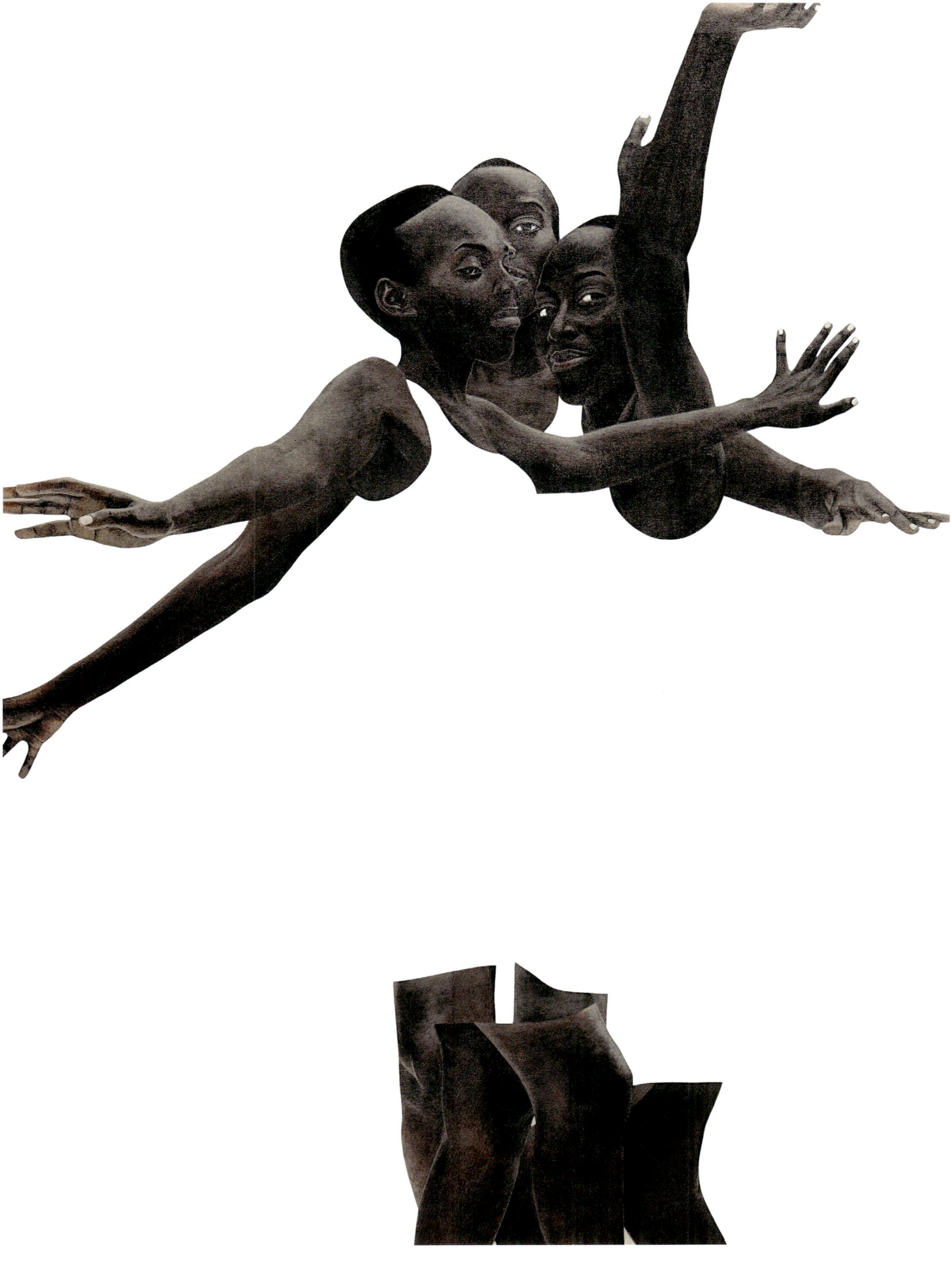

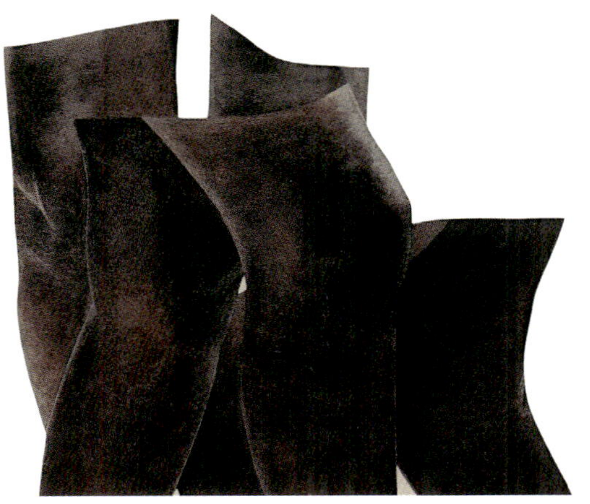

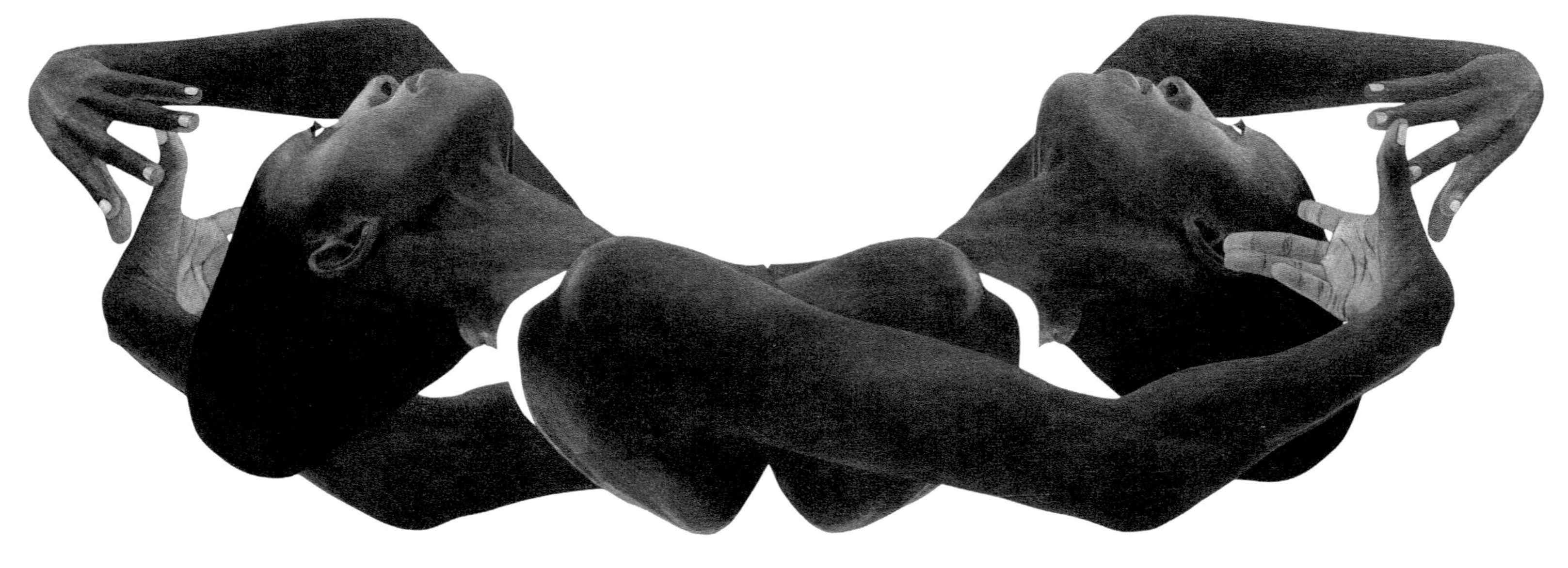

Kushoto Kulia, 2022
acrylic on canvas
150 × 140 cm

Hapa na Pale, 2022
acrylic on canvas
200 × 150 cm

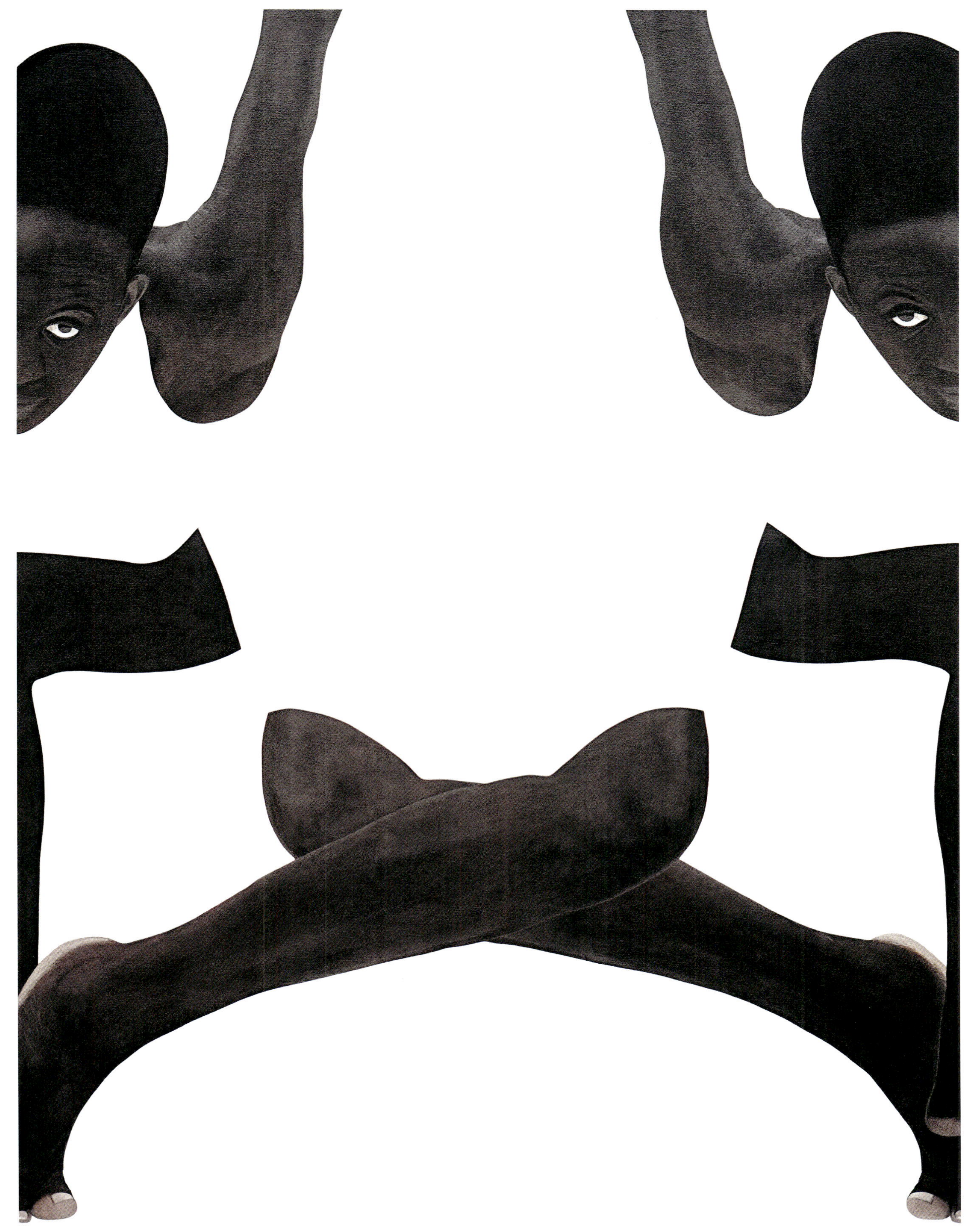

Come, 2022
acrylic on canvas
200 × 140 cm

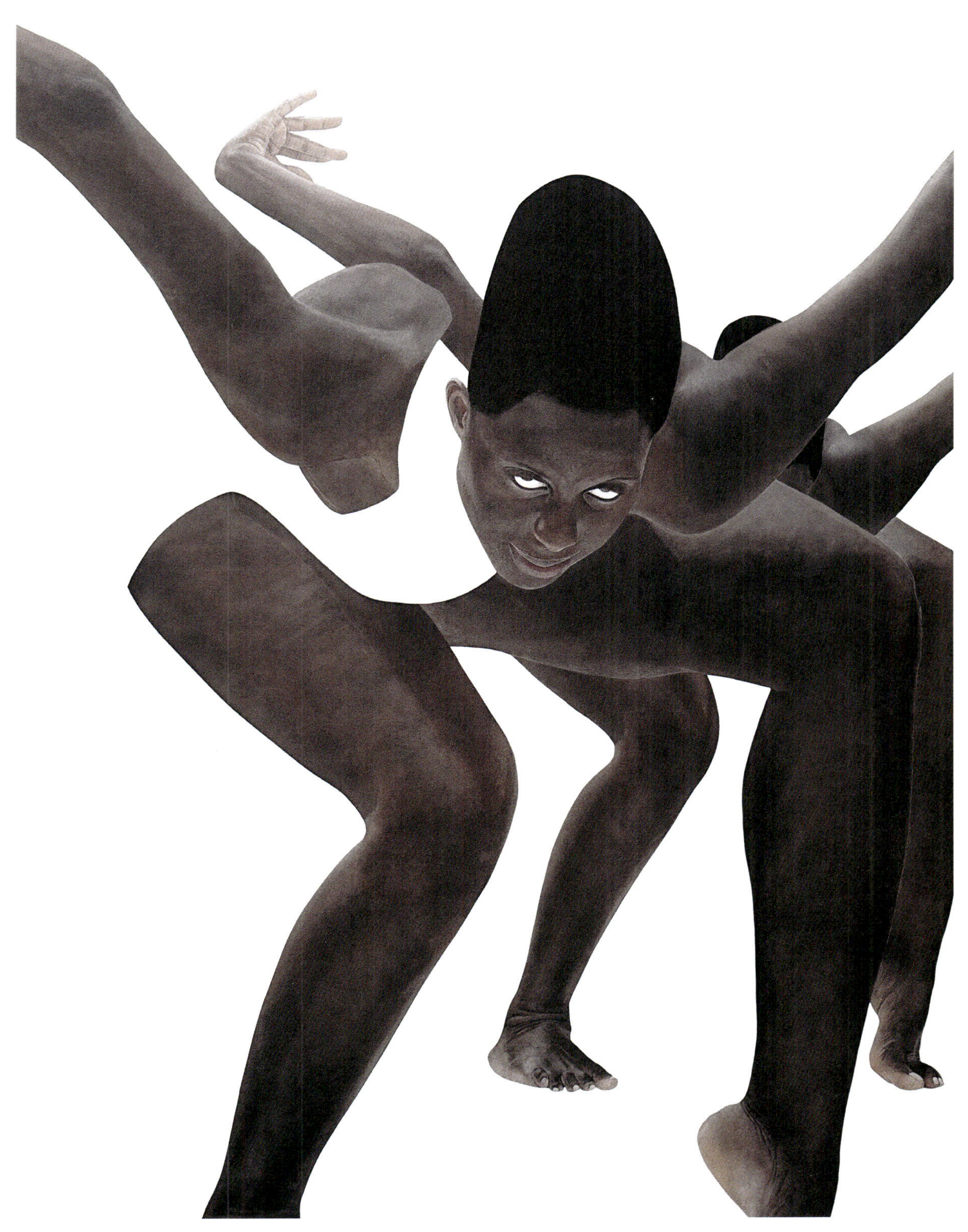

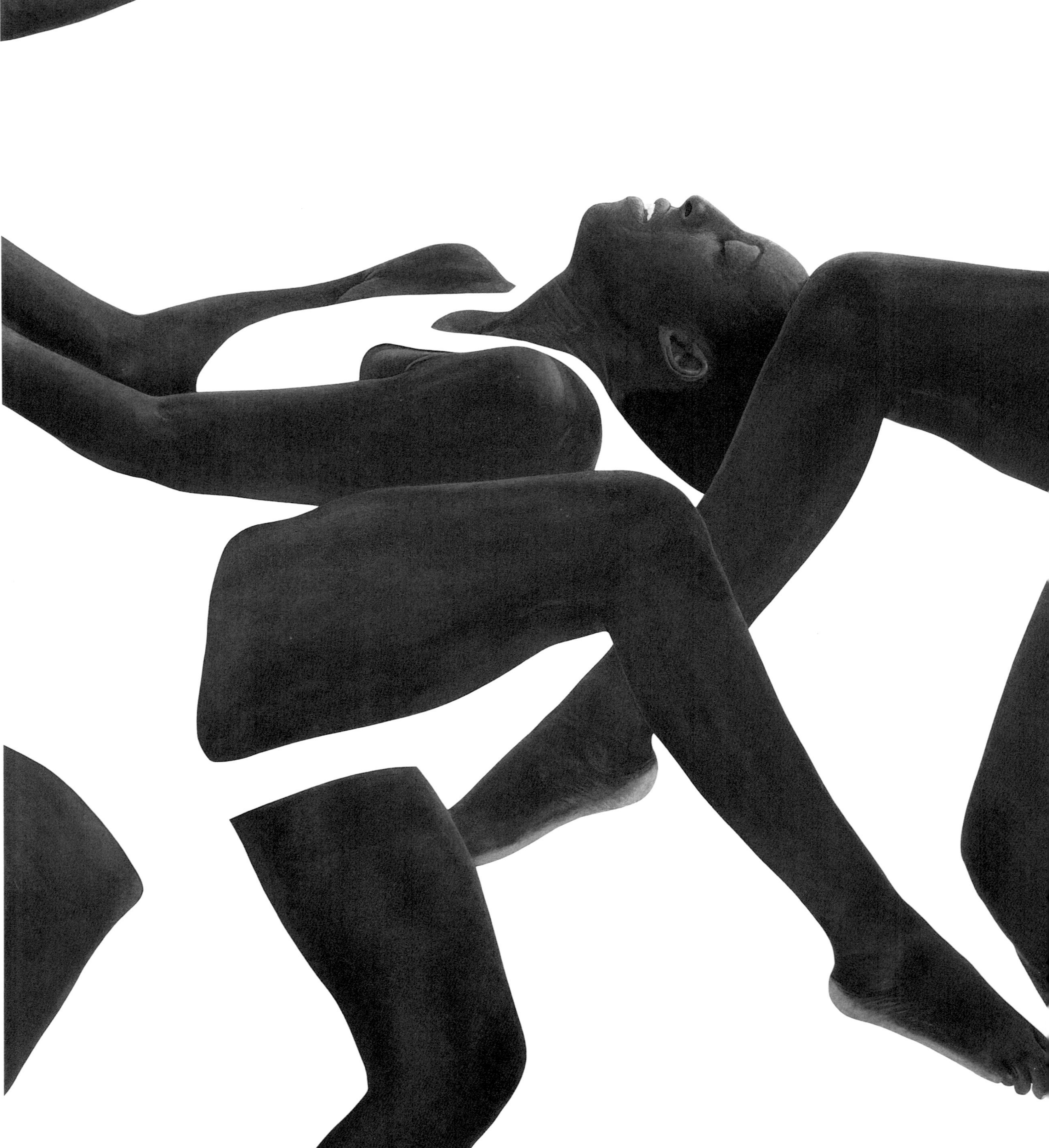

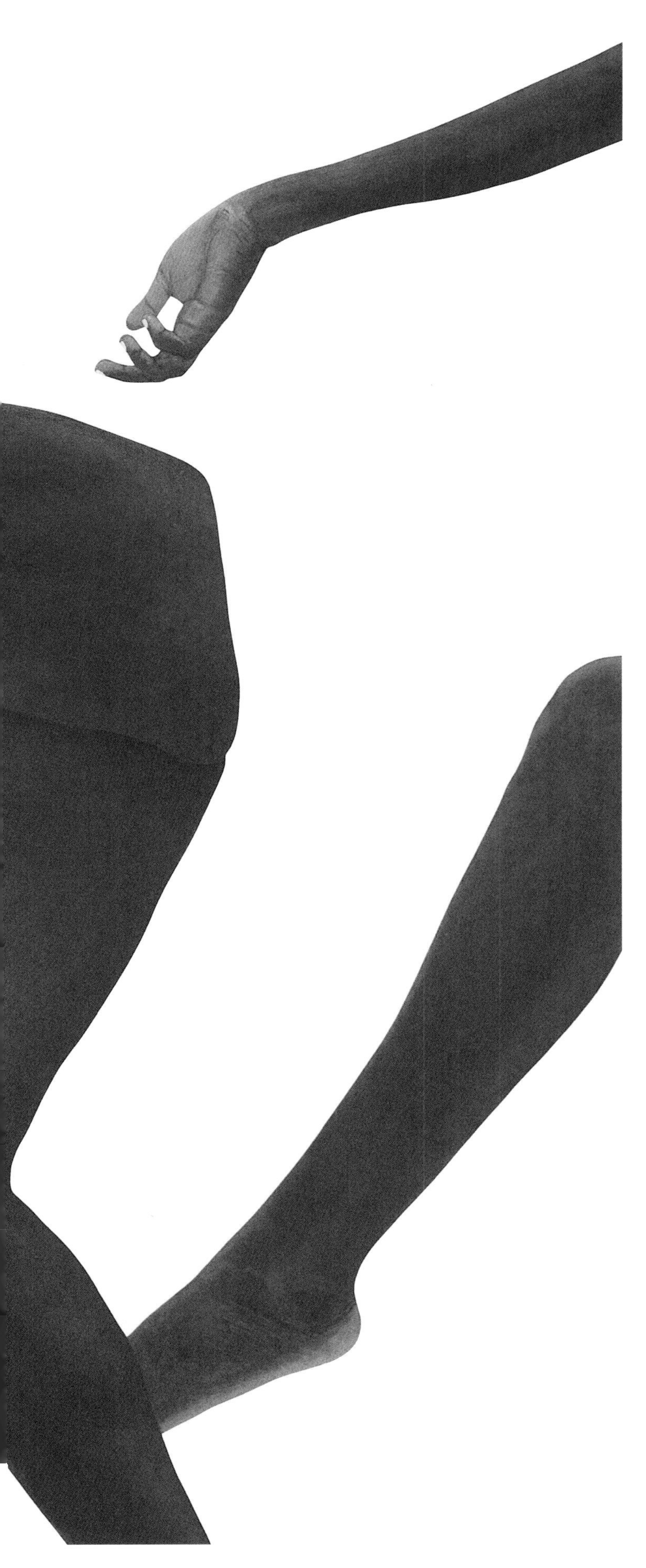

Flow, 2023
acrylic on canvas
200 × 150 cm

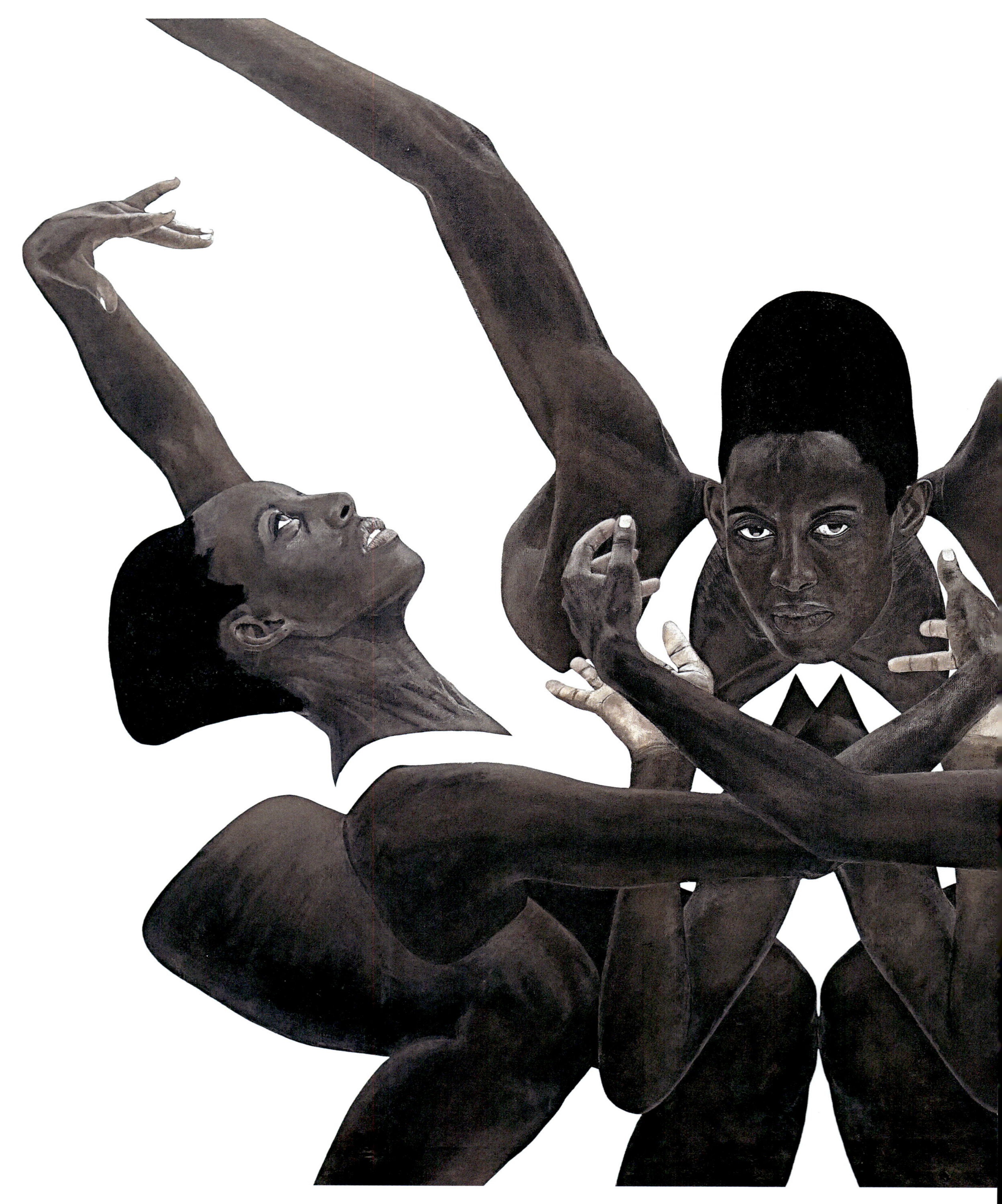

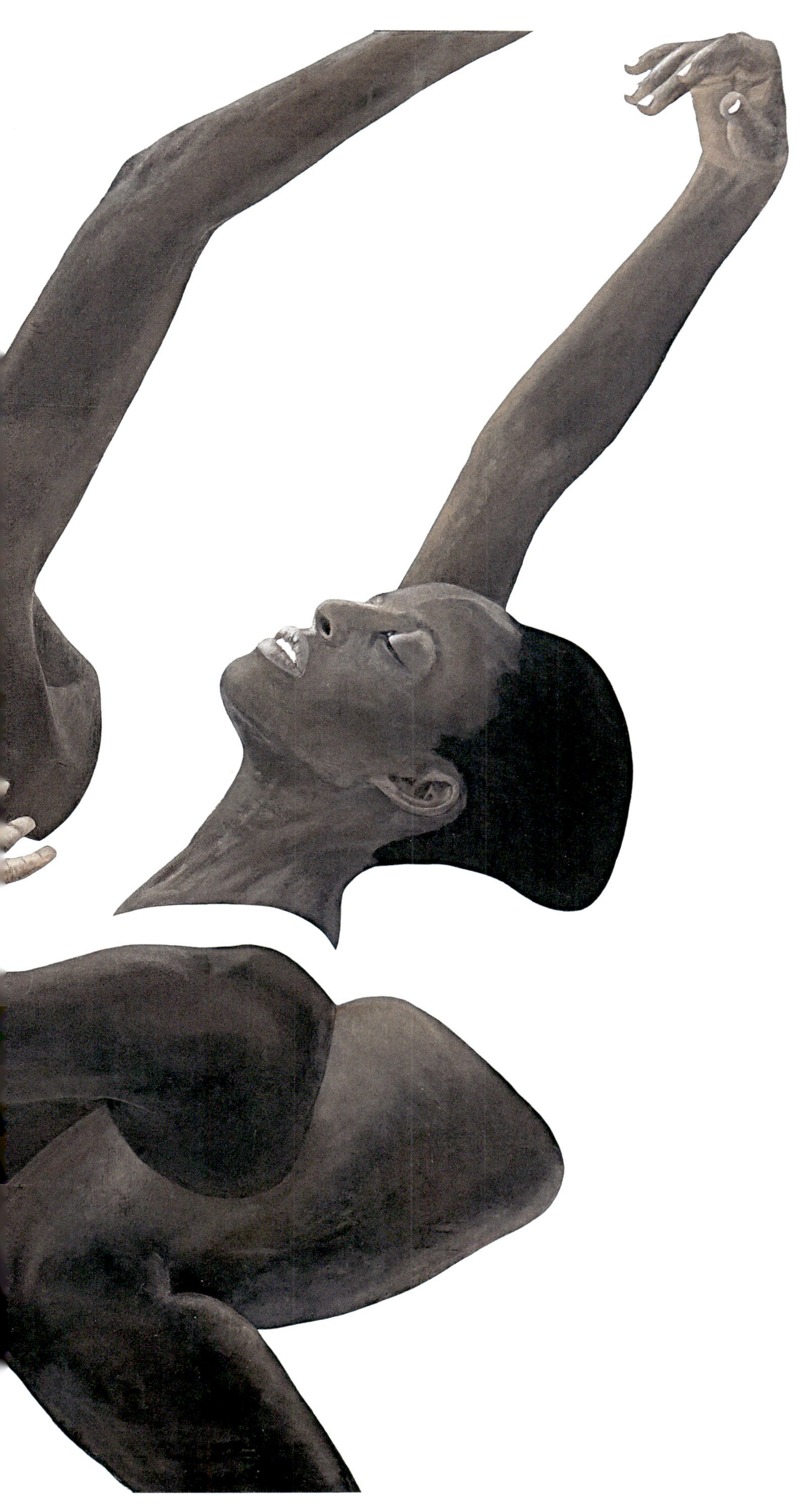

Swish Swash, 2023
acrylic on canvas
150 × 225 cm

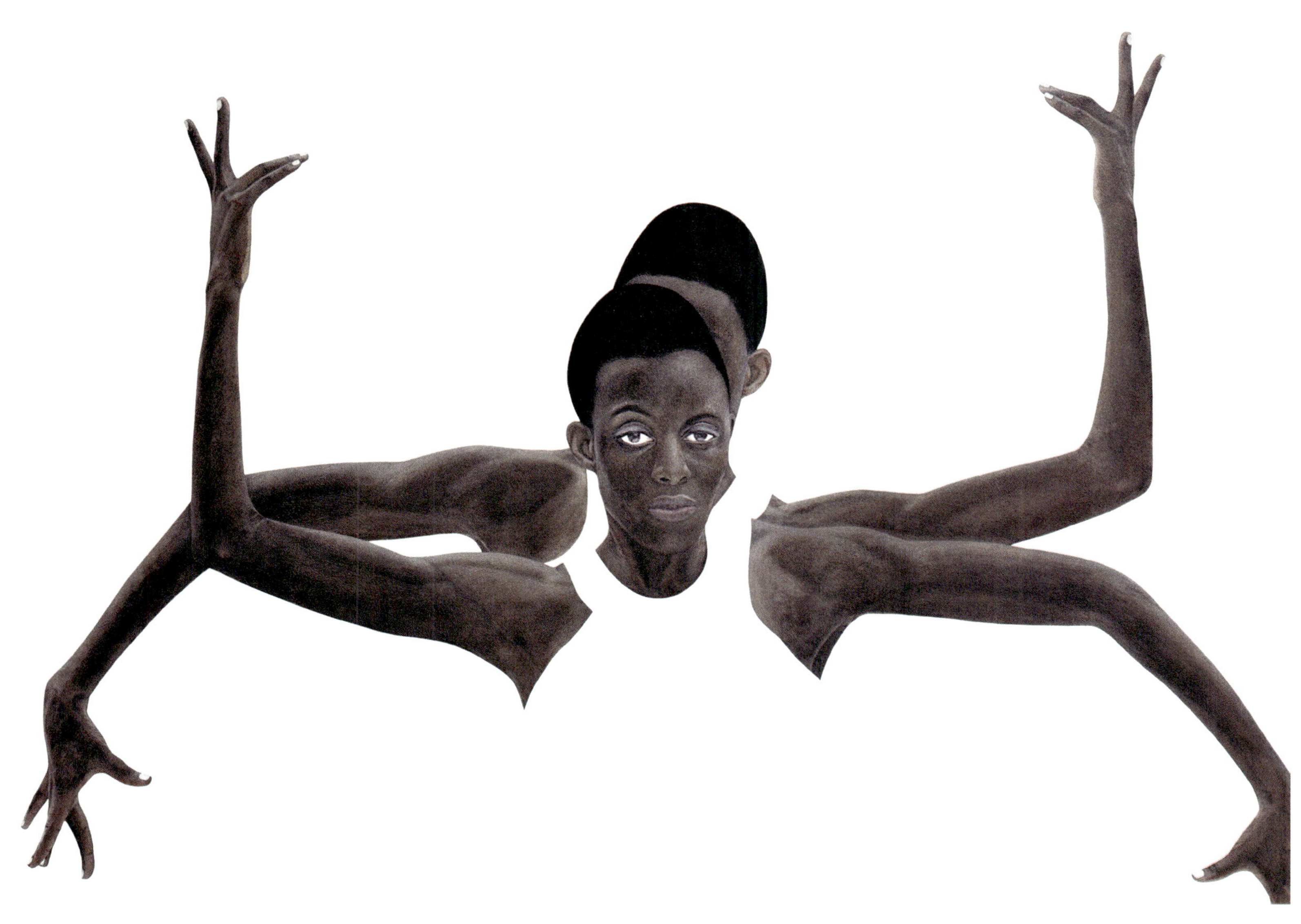

Emergence, 2023
acrylic on canvas
150 × 140 cm

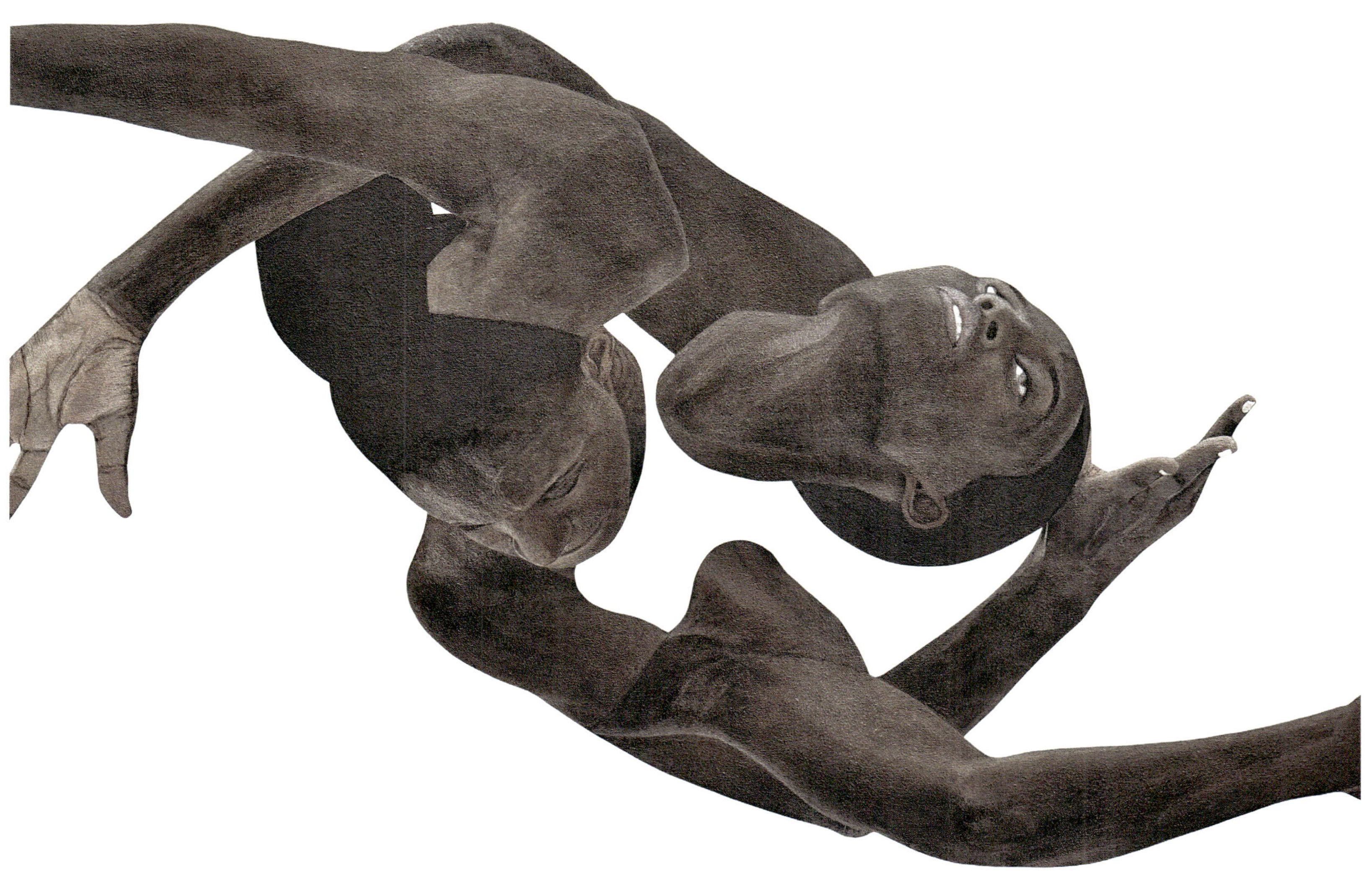

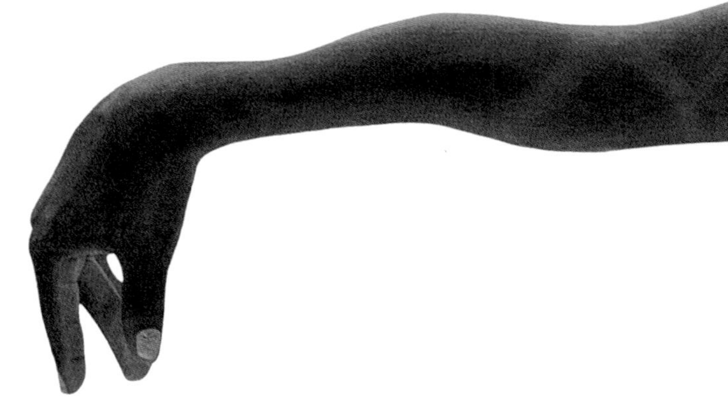

Ripple, 2024
acrylic on canvas
140 × 200 cm

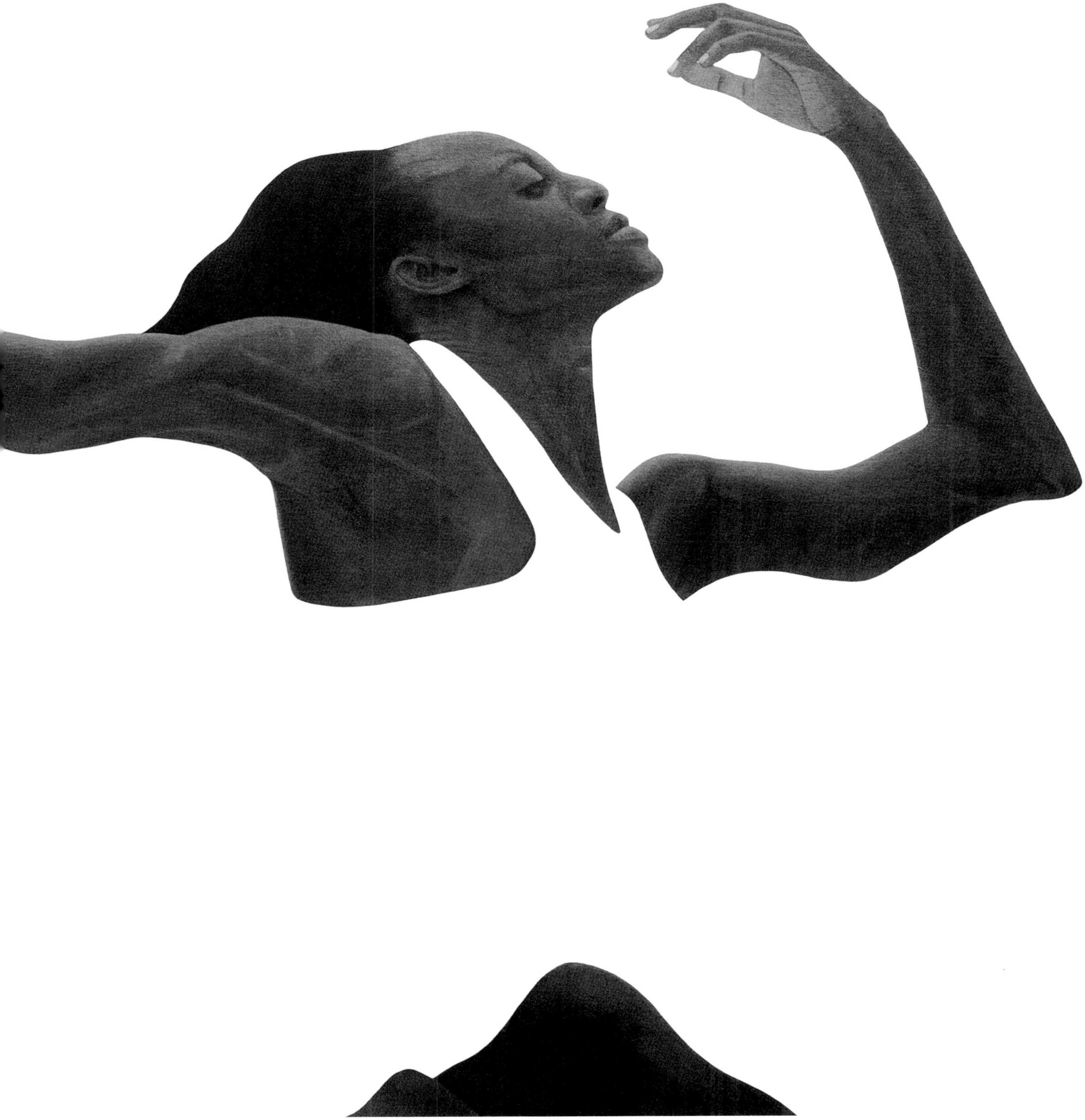

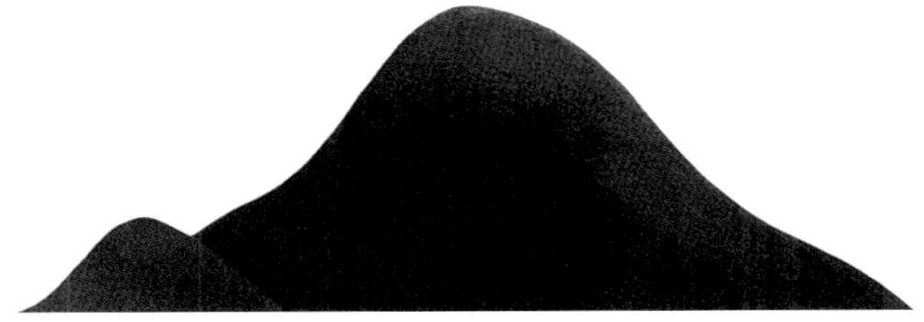

Reflections, 2024
acrylic on canvas
150 × 140 cm

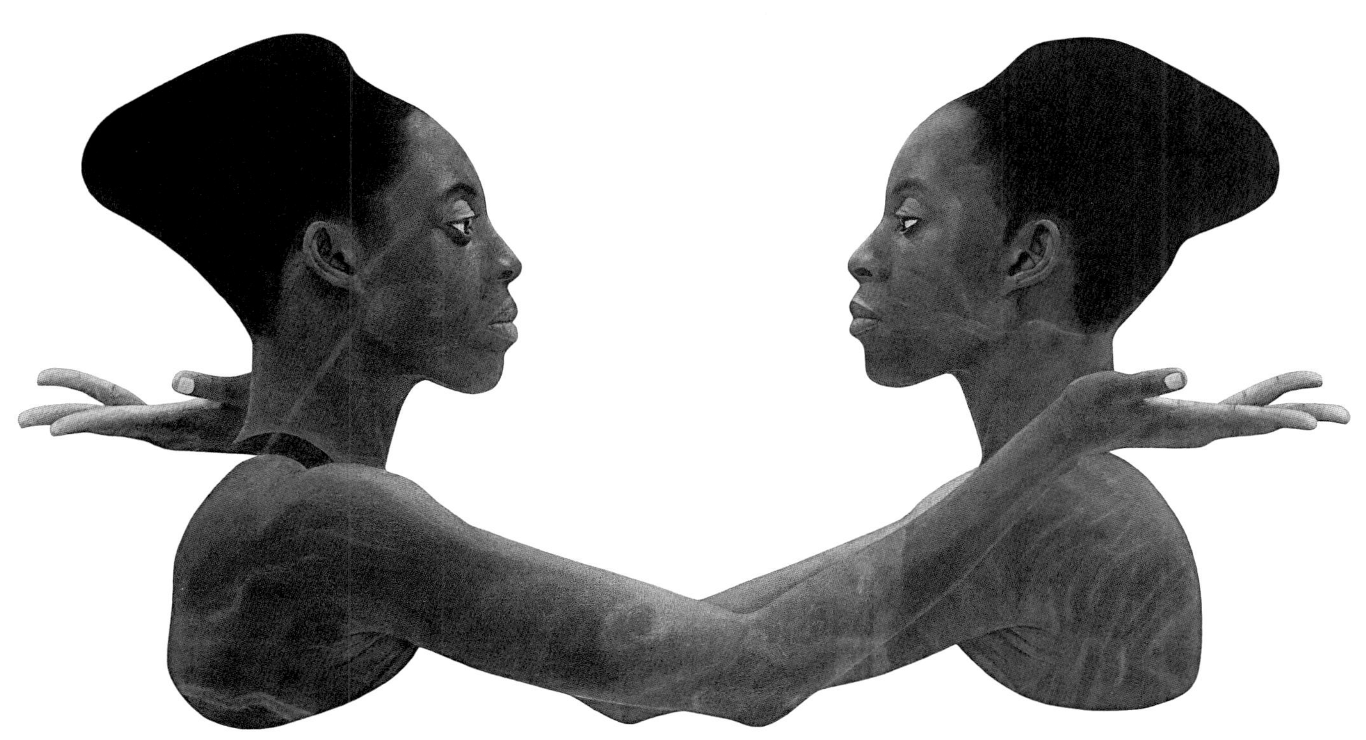

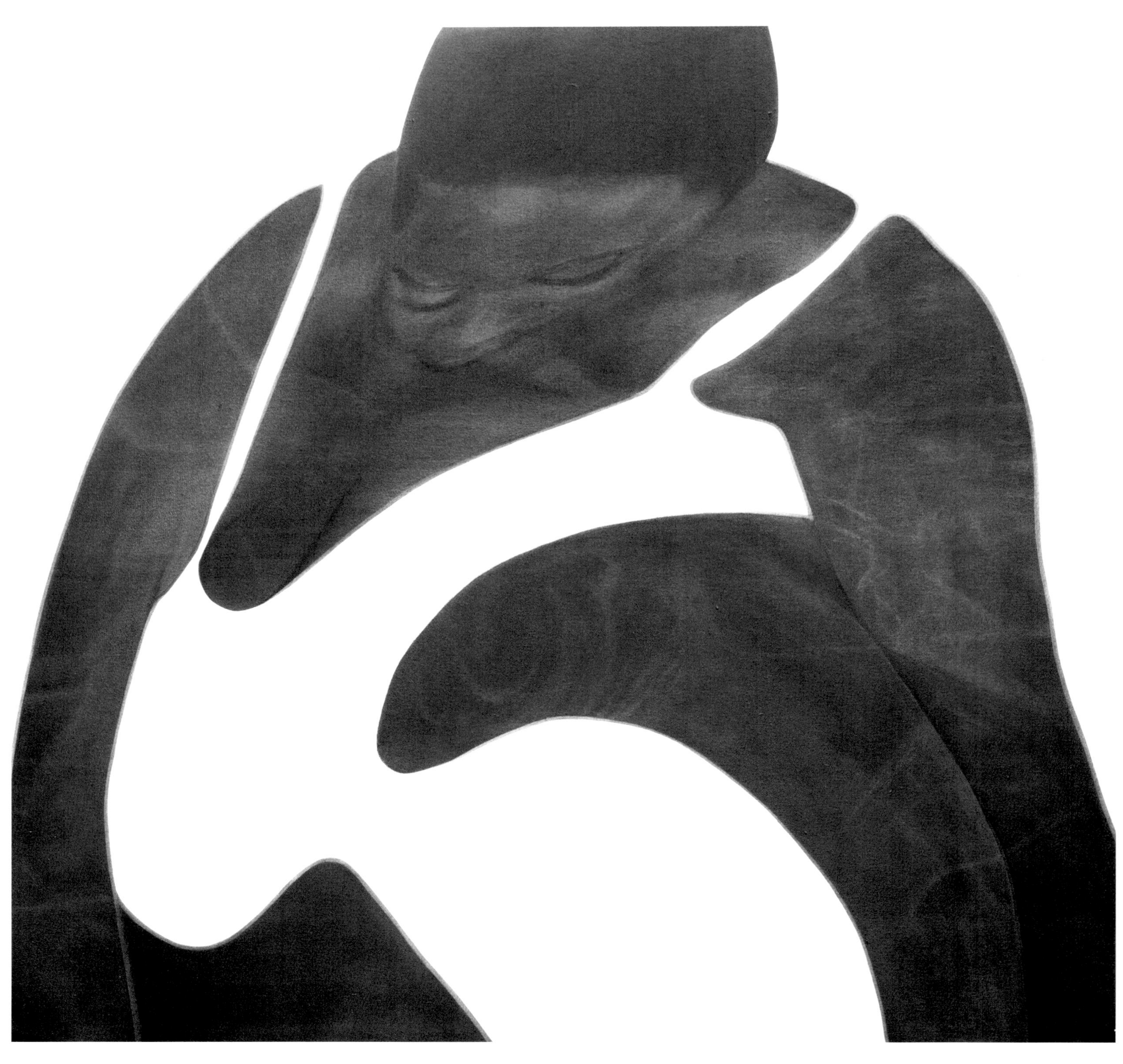

In the Depths, 2024
acrylic on canvas
150 × 140 cm

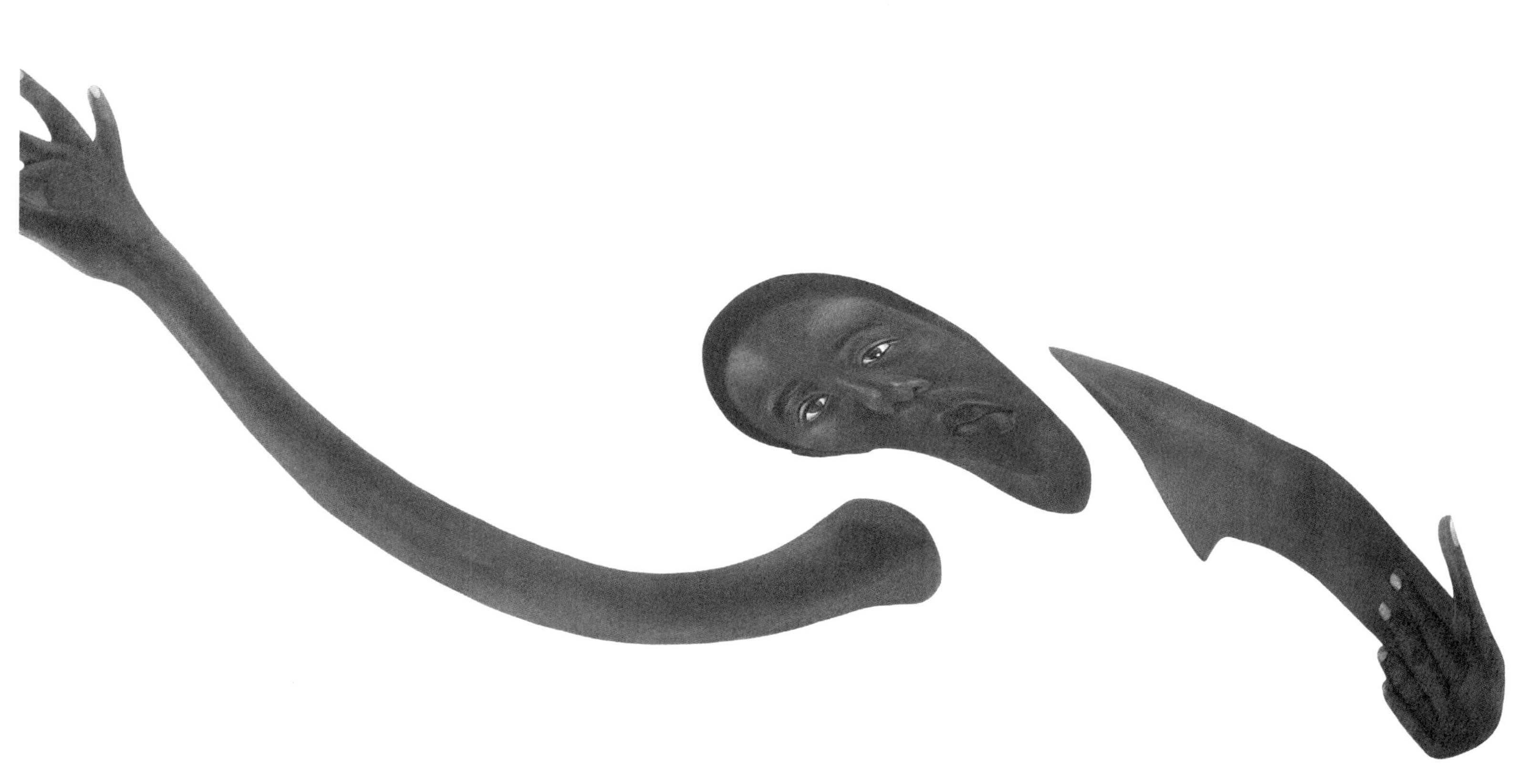

Swimmer, 2024
acrylic on canvas
150 × 200 cm

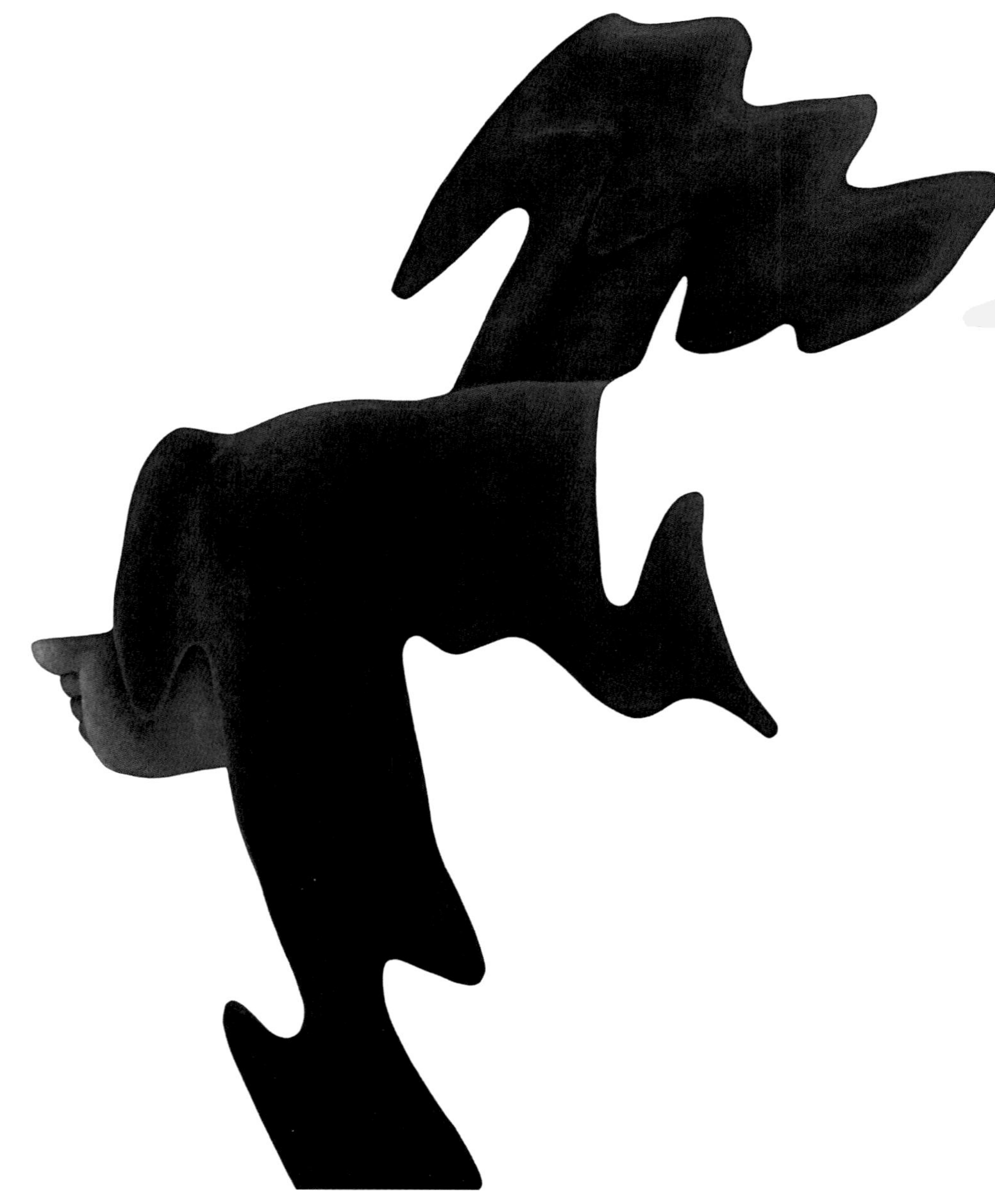

Afloat, 2024
acrylic on canvas
200 × 150 cm

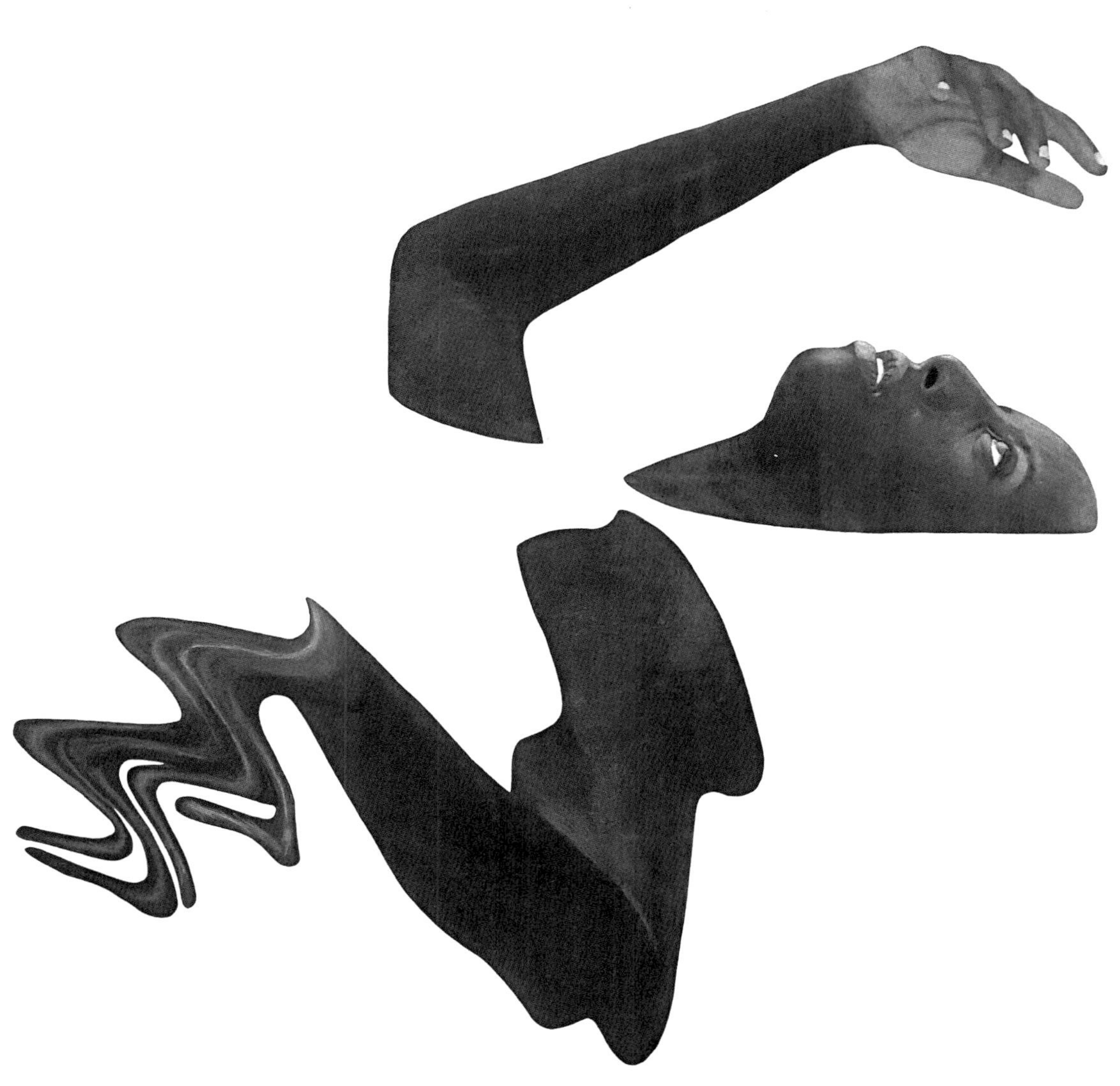

Still Waters, 2024
acrylic on canvas
150 × 140 cm

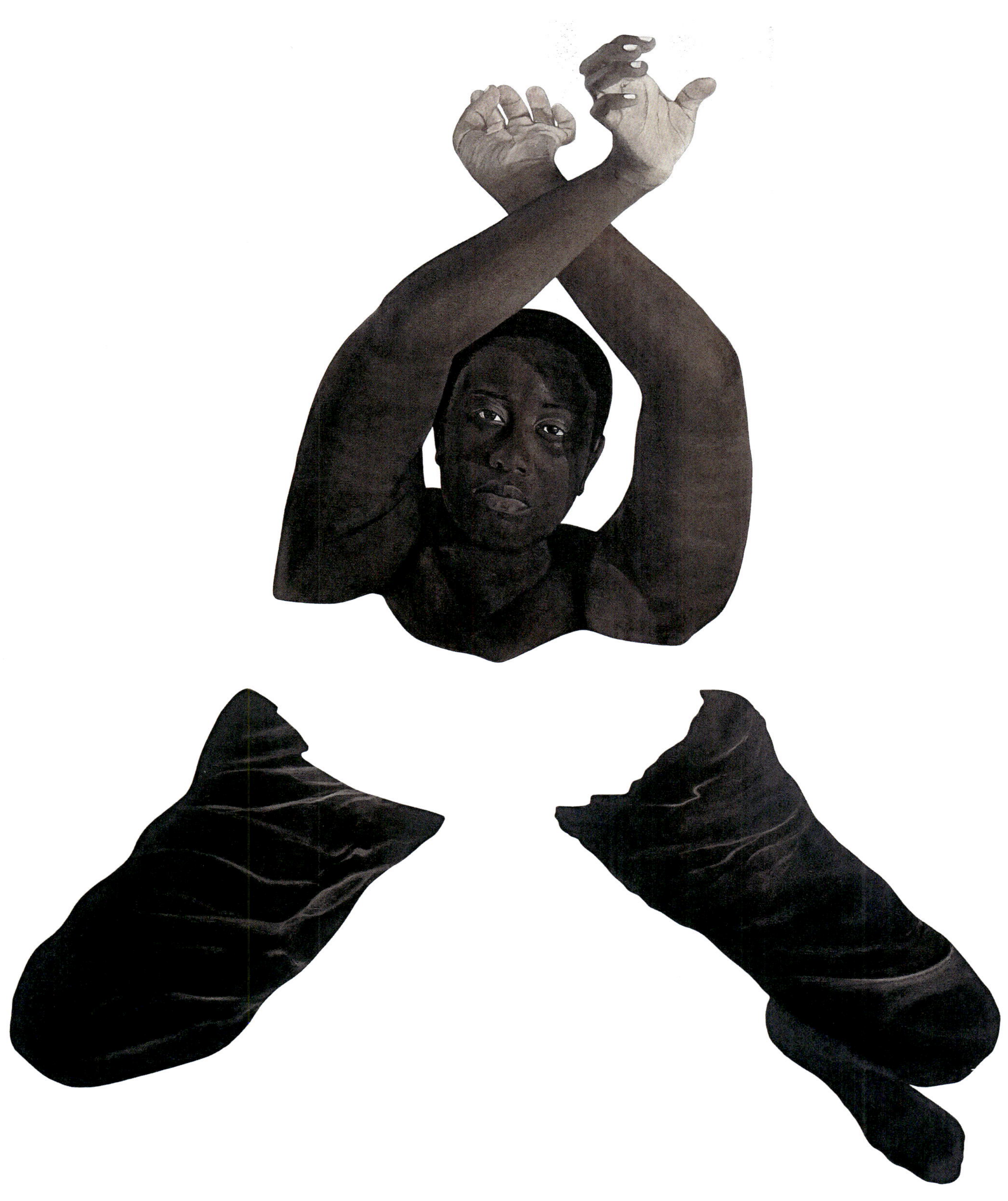

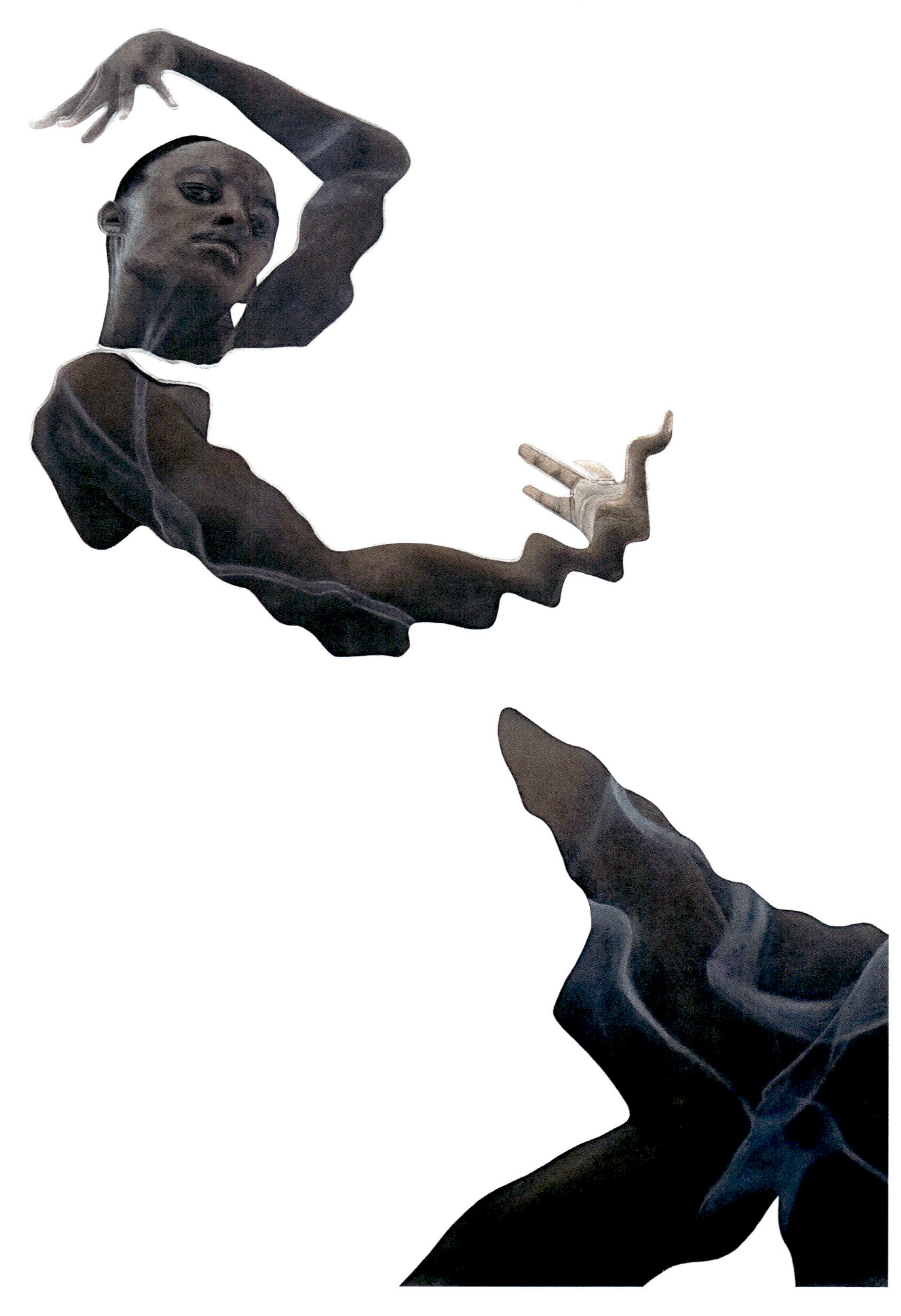

Swirl, 2024
acrylic on canvas
200 × 150 cm

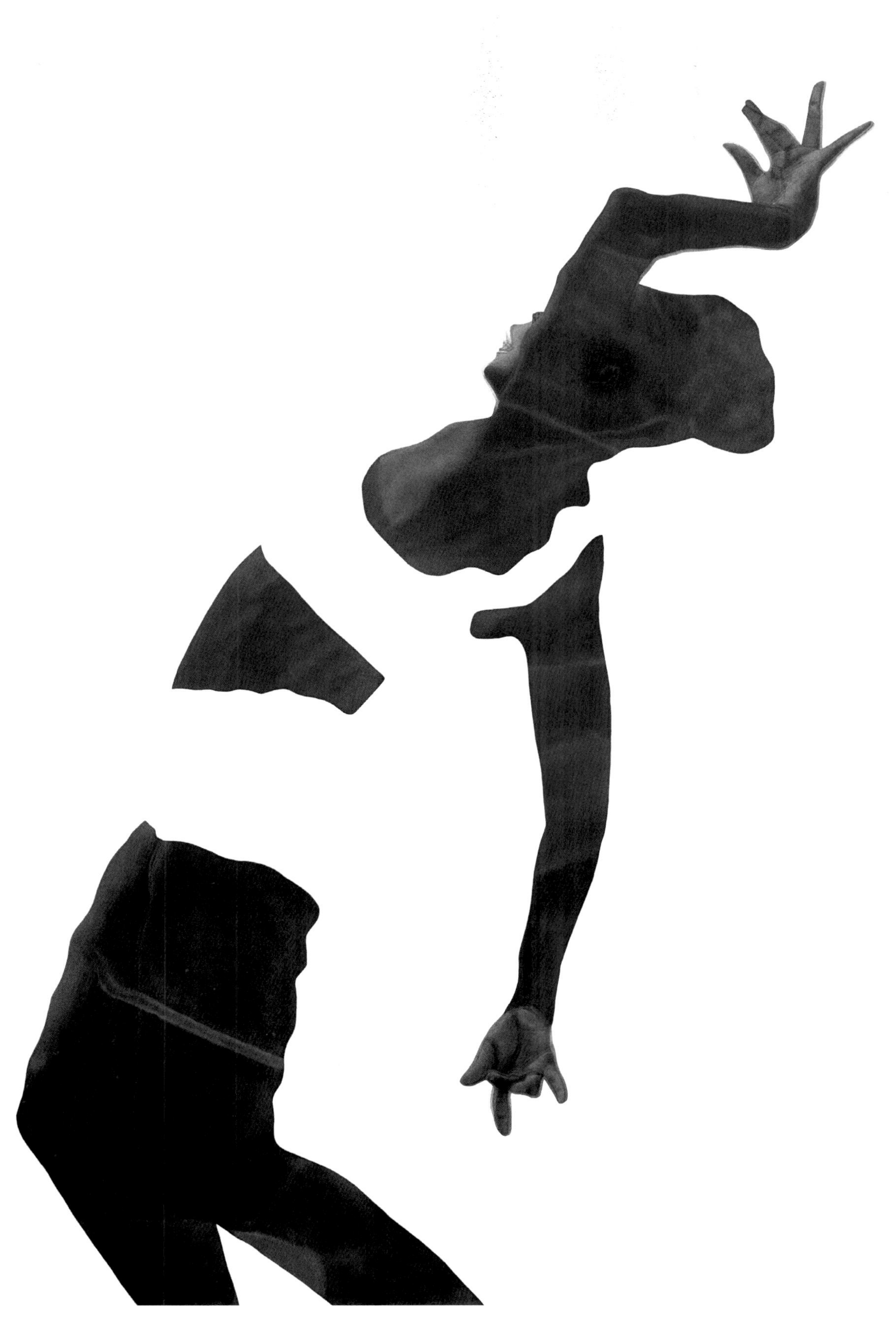

Water Dance, 2024
acrylic on canvas
200 × 140 cm

Laze, 2024
acrylic on canvas
200 × 150 cm

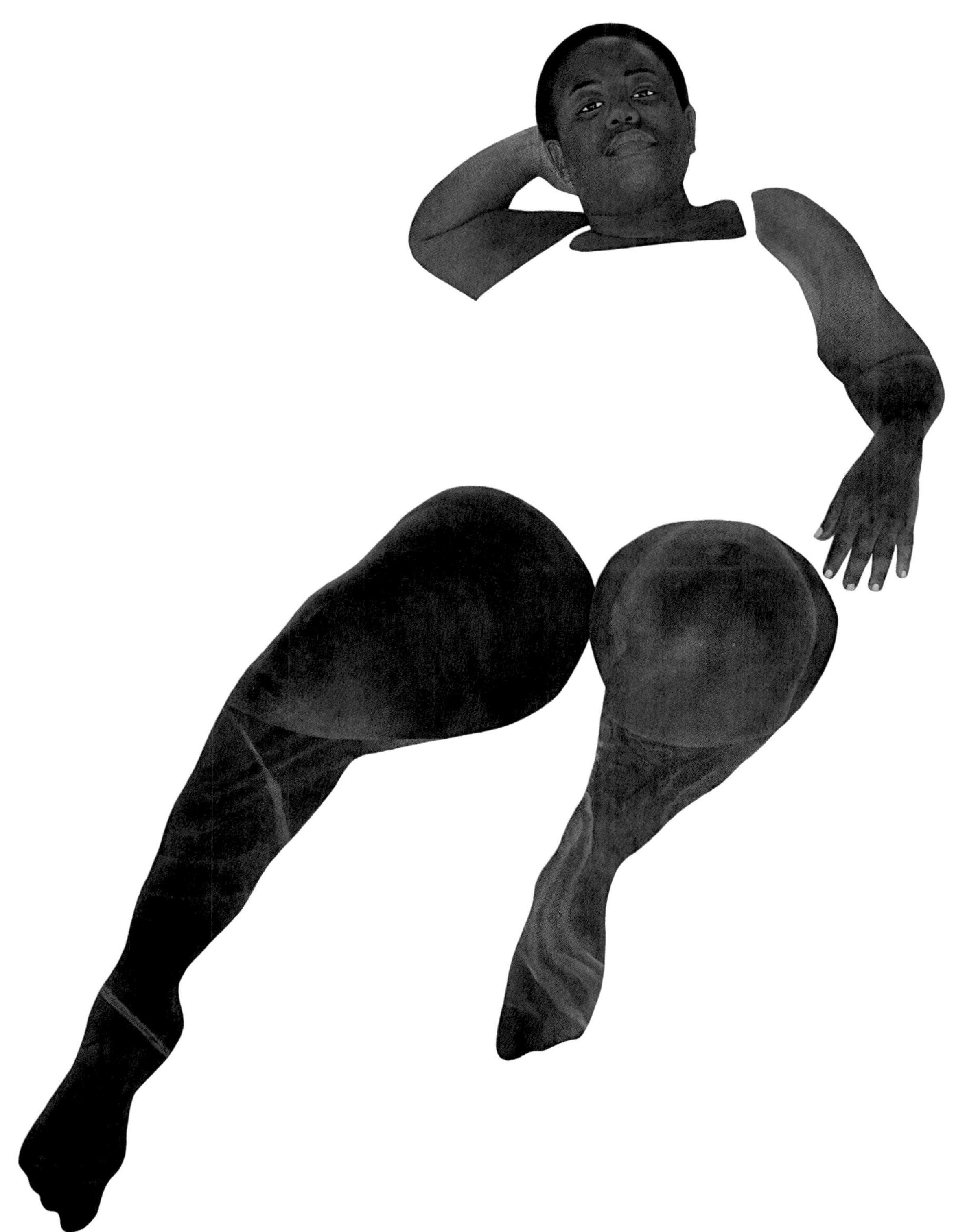

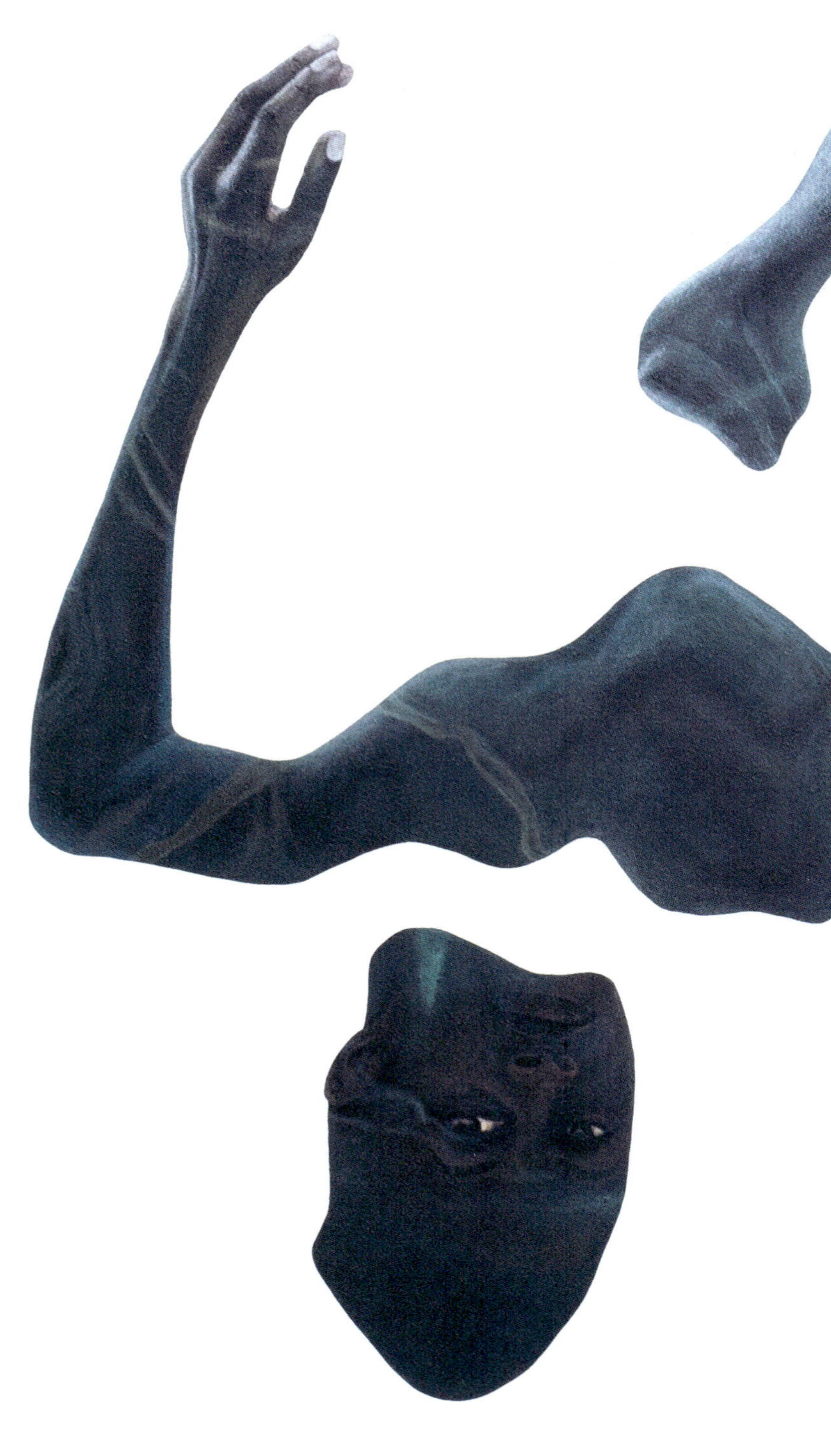

Surge, 2024
acrylic on canvas
150 × 200 cm

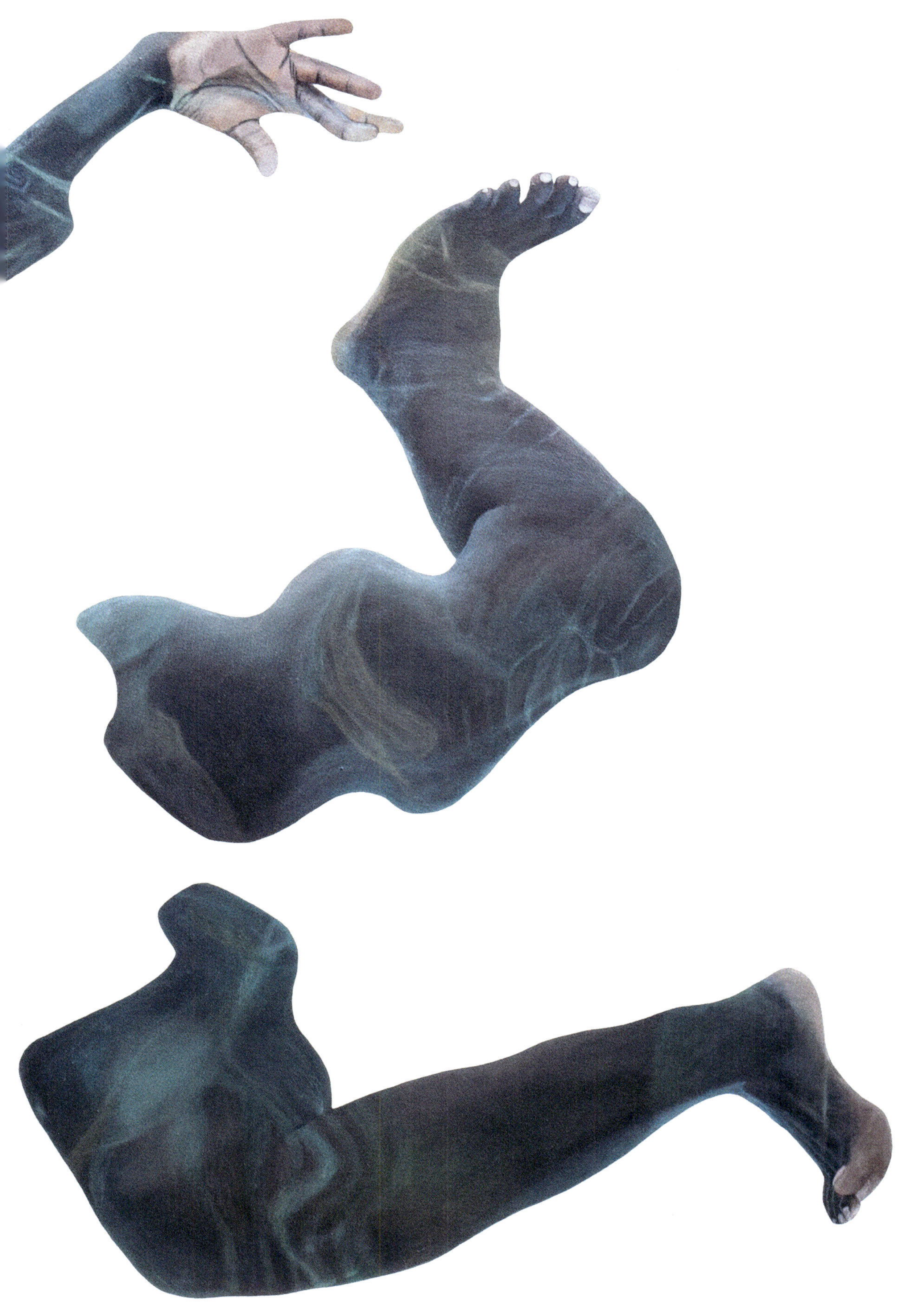

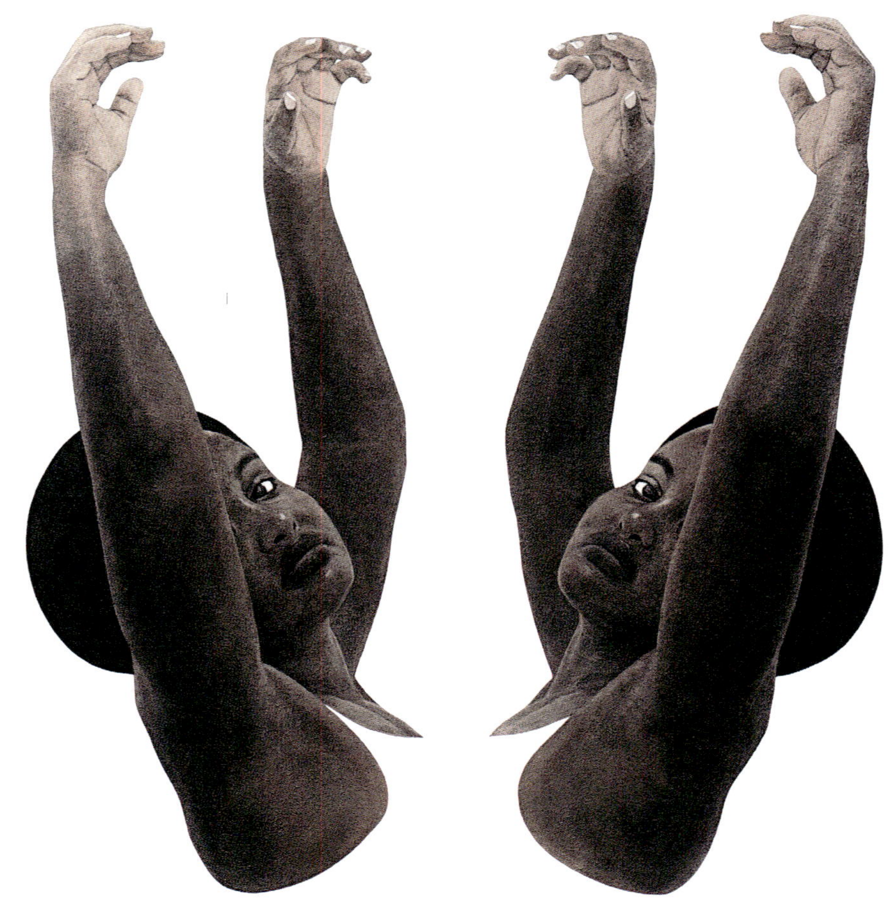
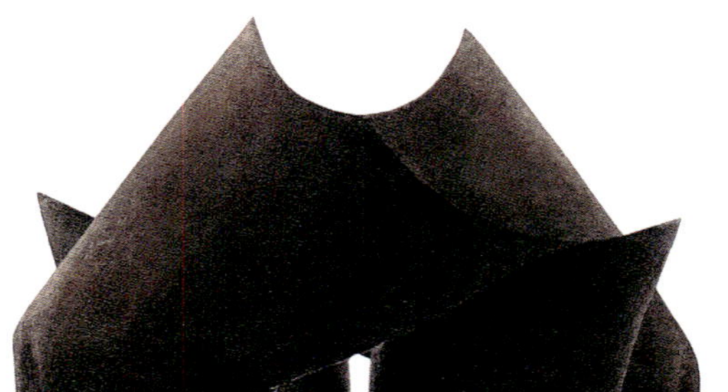

Zone, 2022
acrylic on canvas
150 × 140 cm

In Conversation with Sungi Mlengeya

Sungi Mlengeya – Jemima Michael

Sungi and Mima met in their teenage years in Arusha, Tanzania, where they shared memories of years spent in separate high schools, mischievous holidays and youthful ambitions. Today, they live over 6,000 kilometres apart—Sungi in Arusha, Tanzania, and Mima in Accra, Ghana. Sungi, who periodically turns to Mima as a subject in her work, finds in her friend a muse, one whose presence is both a celebration of their shared past and a vessel for reimagination. In this vivid, spontaneous conversation, they open up about their fears and dreams, exploring how these moments have shaped the women and artists they became.

Mima: We used to talk a lot. We would daydream and talk forever. Do you remember what we hoped for then?

Sungi: Oh, we did daydream. I was so comfortable sitting alone and just imagining all sorts of things. I yearned for freedom, everyone was just so strict. I couldn't wait to be free, you know. I envied people who would be able to go out, meet friends or do anything and they didn't have to worry about a hard time from their parents. I couldn't wait to have the freedom to do all that. I don't think I loved school either. I couldn't wait to finish and be able to do my own thing. Not to have to pretend for survival. And your boyfriend then, remember? He was an artist.

He was one of the few people I knew then who were painters. He chose to go to an art college and I admired him so much for that. I used to wonder how he could draw and paint so well – I just wanted to be able to do that too. What about you? Do you remember your hopes?

Mima: Oh yes. I really resonate with what you said on freedom, although our experiences were very different. There's a time when it felt like I didn't belong, and for me the immediate plan was to finish school. That was in Ashira. I knew that if I was going to advanced secondary school, I needed to get away from Arusha, from Moshi, and go somewhere far away. When I was preparing for my exams and applying to schools, all I was thinking of was how I needed to get out of that place.

Sungi: I can imagine.

Mima: So freedom for me was going to come through getting a school somewhere else. Whereas you knew you didn't want to do anything else. My journey was a step at a time. I wanted more for myself. But when you don't have examples of people who have done that, you see people but you're not close to them, you can't really understand how they got to where they are. So my priority was just getting away from that environment. I was tired and felt that I couldn't grow there.

Sungi: I think we've gotten what we hoped for. Don't you think?

Mima: I do, totally. On those times when you sit down and think that you haven't done things, and haven't achieved much, it's important to question if this is really true. I have changed, my life has changed so much, everything is different now. As you know, I'm currently working with the Development Programme in Ghana. I feel privileged to support their various projects from sustainable development to gender equality. And I enjoy implementing the empowerment projects most, monitoring trips to the outskirts of Accra to see the progress of the women is so fulfilling. I am content with the way things turned out.

Sungi: You have turned things round.

Mima: And the beautiful thing about this friendship is that we were just kids from Sekei, right? We are dreamers and we wanted things and we've seen each other grow and go out and do things. What do you think? Do you feel like we have?

Sungi: Very much so. So much has happened. It's been a long journey and a fruitful one, even the meagre fact that we had these yearnings and tried to find a way through deserves a cheer, with or without traditional success. Do you remember the tearful phone calls?

Mima: I do! But they are always important, we need those. If I think of it, our journeys have been very different too. I remember when you were actually ready to quit your job. I was very reluctant. We had talked about quitting our jobs for so long, we would quit and travel or quit and do something else. But I didn't know what I wanted to do. I had this job, I was comfortable. I could afford things, and you were talking about quitting that life. You had an idea of what you wanted. Your heart was into this thing and you were all in. I thought you were mad. The money I was getting, I could buy fuel for my car, pay my rent, I could eat, buy a nice pair of shoes.

Sungi: I understand how that might have been difficult for you, it was hard for me to get it at that time.

Mima: I loved writing. I used to write but I wasn't sure about myself. What would I do if I became a writer? You had something to show for that period that you weren't working. You quit your job, you were painting, you were doing things.

Sungi: But you know, I also just wanted to enjoy life, and that meant doing what I enjoyed. There's this perception that hardship and the grind is the only way to live correctly. Study hard, work hard, just try not to sink throughout life. I'm learning, or rather, I'm reminding myself to accept and celebrate the various ways of living; whether we are working or taking it easy, all of that. It's all okay.

Mima: That's a good reminder.

Sungi: What are your aspirations now? Do you still feel a need to move on to the next step? I mean, you wanted to get out of there at that moment. You're in a different place now. Do you aspire to something different?

Mima: I think freedom is key in how I want to live my life. It's a different type of freedom now. I saw people that grew up and lived in Sekei and there was a lot of settling. I didn't want that, and me wanting to get out of there was because I felt that if I stayed there, I would settle. This still drives me. I want my life to be better. Better can mean a lot of things. It could be coming back home but doing better. I just want to continue growing and to move forward in life. It can be here; it can be somewhere else. It can be moving jobs or something else. But what I'm aspiring towards now is growth and a better life. How about you?

Sungi: I doubt the underlying need for freedom has changed for me either. I've tasted freedom and I love it. I don't think I would want to give it up. People say you compromise that as you get older, I don't want that to be the case, I want to maintain a level of choice in whatever I do.

Mima: Speaking of hopes, and your hopes on art, you must feel so content.

Sungi: Oh I'm so happy I got into that and I hope I'll be creating for a very, very long time – I feel at peace in this path. And with my current technique, I get to celebrate people like you, that's a great bonus.

Mima: Aaaaaw!

Sungi: I've made several paintings of you. What's your favourite?

Mima: The first one you made of me, the one in your first solo show in Kampala.

Sungi: Oh interesting. Can I ask why? How did it make you feel?

Mima: I felt seen, I had never seen myself on a canvas before. When you asked me to model, I was really, really excited because I had seen some of the paintings you did, and I loved them. The whole process, you asking me to model, the photography session was so exciting. It was you also that painted me. You know me well, we are close, we are friends. We are sort of like sisters. I felt vulnerable too. When I saw the final piece, I couldn't believe it was actually me. And I remember it was in your room in Kampala for a while.

Sungi: It was. Oh, thank you! You are always a great model.

Mima: And you were really focused when you painted, you are always focused when you paint. What goes through your mind?

Sungi: Well, I think it's different every time. I work in silence and I only play music or a podcast at the end of the day when I'm getting tired and need motivation to finish something. But otherwise, especially in the morning and afternoon, it's mostly silence and that allows me to really be calm and for my mind to roam. Sometimes I tell myself to think about something specific, but that hardly happens, and I think of all sorts of things. It's much needed when life is busy, I can really slow down and let my thoughts unravel. Everything catches up with me, and I let it all come.

Mima: Oh that's a rewarding process. Life can be so busy sometimes that we hardly have time to react to it.

Sungi: Completely.

Mima: So the models you paint, is it the same with everyone? Or do you feel more pressure when you paint someone you know so well?

Sungi: Not all the time. With models who are peers, it has been me putting out my thoughts and ideas or beliefs through you guys. For instance, I love dance so I would ask you to dance and paint you dancing. It is a mirroring of the things and ideas that I resonate with, portraying that on you as well. But it's hardly a one-way process, I'm also guided by something about the individual model. I've painted my sister Ngollo in a lot of "don't mess with me" poses. I feel like she has that energy.

Mima: Yeah, she does.

Sungi: And I love it, she looks so powerful. I do want to exude power, and make anyone think twice before they act inconsiderately. Not sure

I can pull it off in her exact manner, but it's something I look for in myself, and it's thrilling to see that unapologetic autonomy in the women around me.

Mima: Life would be so much smoother.

Sungi: It would. Recently, I painted my mom again. I had this strong urge to do that quickly so that I could celebrate her with everyone who would come across this book. Painting her was a different experience. I used a photo from her thirties, so she was around our age and I was around two or something at that time. The process was deeply reflective and emotional, I thought of her at that age, my perception of her then. How much she changed throughout her life. Her influence on my life as someone I care for so much. And I did feel the pressure to capture her essence. I wanted her to look at it and be proud, see herself. I wanted that tap on the back.

Mima: That's beautiful, did you manage to show it to her?

Sungi: I did. She loved it, phew!

Mima: Haha! Of course.

Sungi: My favourite painting of you is *Zone.* You're dancing, your hands are above your head, it's a mirror image. I made it when I was getting freer in my technique and didn't feel the need to make paintings that only made logical sense. I think it was also one of the first paintings that I did in the theme of dance.

Mima: That's special, I didn't know that. By the way, I hope you still dance?

Sungi: In my head. But I seriously want to put it on my priority list.

Mima: Please do, I'll hold you accountable. These things, they are the whole point of life.

Sungi: *Kabisa.*[1] So, when you look at yourself in *Zone* or your favourite painting, do you feel like it captures who you are or is there a part of yourself you wish I could focus on more? Something that you feel defines you?

Mima: That's a very deep question, actually. I think I'm all things with you, right? I feel seen. And I think a lot of people don't see this side of me where I'm very playful, I am unserious, I am free. I think that comes out when I'm surrounded by people that I love, people that I trust. That comes out when I'm with you, I feel like you see me that way and I see that in the paintings.

Sungi: Aaaaaaaw, thank you! Seriously, that means a lot. Also, we keep growing and evolving. Having that in mind, maybe there's always going to be something else to be captured. Do you ever think we ever truly see ourselves the way others do?

Mima: That's a difficult one. I'll just give you an example. A lot of people think that I'm harsh. I don't know if harsh is the word. But there are people who do not see me that way. And I don't see myself that way. If I had to list everything I think about myself or how I see myself, harsh won't be there. It won't be on top of the list anyway. I feel like we have these pieces of ourselves that we let people see. Who I am with you or who I am with my close friends is not the same person I am with just anyone else, they all see me differently.

Sungi: I agree with you. I think we are different people to different people. And sometimes we know ourselves best. There are parts of us that only ourselves can know. And then there are parts that other people know better than us. I think if we took ourselves out of our bodies and observed ourselves from a corner of a room, we'd be surprised.

Mima: True. Do you ever worry that portraying me, or anyone else really, might reveal more about you than me? Do you learn anything from the process?

Sungi: Yes. I don't think it's something I worry about but it's something that happens in different ways as my subjects expand. Painting someone so profound as Mama forces me to think of them deeply, it's a time of contemplation that can open doors of questioning and new understanding about her and myself, as somebody who brought me into this world and has been with me all my life. Painting you also makes me discover things, the things that I find meaningful can show themselves to me in the work.

So of course, there are the women, who sum up all those moments with you or a good friend, my sister, mother or aunty; the real constants in life, the comfort and blissful circles. And then there are the things they're doing in the paintings, their actions or poses, whether they're standing still or dancing, they all could give away something.

Recently I've been looking at water, trying to incorporate the peace and joy of the sea into the canvas. So with each painting, I ask myself what to put out, and it should make me at least excited at that moment, this then is a revelation of something, of what moves me. And this could change as I change, it's all a process of exploration and discovery.

Mima: Wonderful.

Sungi: Speaking of freedom, this has come up a lot and it obviously matters to both of us. What does it mean to you now? If you had to loosely define it.

Mima: It's such a huge word! But I think it's about living authentically, having choices. Doing things because I choose to do them. There are a lot of expectations from people but living truly and not giving into that pressure is important. One thing that I've learned throughout this journey is we know ourselves well. I wouldn't go about and do something that would intentionally harm me, I want what's best for myself and I'm the best person to make those decisions, you know. What about you? Do you think you're free?

Sungi: I am deep down, I just need to channel my freedoms more. I'm realising that it's all tied to allocation of time, what you choose to spend your time doing, who you choose to spend your time with. It's refreshing when I actually remember to choose after I have been caught up reacting to life, then there is this fresh excitement of the new possibility, new doors and a possible shift of things.

Mima: It's so easy to get swept up in things and forget.

Sungi: Yeah. And what is your greatest dream now?

Mima: Well, for the last two years or so I've really taken time to write. And like with anything, the more you practise, the better you become at it. I want to publish a book, a poetry book. It's on top of my list right now. I've been reading more poetry, I want to understand how other writers write. That's one of my biggest dreams. Now, I do have other dreams. The other things are just what we talk about all the time; travelling, settling down. I'm still doing 9 to 5. I don't know how I feel about where I am now, but I know that I want to continue. I love what I do. I can see that I'm making a difference. And one of my core beliefs is creating impact. The work I do now allows me to do that. So it's bits and pieces.

Sungi: Oh wow, beautiful. The book is exciting! I'm sure you'll make it happen.

Mima: Thank you!

Sungi: I relate with the bits and pieces. At the moment, I don't think I have that all-encompassing dream that is the purpose of my life. What I want now is probably different from what I wanted five years ago and that will change in ten years. But one thing that has stuck with me for a while is creating. What I want now is to indulge even further into making, maybe take it beyond the canvas into other mediums or spaces. I just want to be surrounded by beautiful pieces and spaces. I also want to have fun. Just enjoy life. I don't think there are moments when life understands that you have just finished dealing with something and decides to give you some chill time. Life just happens, so I want to intentionally make time for enjoyment, in big or small ways.

Mima: And what makes it more fun is that you can change your mind. You can make new choices as you pursue these things.

Sungi: Oh yes. It's not set in stone. We will learn new things. Unlearn other things. I could have

new experiences that change me, you know? And I think that's part of freedom. Otherwise wouldn't we be the ones holding ourselves back? But there's a thin line between this and running away, it's important to figure out what is meaningful.

Mima: I feel the same way. I don't know if this happens to you, when you set out to do something and envision everything, you invest your time and resources. Then you change your mind and there's this feeling of guilt. It's hard letting go of something that you thought you wanted for a long time.

Sungi: I do get that feeling, but sometimes there is a relief after the guilt.

Mima: That's true.

Sungi: So how do you do life your way?

Mima: I think one thing about me is that I won't do something I don't want to do. This has come from independence and people letting me do things on my own from a young age. I had to exercise my muscles to make sure that I am safe and on the right track, I've always had to avoid peer pressure.

Sungi: I wish it came from a nurturing space, but that's an invaluable experience.

Mima: What about you though?

Sungi: It's doing what makes sense to me. I've always been very strong-minded. At the end of the day, it's really important to ask myself, does this matter to me? Even if it's an unpopular opinion, I need to be true to myself. Maintaining a community that inspires me is very important, good examples are good motivation, if I need the validation I'll get it from there.

Mima: I'm not sure if you're a perfectionist, but I've seen you paint even after the work seems finished. How do you know when a painting is done?

Sungi: I think when I start to slow down, I also need to tell myself that there is no perfection. That's when I let go and allow myself to declare a painting done at any moment.

Mima: Have you forced yourself to step away?

Sungi: Yes, many times.

Mima: Any hopes for this book?

Sungi: I get to share my paintings, I get to celebrate the women, movements, and ideas in these works with more people.

Mima: I love that.

Sungi: Just one more question. What is a possibility for you?

Mima: It's knowing that I can go after things, having the courage to do so, even without knowing the outcome.

Sungi: Well, if you haven't heard me say this a million times already, I want you to think of a fresh piece of paper, and you have a pencil in your hand. You are about to draw or write something, you're thinking of what this could be, and it could be anything, as boundless and infinite as the boundaries of your mind. When you see yourself on the canvas, I would like you to imagine being surrounded by this sense; endless possibility, choices, freedom.

Mima: Beautiful. Thank you for reminding me.

Sungi: Thank you for inspiring me.

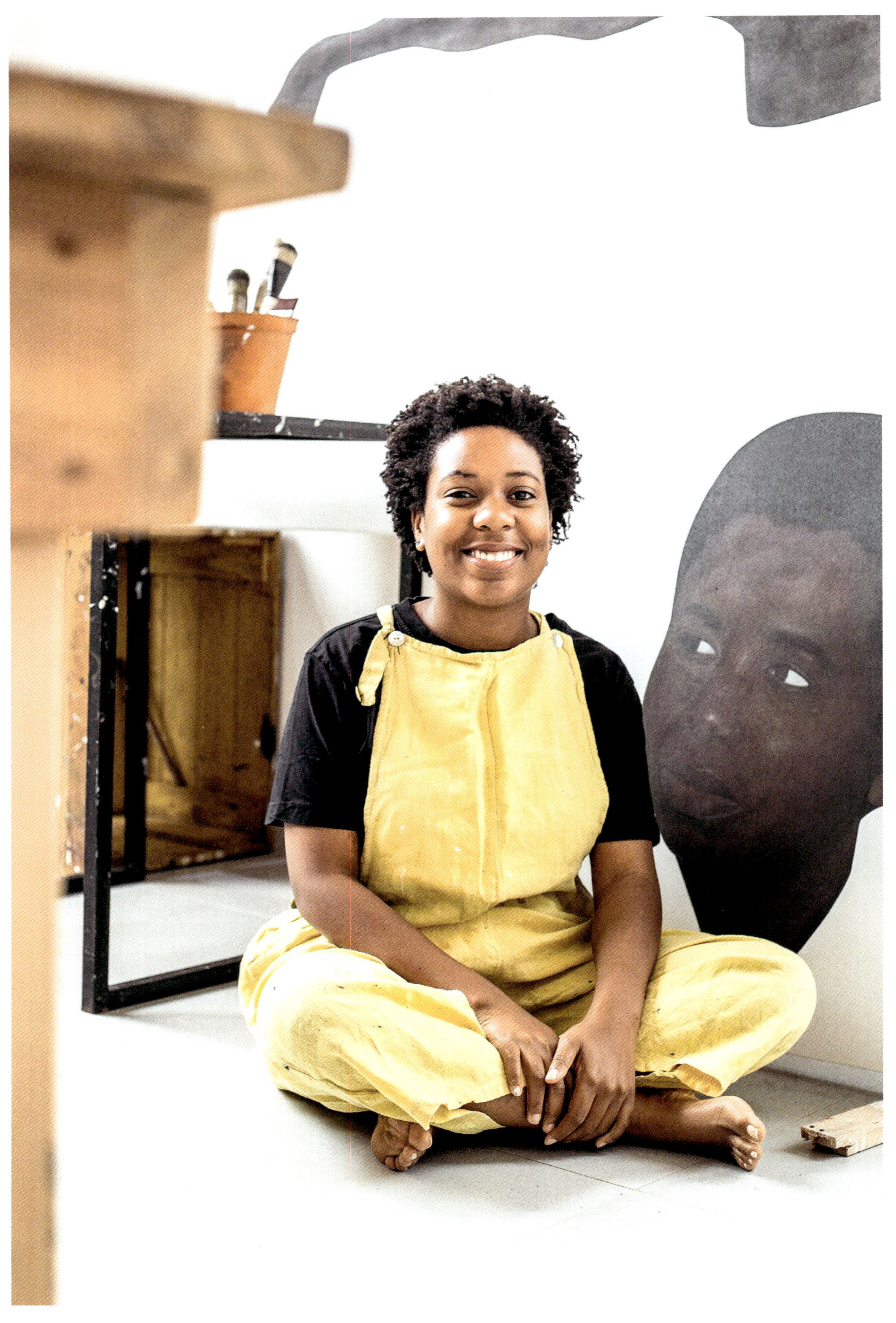

Biography

Born in 1991 in Dar es Salaam, Tanzania, Sungi Mlengeya has gained recognition for her distinctive visual language, characterized by monochromatic portraits of Black women. Her meticulously painted figures are set against minimalist white backgrounds, creating a striking contrast that emphasizes skin texture and form. Mlengeya's figurative portraiture serves as a tribute to the women in her life, depicting them in states of movement and stillness; strength and calm; resilience and repose. Through the interplay of light and expansive negative space, she conveys a sense of boundless possibility, inviting viewers to reflect on the inherent freedom and power of those she paints.

Mlengeya's work has garnered international attention and is featured in prominent private and public collections. Following her debut solo exhibition, *Just Disruptions* at Afriart Gallery in Kampala, she presented *Unsettled Minds*, a solo booth at Art Basel Miami Beach in 2021. In 2022, her solo exhibition *(Un)choreographed* marked the re-opening of The Africa Centre in London, and her work was also the focus of *Don't Try, Don't Not Try*, a solo show hosted by the B.LA Art Foundation in Vienna, Austria.

Her work has been included in *When We See Us: A Century of Black Figuration in Painting*, a groundbreaking travelling exhibition presented at the Zeitz MOCAA in Cape Town, Kunstmuseum Basel, and Bozar Brussels (2022–25). In 2024, Mlengeya's work was featured in *The Beauty of Diversity* at the Albertina Modern in Vienna.

In 2023, she participated in *Insistent Presence: Contemporary Art from the Chazen Collection* at the Chazen Museum of Art in the United States and *Africa Supernova* at Kunsthal KAdE in the Netherlands. Her other notable group exhibitions include *A Force for Change* at Agora Gallery in New York, an exhibition and auction hosted by UN Women in 2021 to support Black women globally, and *Black Voices: Friend of My Mind* at Ross-Sutton Gallery. Mlengeya has also exhibited at Unit London in *The Medium is the Message* and *Drawn Together*, and her work was showcased in *1-54 Highlights* at Christie's London. Her participation in *Playing to the Gallery* in 2020 and *Surfaces II: Gender Identity Rebellion* in 2019 at Afriart Gallery acclaimed her mark on the contemporary art scene.

Mlengeya was named one of Apollo's *40 Under 40 Africa* in 2020, recognizing her as one of the most influential young figures in African art. In 2023, she was honoured as a resident at the Rockefeller Foundation Bellagio Center, and she was also included in the inaugural *Keep Walking: Africa Top 30 List*.

Portrait of the artist
in her studio
October 2024

Pages 132-133:

Solo presentation
by Sungi Mlengeya
at Art Basel Miami Beach
2021

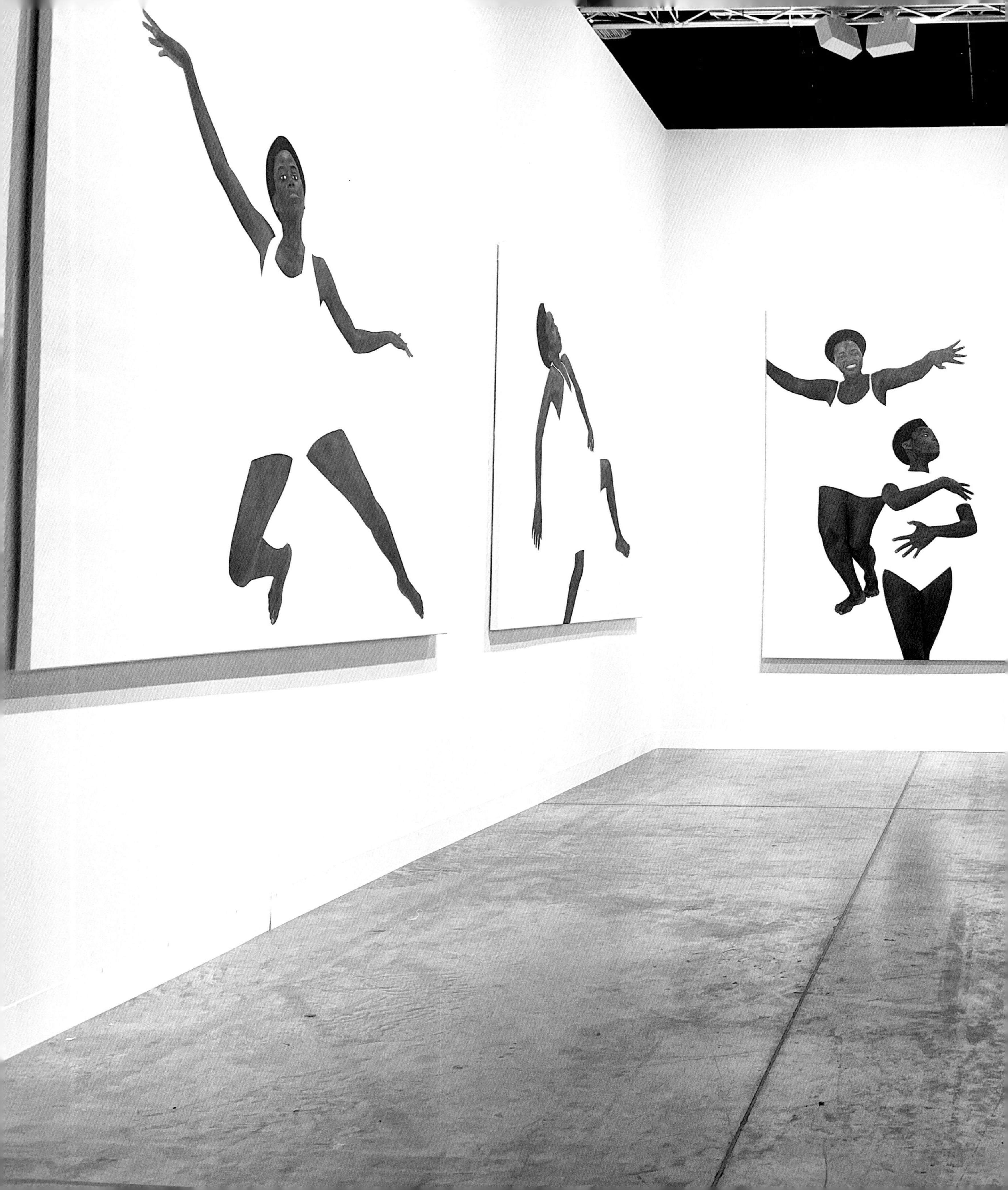

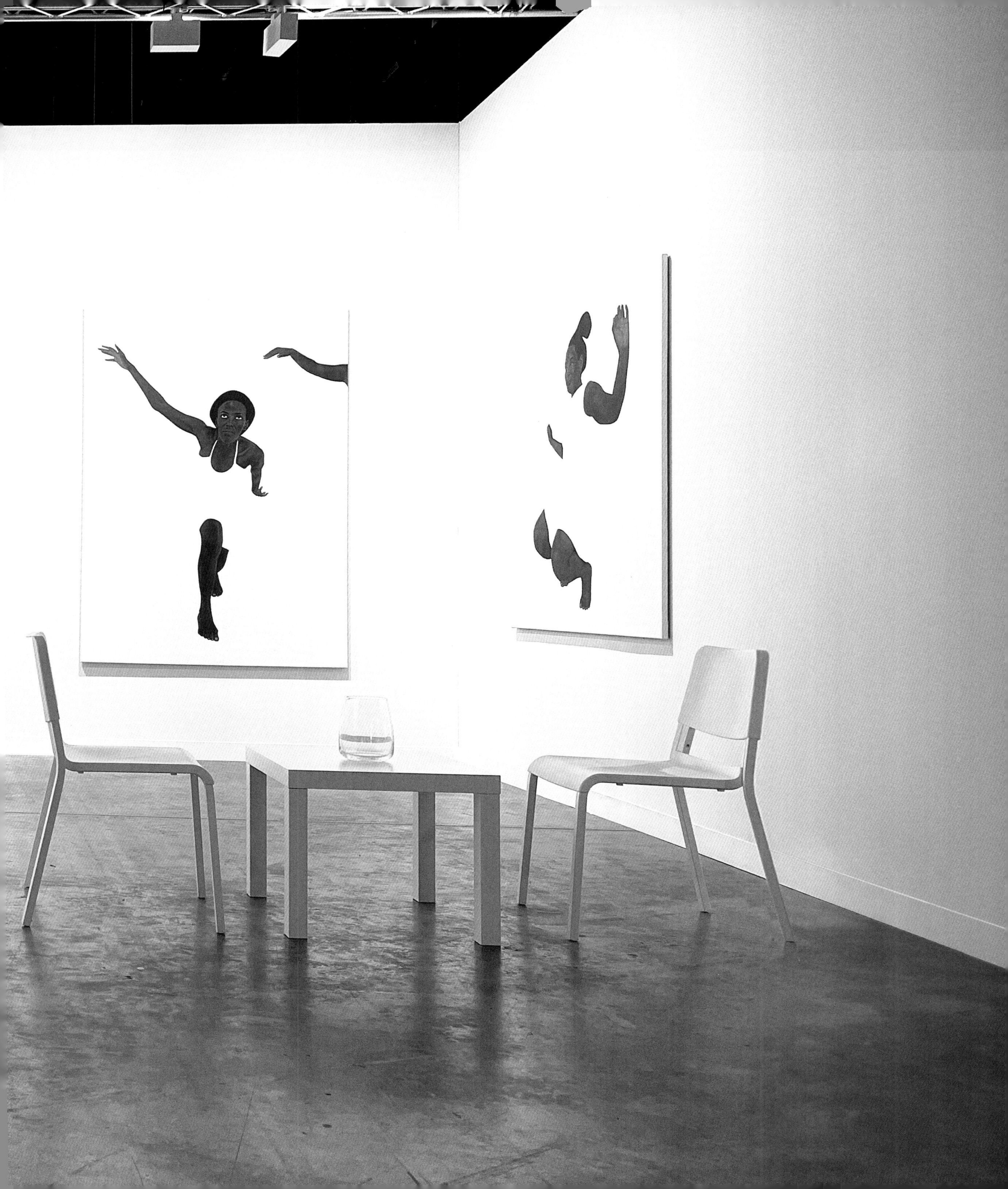

List of Works

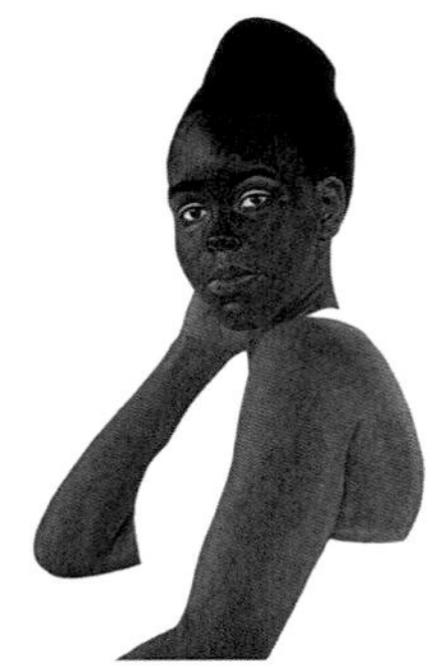

Page 10
Liirwa I, 2020
acrylic on canvas
86 × 60 cm

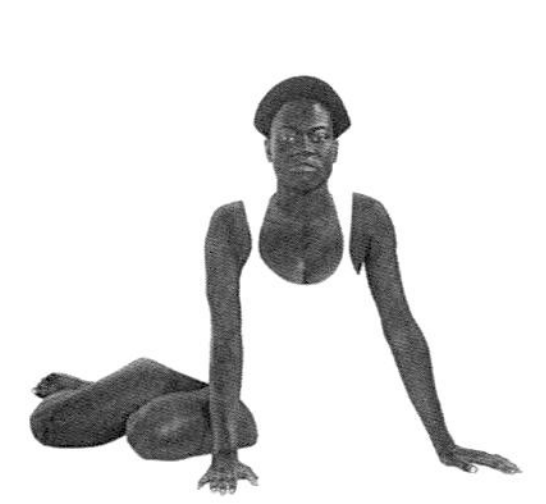

Page 12
Mdada, 2020
acrylic on canvas
150 × 140 cm

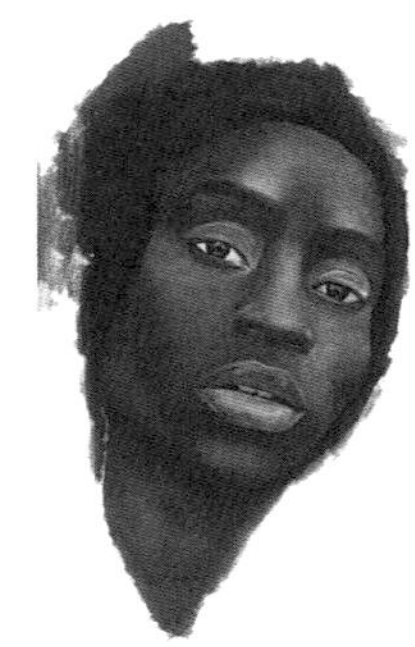

Page 14
Whitney II, 2018
acrylic on canvas
90 × 60 cm

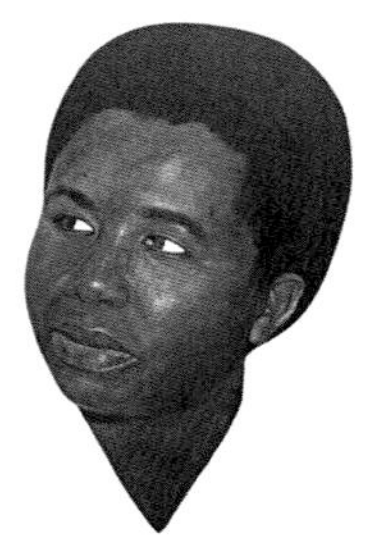

Page 17
Nyamgana, 2024
acrylic on canvas
90 × 82 cm

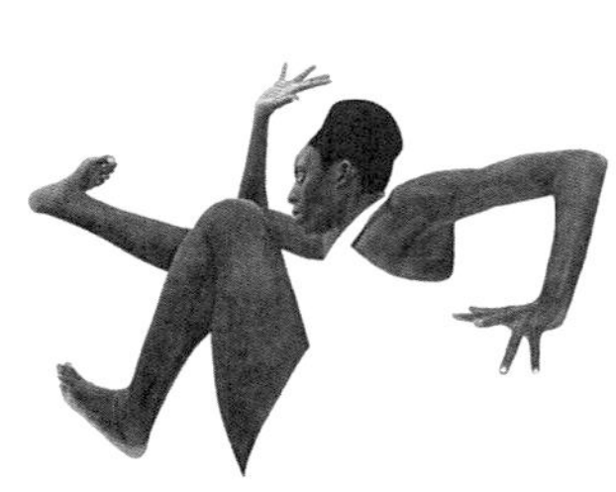

Page 20
Crossroads, 2022
acrylic on canvas
150 × 200 cm

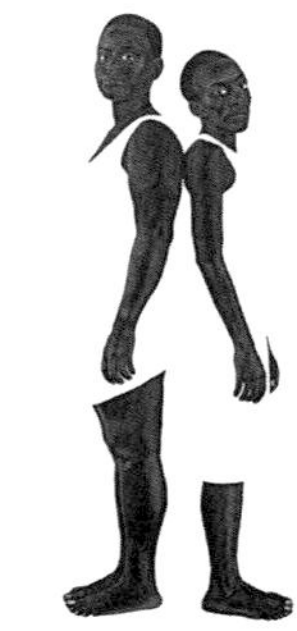

Page 22
Back, 2019
acrylic on canvas
150 × 110 cm

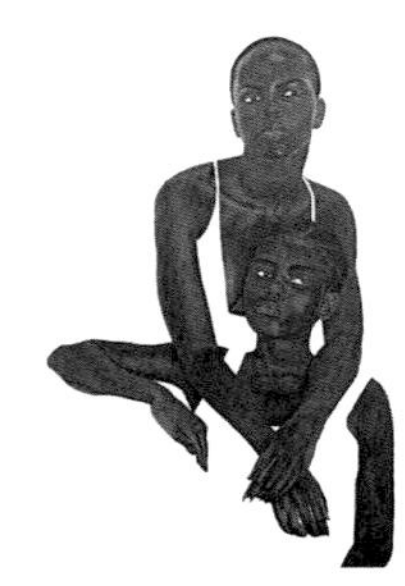

Page 23
Constant III, 2019
acrylic on canvas
140 × 140 cm

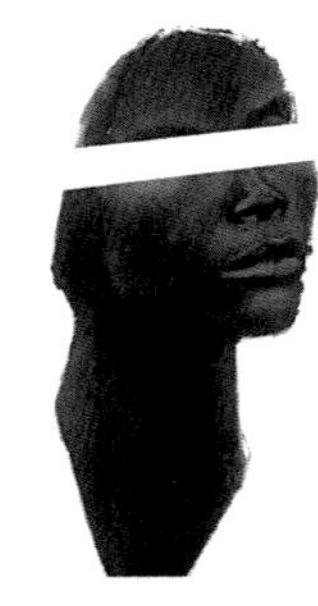

Page 24
Blind, 2019
acrylic on canvas
90 × 60 cm

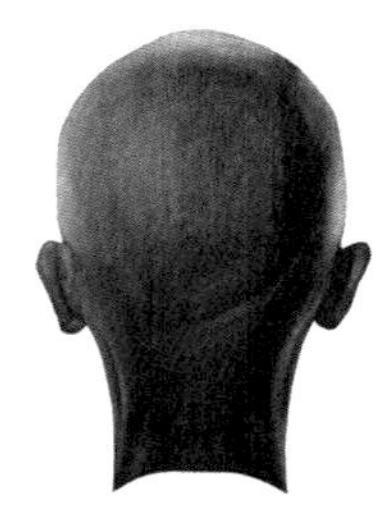

Page 25
Breathless, 2019
acrylic on canvas
86 × 61 cm

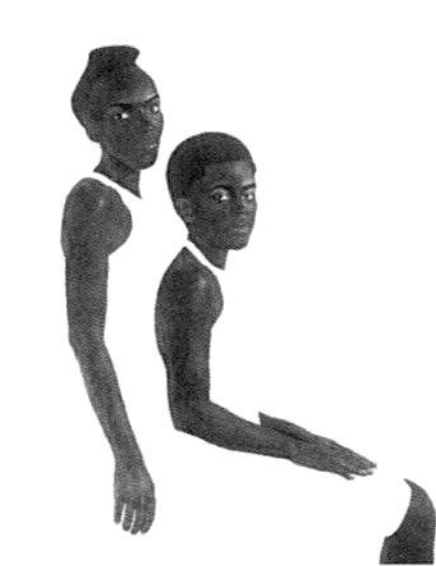

Page 26
The Hems of Our Skirts, 2020
acrylic on canvas
140 × 130 cm

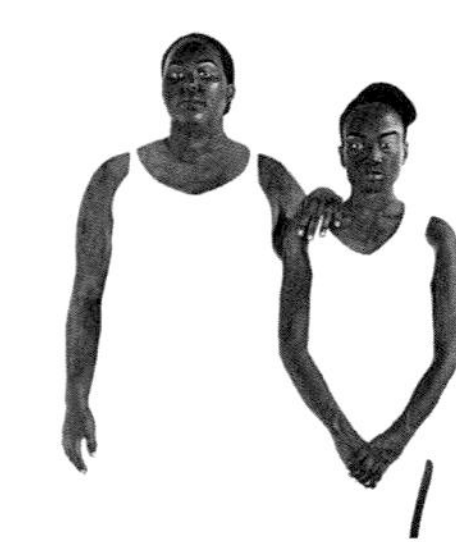

Page 27
At Heart I, 2020
acrylic on canvas
140 × 130 cm

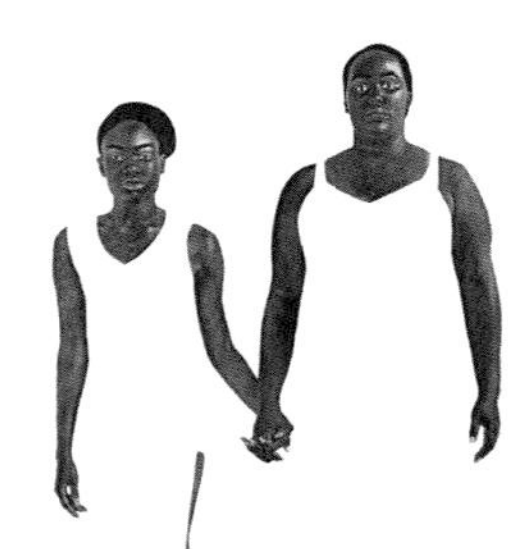

Page 29
At Heart II, 2020
acrylic on canvas
140 × 130 cm

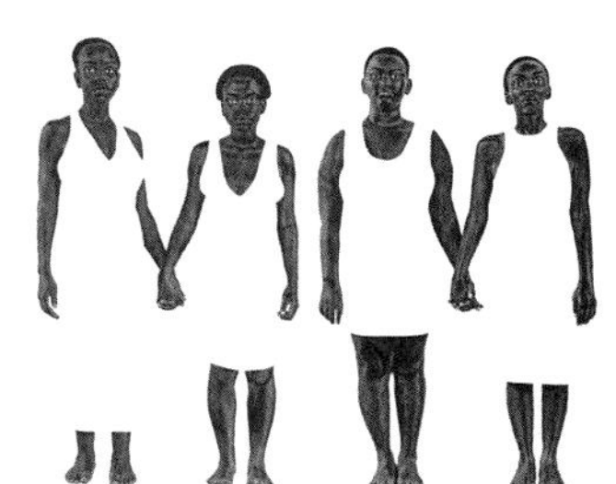

Page 30
Across, 2020
acrylic on canvas
140 × 200 cm

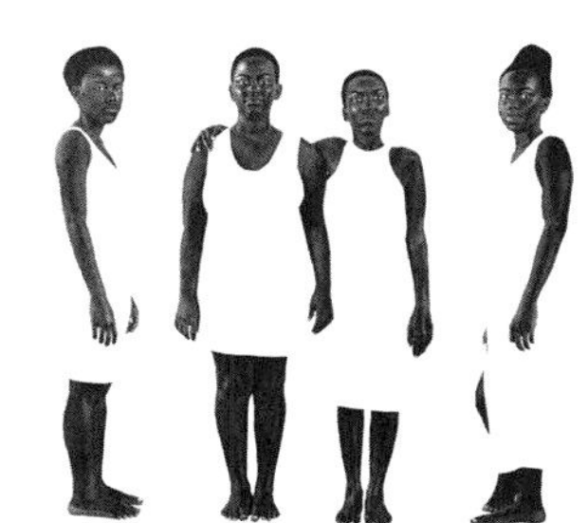

Page 33
At the End of the Evening, 2020
acrylic on canvas
140 × 200 cm

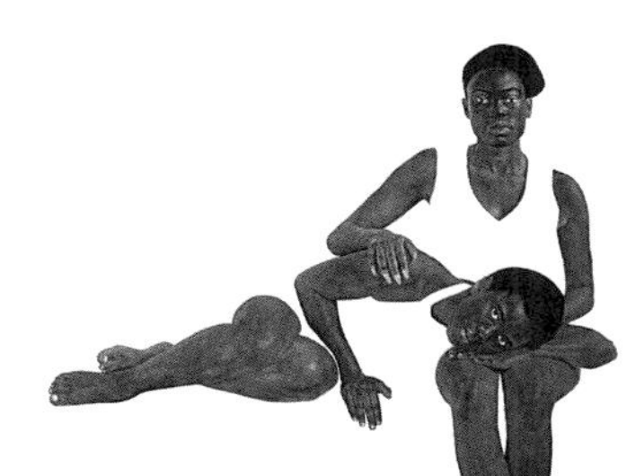

Page 34
Unclench, 2020
acrylic on canvas
140 × 200 cm

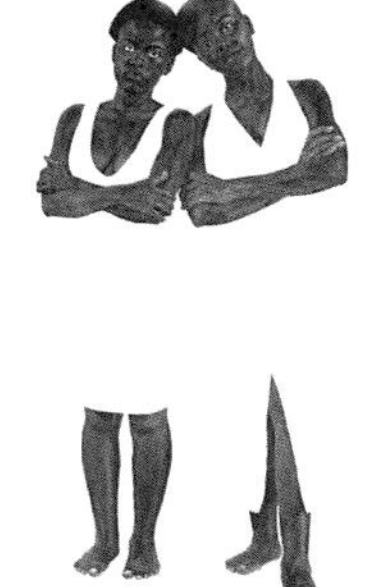

Page 36
In Our Long Dress, 2020
acrylic on canvas
150 × 110 cm

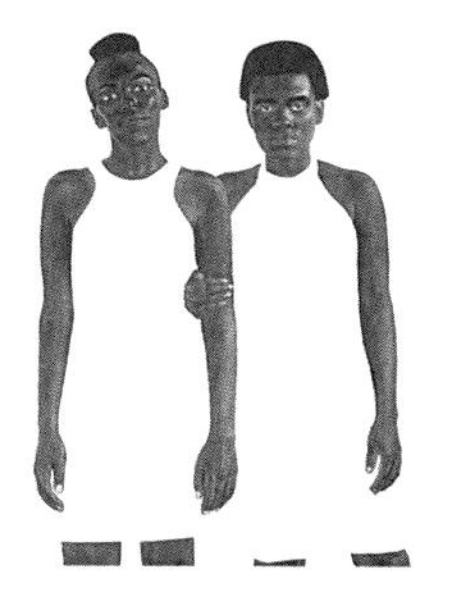

Page 37
The Secrets in Our Hems, 2020
acrylic on canvas
140 × 130 cm

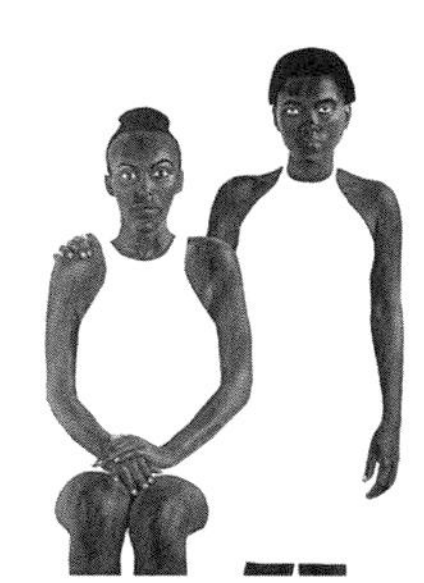

Page 39
Still, 2020
acrylic on canvas
140 × 130 cm

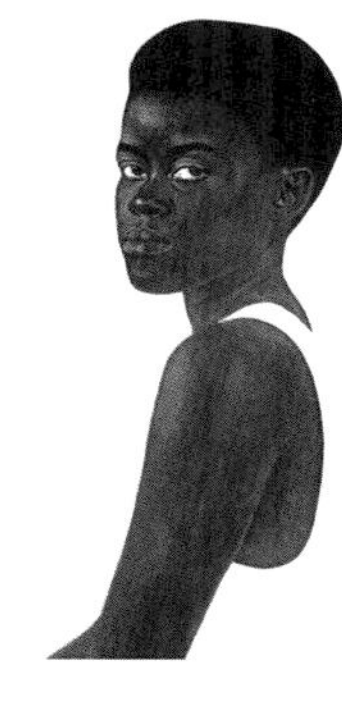

Page 41
Kyomu, 2020
acrylic on canvas
86 × 60 cm

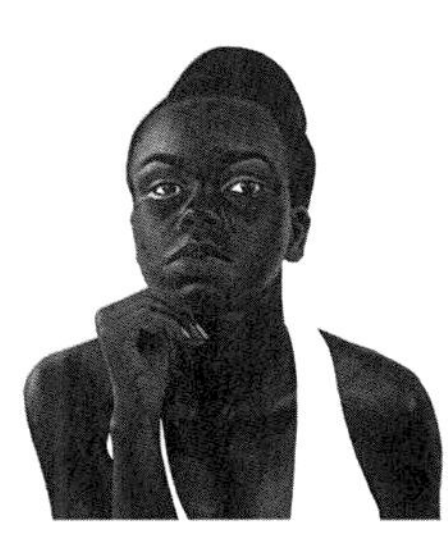

Page 42
Liirwa II, 2020
acrylic on canvas
60 × 75 cm

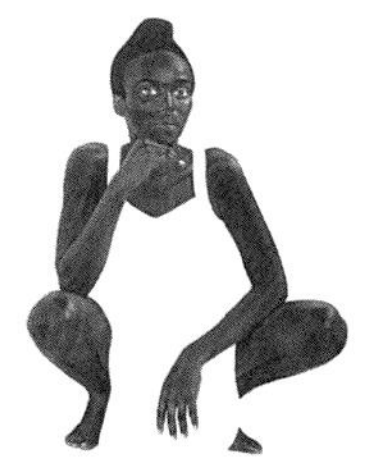

Page 43
Ahueni, 2020
acrylic on canvas
150 × 140 cm

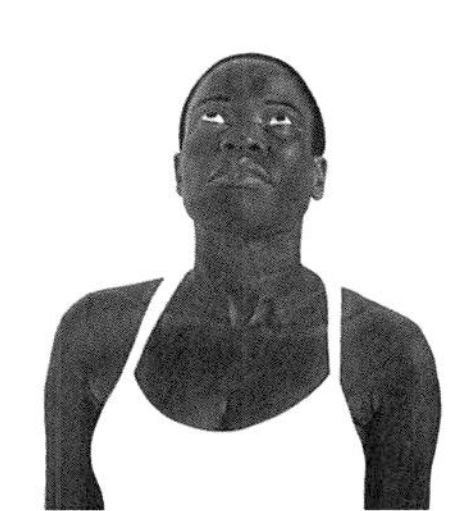

Page 44
Up, 2020
acrylic on canvas
140 × 130 cm

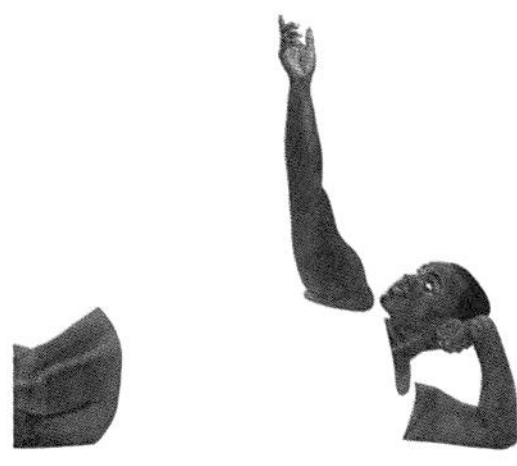

Page 45
Ascend, 2020
acrylic on canvas
150 × 140 cm

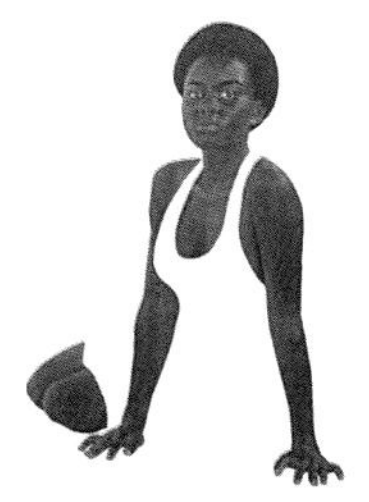

Page 47
Kaa, 2020
acrylic on canvas
140 × 130 cm

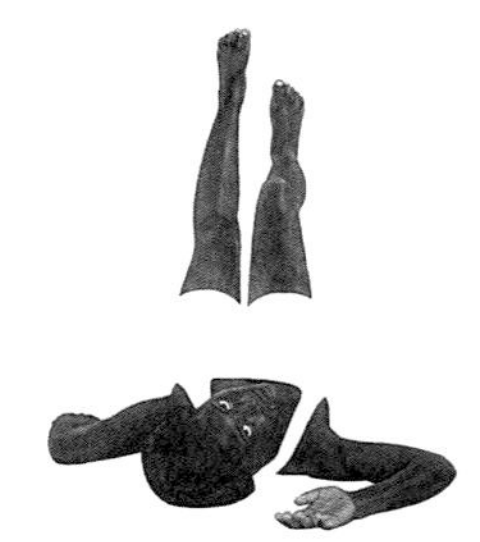

Page 48
Molten, 2020
acrylic on canvas
150 × 140 cm

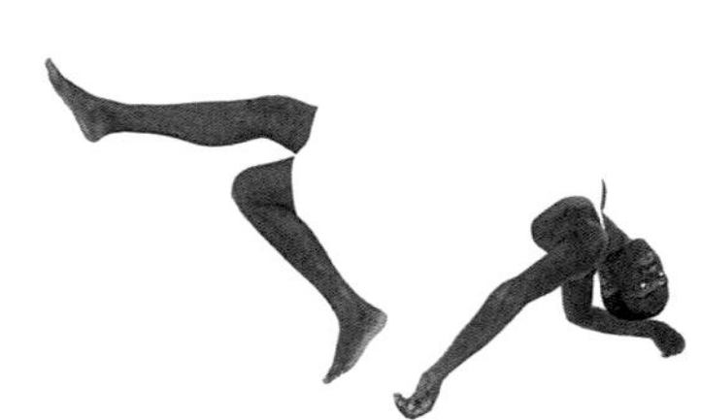

Page 49
Precontemplation, 2020
acrylic on canvas
140 × 200 cm

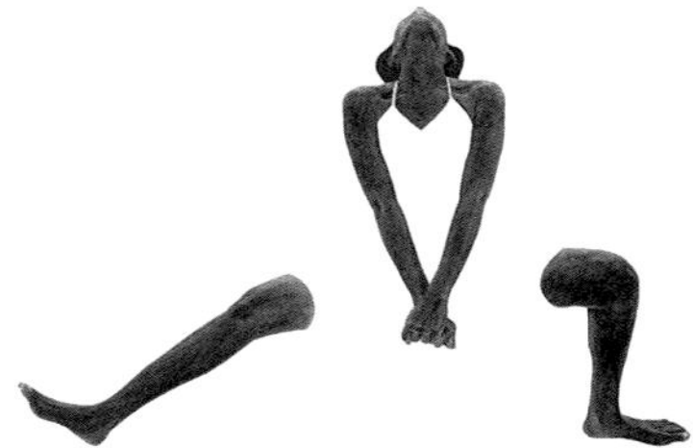

Page 50
Ruka, 2021
acrylic on canvas
140 × 200 cm

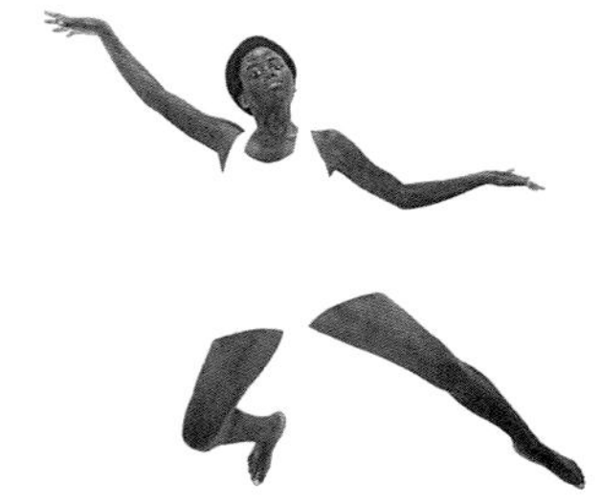

Page 52
Huru, 2021
acrylic on canvas
150 × 200 cm

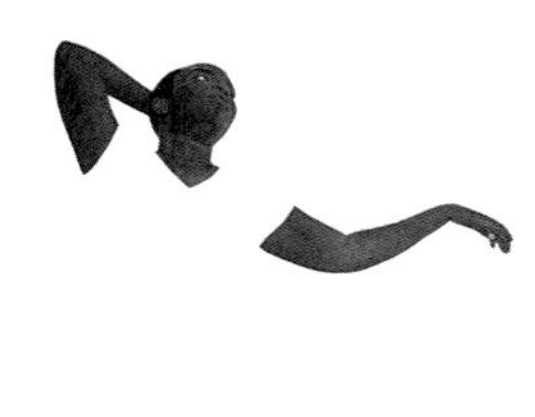

Page 55
Dance, 2021
acrylic on canvas
150 × 140 cm

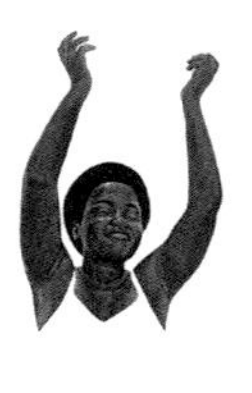

Page 57
Mafeelings, 2021
acrylic on canvas
150 × 140 cm

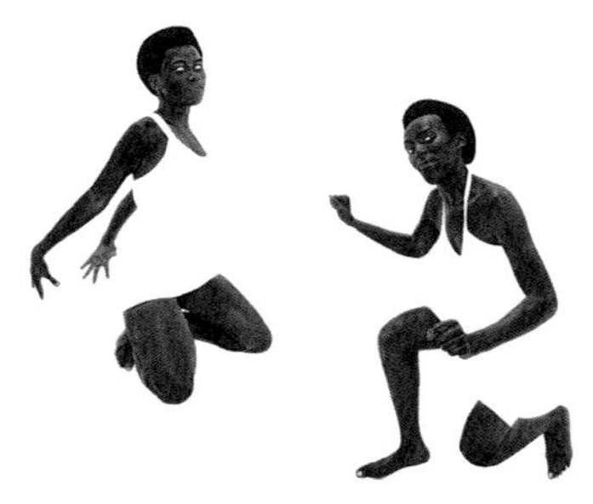

Page 58
Ngoma, 2021,
acrylic on canvas,
150 × 200 cm

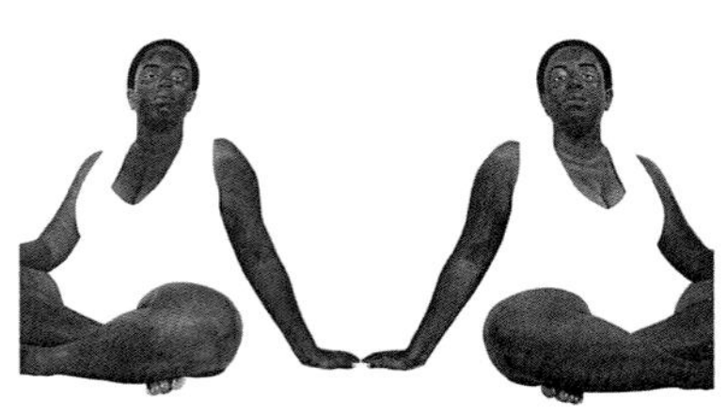

Page 60
Continuity, 2021
acrylic on canvas
140 × 200 cm

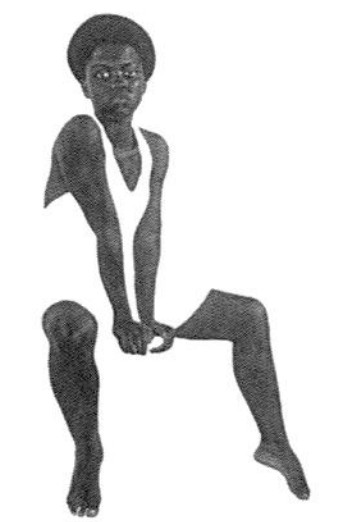

Page 63
Dare, 2021
acrylic on canvas
150 × 140 cm

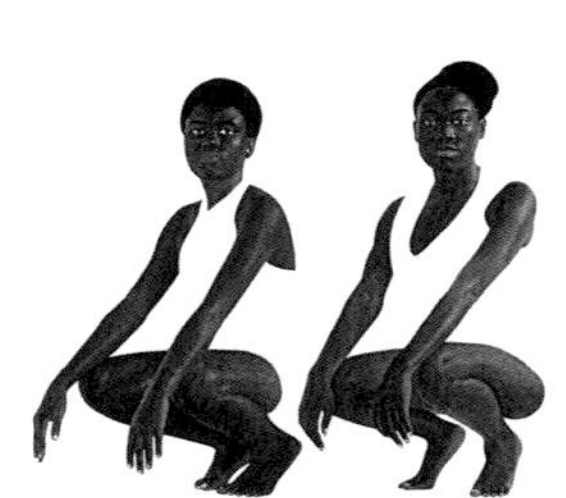

Page 64
Influence, 2021
acrylic on canvas
140 × 200 cm

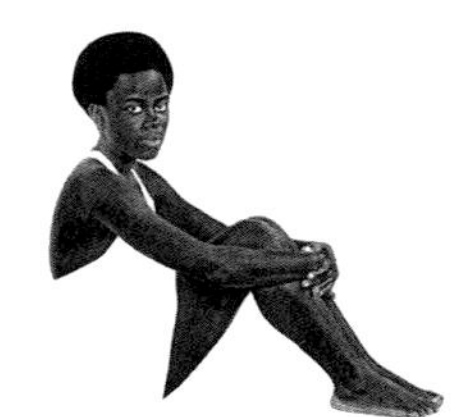

Page 66
Naked Eye, 2021
acrylic on canvas
150 × 140 cm

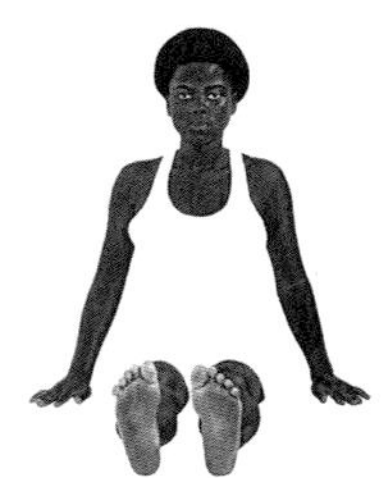

Page 67
Chaotic Disposition, 2021
acrylic on canvas
140 × 130 cm

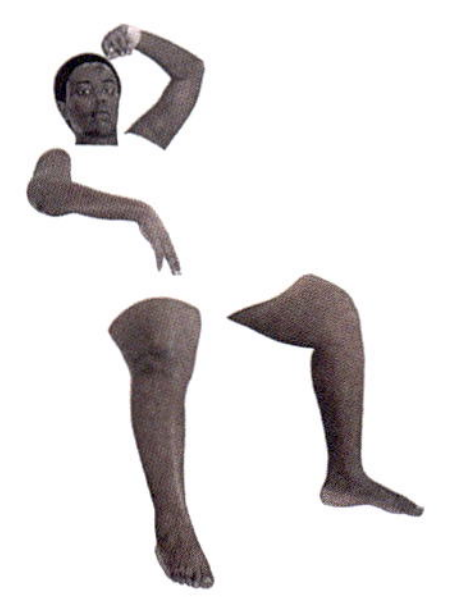

Page 69
Outcome, 2021
acrylic on canvas
200 × 140 cm

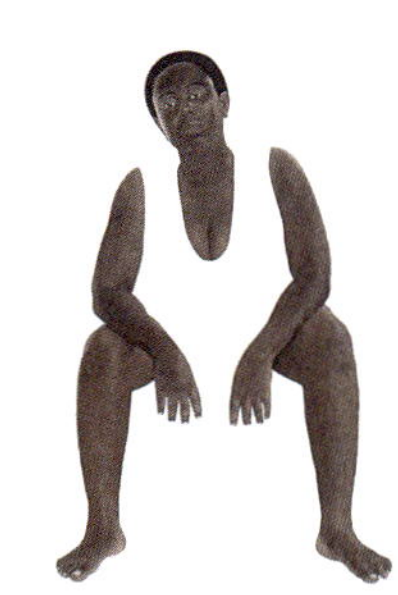

Page 70
Prepared, 2021
acrylic on canvas
150 × 140 cm

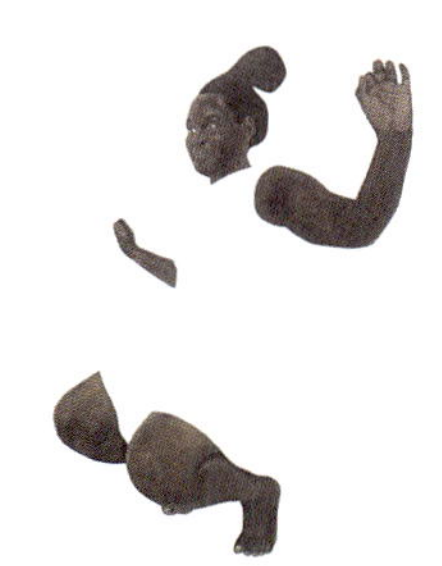

Page 71
Play, 2021
acrylic on canvas
150 × 140 cm

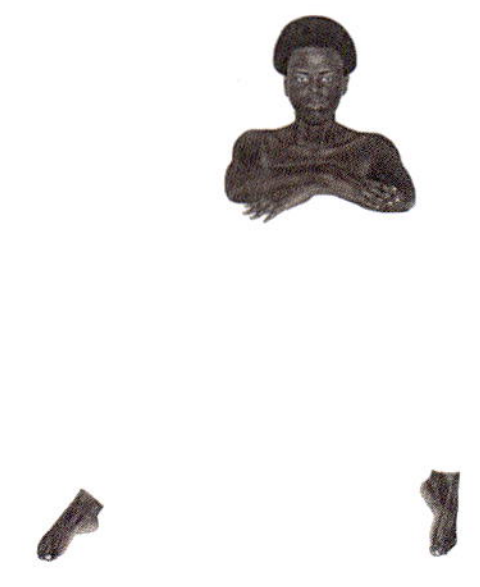

Page 73
Ready, 2021
acrylic on canvas
200 × 140 cm

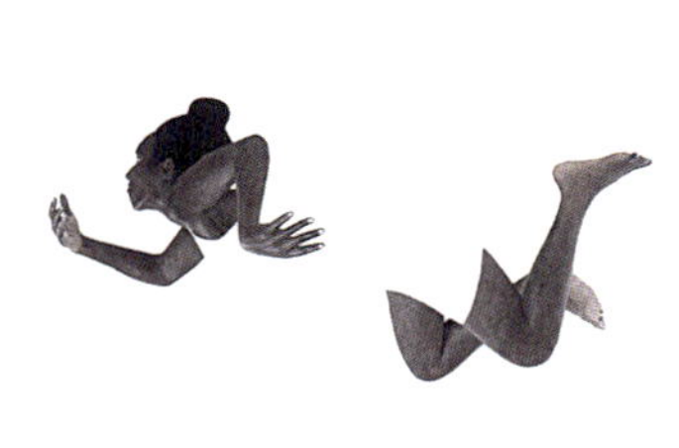

Page 74
Contemplation, 2021
acrylic on canvas
140 × 200 cm

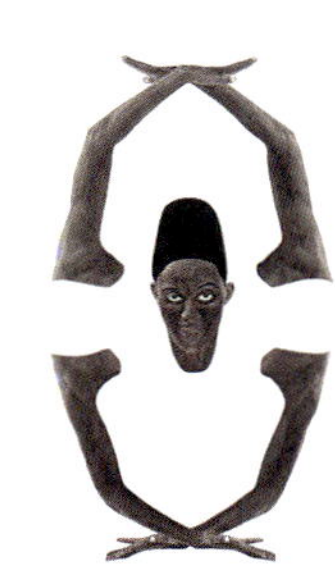

Page 77
All Ways, 2022
acrylic on canvas
200 × 150 cm

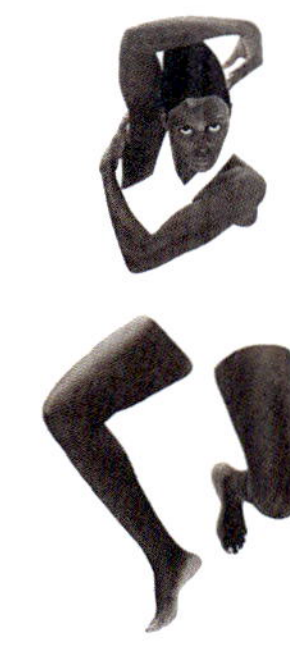

Page 79
Dust Rising, 2022
acrylic on canvas
200 × 140 cm

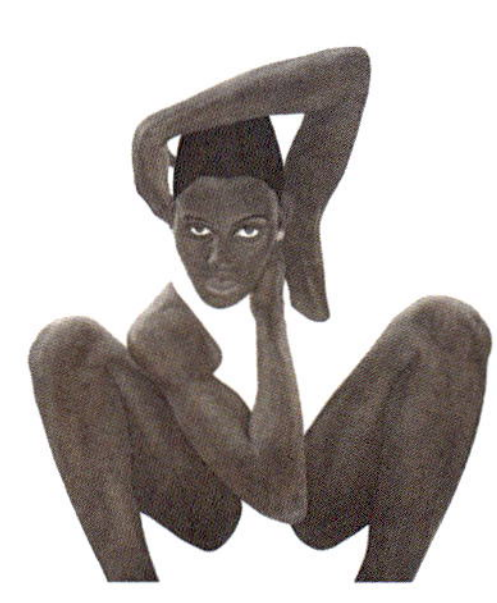

Page 80
Wallow, 2022
acrylic on canvas
150 × 140 cm

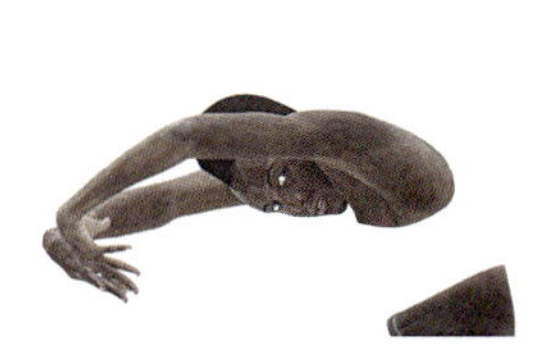

Page 81
Wear Down, 2022
acrylic on canvas
140 × 150 cm

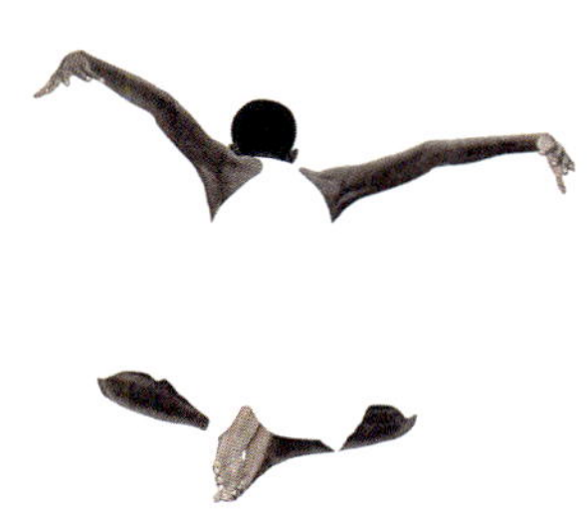

Page 83
Spring, 2022
acrylic on canvas
140 × 150 cm

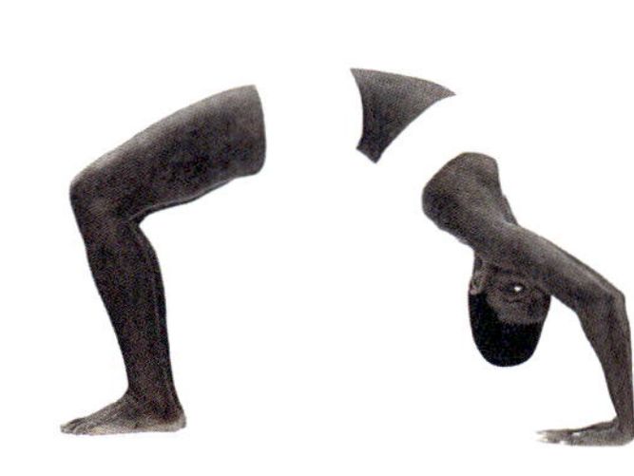

Page 84
Eye-Side Down, 2022
acrylic on canvas
150 × 200 cm

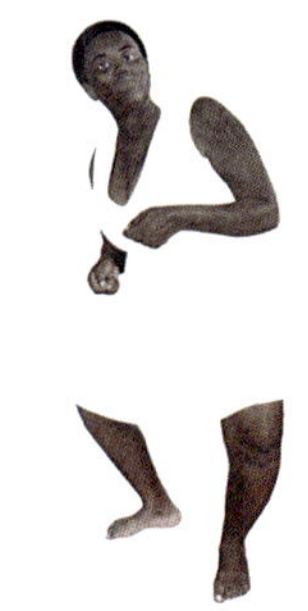

Page 86
Kidada, 2022
acrylic on canvas
200 × 140 cm

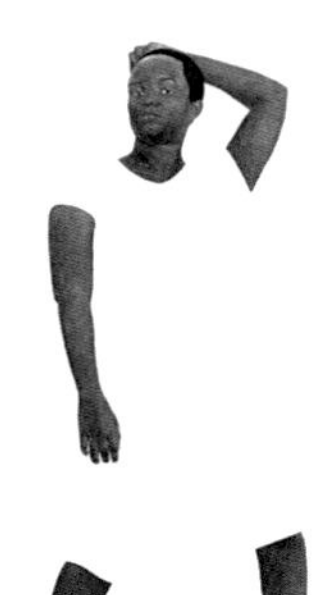

Page 87
Still, 2022
acrylic on canvas
140 × 130 cm

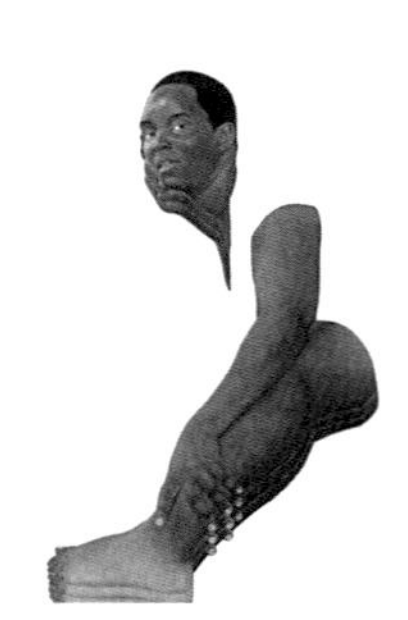

Page 88
Vibration, 2022
acrylic on canvas
150 × 200 cm

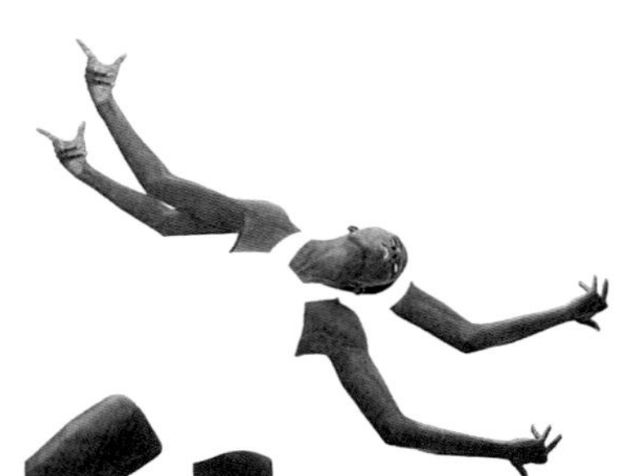

Page 91
Transcendence, 2022
acrylic on canvas
150 × 200 cm

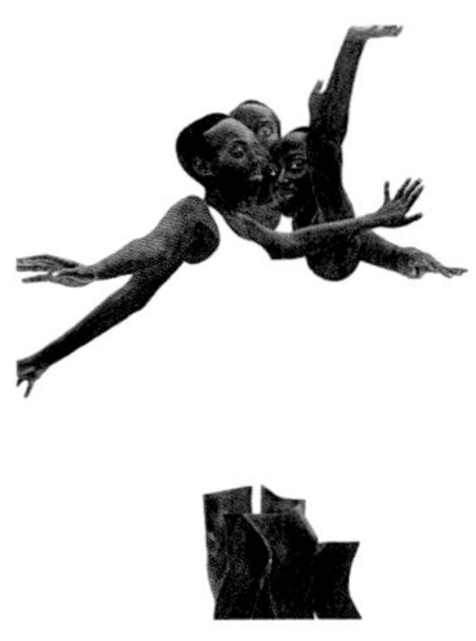

Page 93
Njia Tatu, 2022
acrylic on canvas
200 × 150 cm

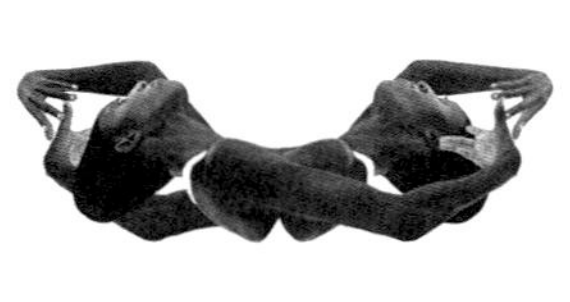

Page 94
Kushoto Kulia, 2022
acrylic on canvas
150 × 140 cm

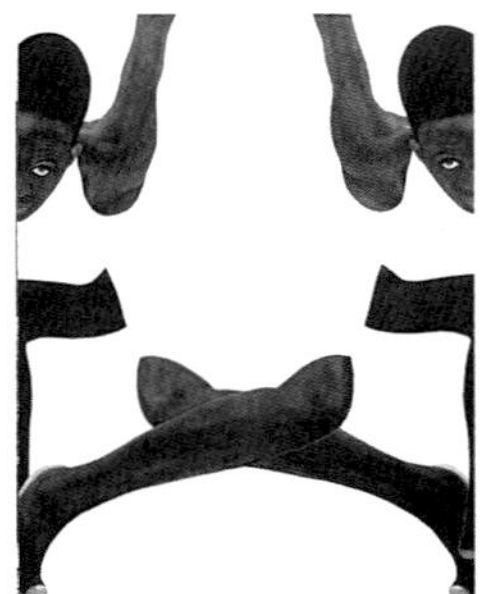

Page 95
Hapa na Pale, 2022
acrylic on canvas
200 × 150 cm

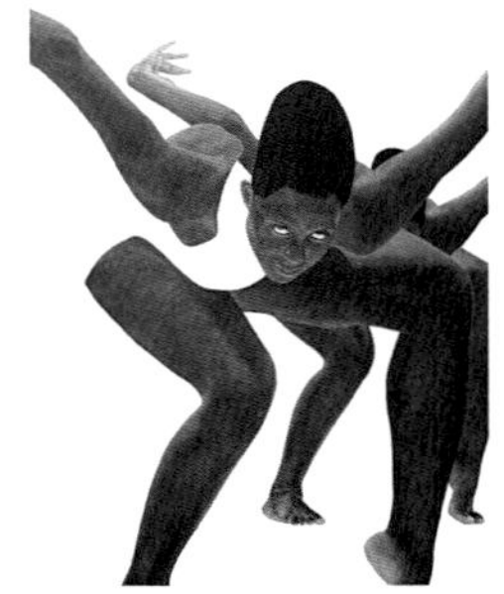

Page 97
Come, 2022
acrylic on canvas
200 × 140 cm

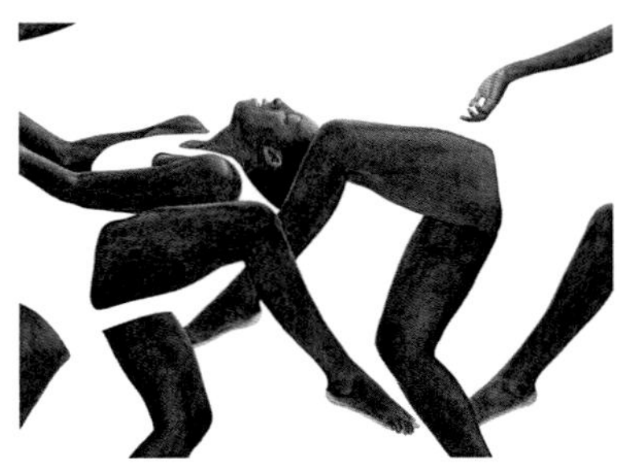

Page 98
Flow, 2023
acrylic on canvas
200 × 150 cm

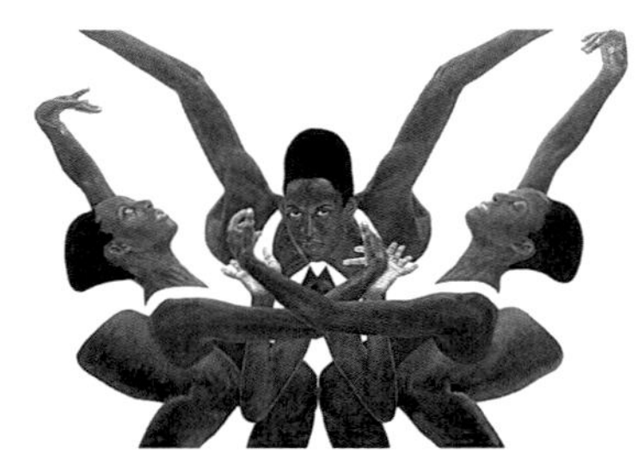

Page 100
Swish Swash, 2023
acrylic on canvas
150 × 225 cm

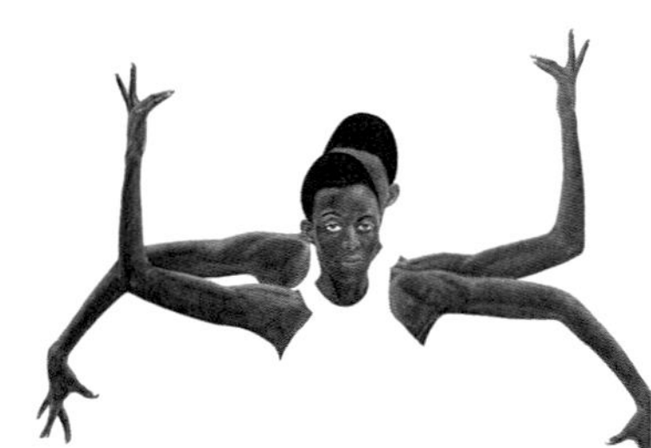

Page 103
Roots, 2023
acrylic on canvas
200 × 140 cm

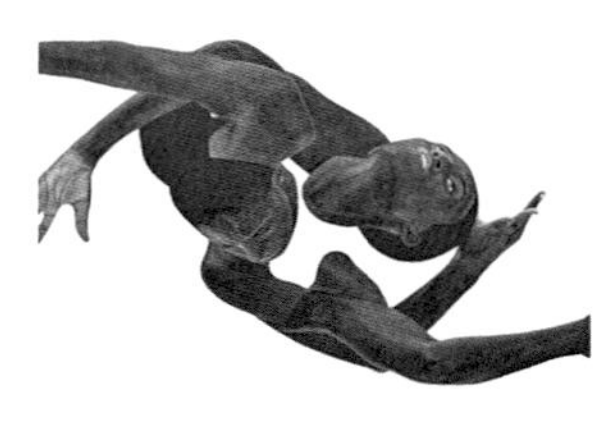

Page 105
Emergence, 2023
acrylic on canvas
150 × 140 cm

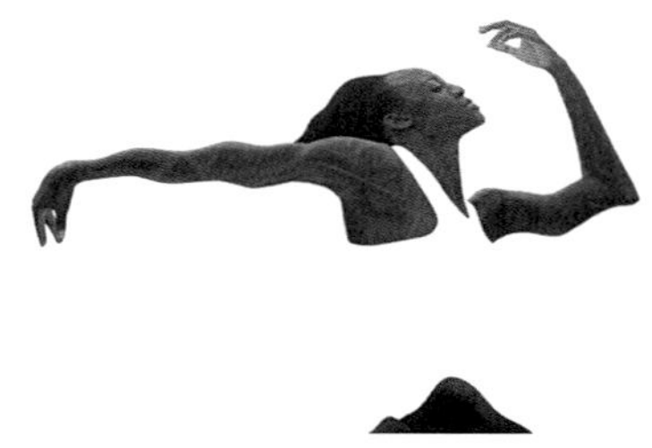

Page 106
Ripple, 2024
acrylic on canvas
140 × 200 cm

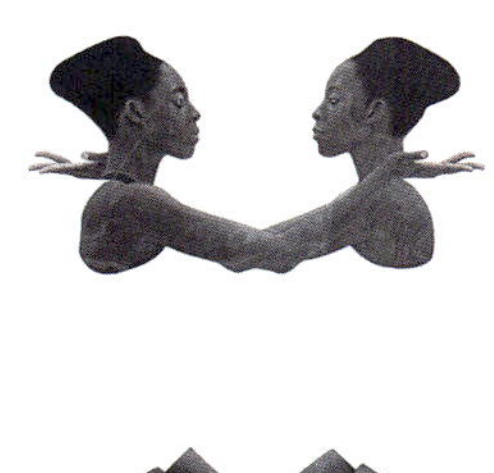

Page 109
Reflections, 2024
acrylic on canvas
150 × 140 cm

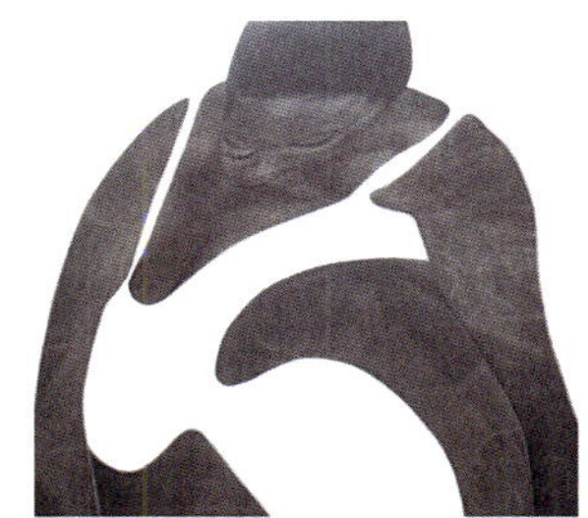

Page 110
In the Depths, 2024
acrylic on canvas
150 × 140 cm

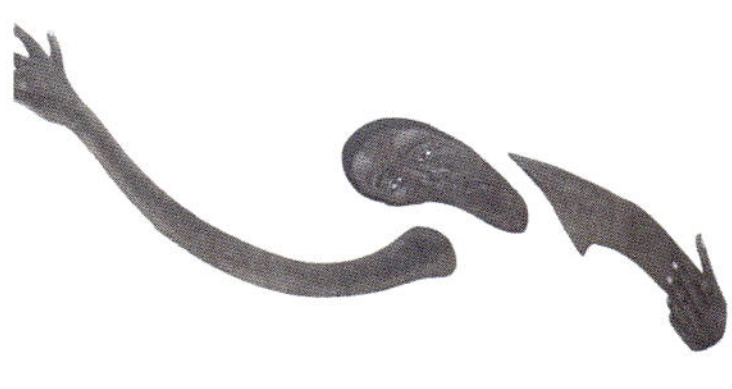

Page 111
Swimmer, 2024
acrylic on canvas
150 × 200 cm

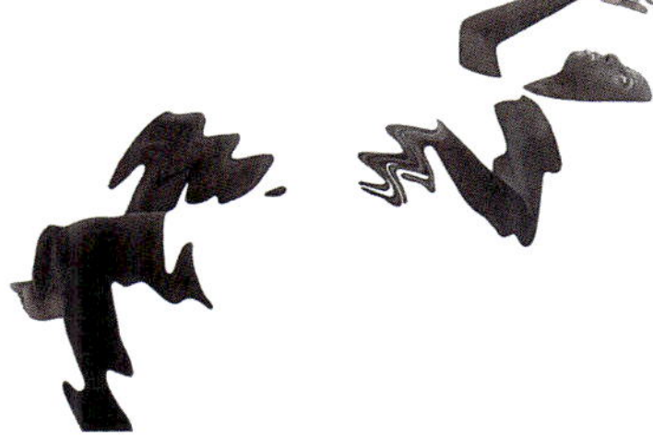

Page 112
Afloat, 2024
acrylic on canvas
200 × 150 cm

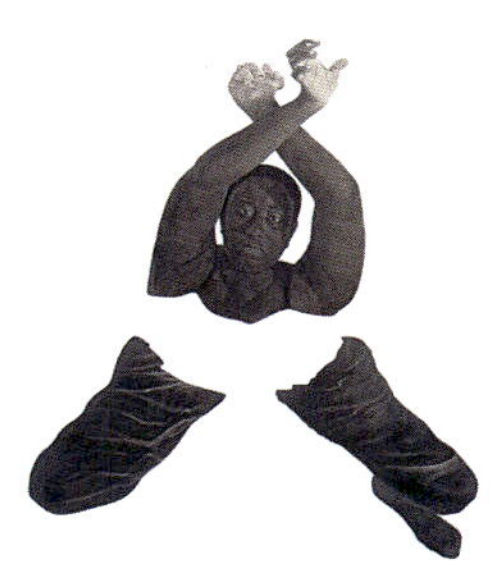

Page 115
Still Waters, 2024
acrylic on canvas
150 × 140 cm

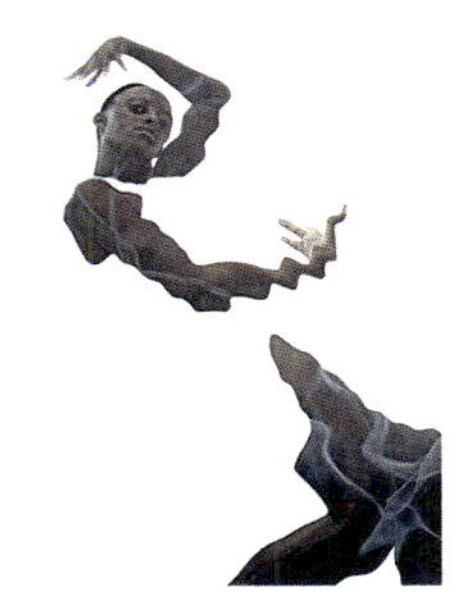

Page 116
Swirl, 2024
acrylic on canvas
200 × 150 cm

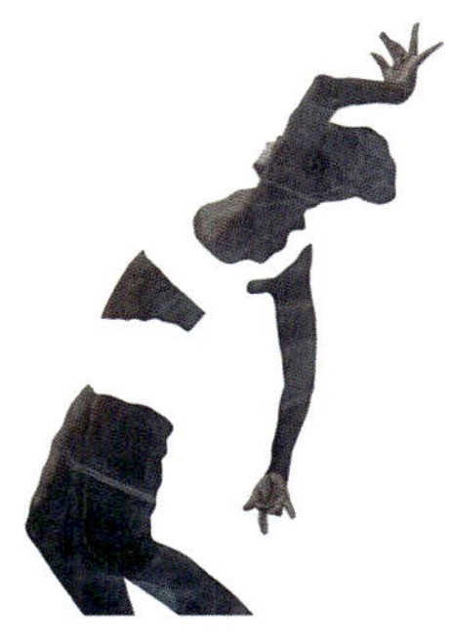

Page 117
Water Dance, 2024
acrylic on canvas
200 × 140 cm

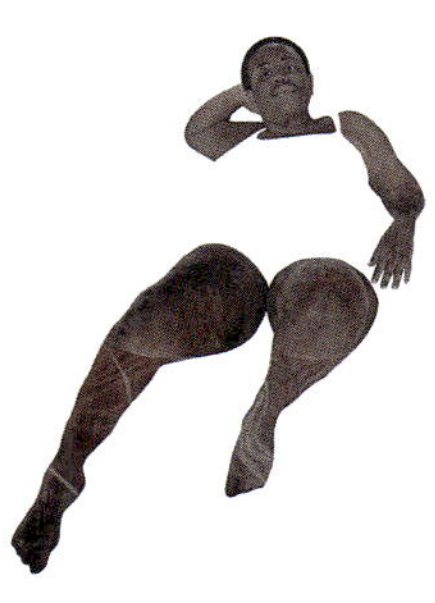

Page 119
Laze, 2024
acrylic on canvas
200 × 150 cm

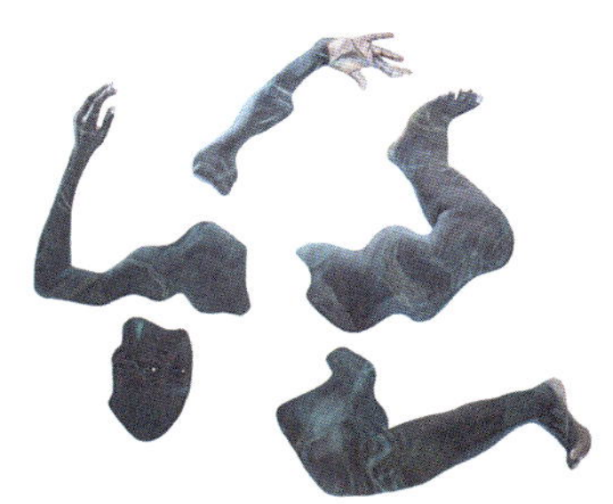

Page 120
Surge, 2024
acrylic on canvas
150 × 200 cm

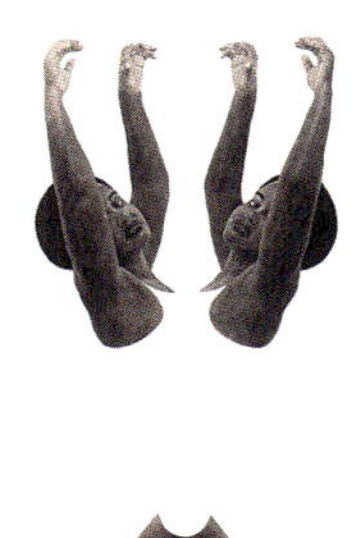

Page 122
Zone, 2022
acrylic on canvas
150 × 140 cm

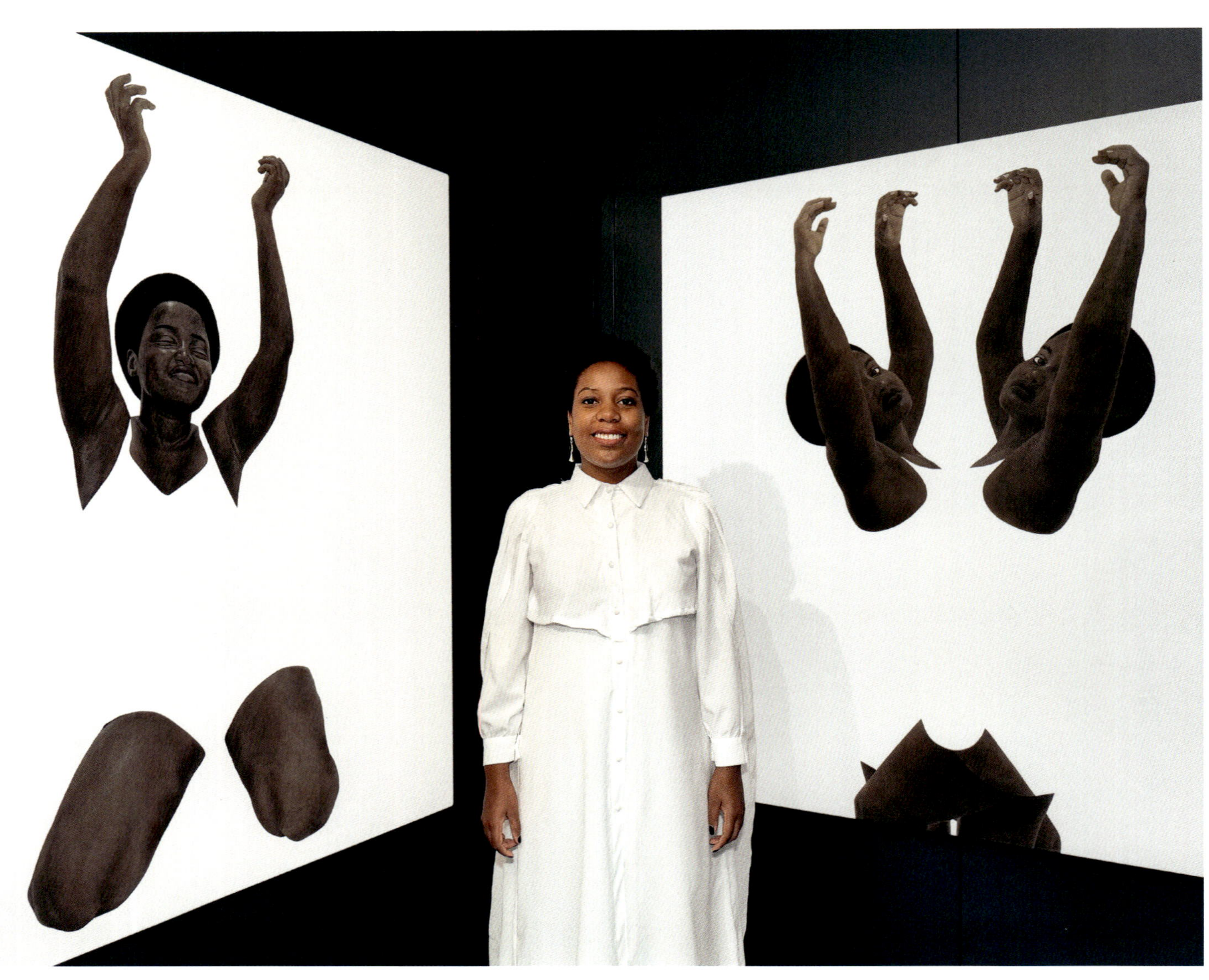

(Un)choreographed
Solo exhibition
The Africa Centre, London, UK
2022

Acknowledgements

Éditions Skira Paris and the Afriart Gallery would like to thank Sungi Mlengeya for her contribution and her commitment throughout the production of this monograph.

Our gratitude also goes to Tandazani Dhlakama and all those who have contributed: Suzanne McFayden, Katherine Alcauscas, Birgit Lauda and Jemima Michael.

We also extend our sincere appreciation to the collectors and the institutions that have exhibited Sungi Mlengeya's work.

And the artist would like to thank all those who have supported her since the start of her career.

Creating this book has been a dream come true — a way to share my work with the world and reflect on the journey that has brought me here. While I believe I would always have turned out to be an artist, the version of me who shares this book with you exists because of particular people and moments.
To my mum and dad: thank you for nurturing our curiosity and encouraging us to explore the world through all our peculiar hobbies. Your unwavering support eased so many burdens, allowing us the freedom to dream and create.
To my sister Ngollo: you have been my partner in creativity from the days of cutting paper in our little "office" in Serengeti to swinging ideas in adulthood. Here's to a lifetime of play.
To my brother Sabu: thank you for opening my eyes to other art forms and showing me how creativity can extend into space. I am so grateful for your inspiration.

To my soul sister Jemima: thank you for standing by me with unflinching support and for all our shared adventures that continue to inspire my journey.
To Daudi: I am deeply grateful for your mentorship and friendship, which began at that workshop so many years ago and continues to guide me today. My work is deeply influenced by women — both constants in my life and fleeting encounters. To those who fill my world with laughter, joy, and grounding presence, and to those whose brief moments of connection have inspired my thinking and practice; you are reflected in my art. Thank you Nyamgana, Ngollo, Mima, Kyomugisha, Sarah, Lilian, Melba, Meron, Lirwa, Olivia, Rukia, Jennifer, and so many others.
The creation of this book was made possible through the efforts of many collaborators. My heartfelt thanks go to SKIRA and their incredible team, Suzanne McFayden, Tandazani Dhlakama, Katherine Alcauscas, Birgit Lauda, Daudi Karungi, Lara Buchmann, and the Afriart team as a whole. To the collectors who have supported me, shared my work with museums and exhibitions, and to the curators who have brought my paintings to new audiences — I feel deeply honored and thankful for your support.

Finally, to the audience: creating art gives me purpose, but sharing it with you brings it to life. Thank you for being part of this journey.

AFRIART GALLERY (AAG), KAMPALA
110-112 Seventh Street
Kampala, Uganda
afriartgallery.org

Founding Director
Daudi Karungi

Exhibitions & Press
Lara Buchmann

ÉDITIONS SKIRA PARIS
14 rue Serpente
75006 Paris
www.skira-arte.com

Senior Editor
Nathalie Prat-Couadau

Project Manager
Irène Rodriguez

Editorial Manager
Juliette Chambon

Junior Editor
Roxanne Rebours

Editorial Assistant
Louise Coulet (intern)

Graphic design
Claire Luxey

Copyediting & proofreading
Timothy Stroud

Colour separation
Litho Art New, Turin

ISBN 978-2-37074-266-7

Cover:
Ripple, 2024
acrylic on canvas
140 × 200 cm

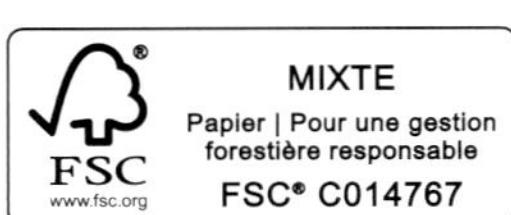

This book has been printed on FSC-certified paper, and all stages of its manufacture have complied with this certification, which supports the environmentally appropriate, socially beneficial and economically viable management of the world's forests, using materials from well-managed forests, recycled materials and other controlled sources. www.fsc.org

Printed in December 2024 by Graphius, Ghent, Belgium.
Legal deposit January 2025.